# WORKPLACE SECURITY ESSENTIALS

## A GUIDE FOR HELPING ORGANIZATIONS CREATE SAFE WORK ENVIRONMENTS

ERIC N. SMITH

T0348528

AMSTERDAM • BOSTON • HEIDELBERG • LONDON
NEW YORK • OXFORD • PARIS • SAN DIEGO
SAN FRANCISCO • SINGAPORE • SYDNEY • TOKYO

Butterworth-Heinemann is an imprint of Elsevier

Acquiring Editor: Brian Romer
Editorial Project Manager: Keira Bunn
Project Manager: Punithavathy Govindaradjane
Designer: Mark Rogers

*Butterworth-Heinemann* is an imprint of Elsevier
225 Wyman Street, Waltham, MA, 02451, USA

Copyright © 2014 Elsevier Inc. All rights reserved.

No part of this publication may be reproduced or transmitted in any form or by any means, electronic or mechanical, including photocopying, recording, or any information storage and retrieval system, without permission in writing from the publisher. Details on how to seek permission, further information about the Publisher's permissions policies and our arrangements with organizations such as the Copyright Clearance Center and the Copyright Licensing Agency, can be found at our website: www.elsevier.com/permissions.

This book and the individual contributions contained in it are protected under copyright by the Publisher (other than as may be noted herein).

**Notices**
Knowledge and best practice in this field are constantly changing. As new research and experience broaden our understanding, changes in research methods or professional practices, may become necessary.

Practitioners and researchers must always rely on their own experience and knowledge in evaluating and using any information or methods described herein. In using such information or methods they should be mindful of their own safety and the safety of others, including parties for whom they have a professional responsibility.

To the fullest extent of the law, neither the Publisher nor the authors, contributors, or editors, assume any liability for any injury and/or damage to persons or property as a matter of products liability, negligence or otherwise, or from any use or operation of any methods, products, instructions, or ideas contained in the material herein.

**Library of Congress Cataloging-in-Publication Data**
Smith, Eric N. (Eric Newell), 1967-
  Workplace security essentials : a guide for helping organizations create safe work environments / Eric N. Smith.
      pages cm
1. Business enterprises–Security measures. 2. Industrial safety. 3. Risk management.
4. Fraud–Prevention. I. Title.
  HD61.5.S65 2014
  658.4′73--dc23

                              2013000588

**British Library Cataloguing-in-Publication Data**
A catalogue record for this book is available from the British Library.

ISBN: 978-0-12-416557-1

Printed and bound in the United States of America
14 15 16 17 18   10 9 8 7 6 5 4 3 2 1

For information on all Butterworth-Heinemann publications
visit our website at http://store.elsevier.com

**Working together
to grow libraries in
developing countries**

www.elsevier.com • www.bookaid.org

# Dedication

To Larry Smith, my father, who helped a dream become reality

# Contents

# Acknowledgments

With the writing of this book, I have realized how much help and support are needed. It is not the work of a lone individual hunkered over a keyboard. It is a team effort.

Thank you, God, from whom all blessings flow.

Much thanks to Keith Karel and Tom Riggs. You both put up with the raw, unedited manuscript and helped turn it into something resembling the English language. You deserve special thanks.

Of course, the manuscript would not have been written without the support of Mary Jane Peluso, my acquisition editor, who championed the idea and helped move the project forward. Elsevier editors Amber Hodge and Keira Bunn both kept me on track and on target with some occasional prodding and reminders.

To my family, Gretchen, Emerald and Alexander, who gave up weekend outings and tolerated the hours I spent in the evenings putting pen to paper, brainstorming, and typing over the last 10 months. Without their love and encouragement, this book would not have been possible.

# About the Author

Eric Smith, CPP, is the leading authority on organizational self-defense. Currently, Eric is the HSS Security Director for the Denver-area Sisters of Charity of Leavenworth Health System locations. Before joining HSS, Inc., he spent more than a decade in law enforcement, including working on a special team focused on street-level drug interdiction. He is experienced in security management, directing the security operations at several locations. He teaches active shooter response for school administrators, faculty, and hospital staff. Eric has developed staff education and security awareness training programs for employees and security staff members. He instructs critical incident command leaders on how to handle emergency procedures.

After authoring various articles on law enforcement and security topics, he has contributed to two books on security program administration and has been cited in the latest edition of *Human Resource Management*. His most recent publication, *Healthy Access to Healthcare: Visitor Management for Hospitals*, is available online through Amazon.com (paperback) or electronically on Kindle. Recently, Eric developed an active shooter guideline for IAHSS after helping to plan and conduct a full-scale scenario involving SWAT, police responders, bomb squads, and negotiators in an urban hospital.

In addition to authoring *Workplace Security Essentials*, as an avid writer and trainer, Eric created the Business Karate Blog. The blog includes security tips and suggestions for business leaders and anyone interested in personal security. Topics range from active shooters, corporate espionage, to suggestions on how to survive a robbery.

Eric obtained his Certified Protection Professional (CPP), the preeminent security management certification, through ASIS International. He holds a bachelor of science degree in International Business and Marketing from the University of Colorado.

# Digital Assets

Thank you for selecting Butterworth-Heinemann's *Workplace Security Essentials*. To complement the learning experience, we have provided a number of online tools to accompany this edition. Two distinct packages of interactive digital assets are available: one for instructors, trainers, and managers; and the other for students and trainees.

## FOR THE INSTRUCTORS, TRAINERS, AND MANAGERS

Qualified adopters and instructors need to register at this link for access: http://textbooks.elsevier.com/web/Manuals.aspx?isbn=9780124165571.

- **Test Bank.** Compose, customize, and deliver exams using an online assessment package in a free Windows-based authoring tool that makes it easy to build tests using the unique multiple choice and true or false questions created for *Workplace Security Essentials*. What is more, this authoring tool allows you to export customized exams directly to Blackboard, WebCT, eCollege, Angel, and other leading systems. All test bank files are also conveniently offered in Word format.
- **PowerPoint Lecture Slides.** Reinforce key topics with focused Power-Points, which provide a perfect visual outline with which to augment your lecture. Each individual book chapter has its own dedicated slideshow.
- **Instructor's Guides.** Design your course around customized learning objectives, discussion questions, and other instructor tools.

## FOR THE STUDENTS AND TRAINEES

Students will need to visit this link in order to access the ancillaries below. http://booksite.elsevier.com/9780124165571.

- **Self-Assessment Question Bank.** Enhance review and study sessions with the help of this online self-quizzing asset. Each question is presented in an interactive format that allows for immediate feedback.
- **Case Studies.** Apply what is on the page to the world beyond with the help of topic-specific case studies, each designed to turn theory into practice, and followed by interactive scenario-based questions that allow for immediate feedback.

# 1

# The Fighting Stance: Security Awareness

## WHAT IS BUSINESS KARATE?

Several years ago, I had a brilliant thought. That is not a very common occurrence, so of course it stands out in my mind. I realized that the whole concept of protecting a business or organization (in my case at the time a large urban hospital) was not that different from a form of self-defense— self-defense on a larger scale. The steps involved in learning a martial art for defense actually did have some comparable real life aspects that translated to how an organization or enterprise could, or should, go about protecting itself. Martial arts students have to learn to block, kick, punch, and even how to break out of holds or fight after being knocked down to the ground.

Karate students have to learn what parts of their bodies need the most protection and are vulnerable to different attacks. Enterprises have to learn what parts of its businesses need the most protection and are the most vulnerable to different threats. Both have to learn how to protect themselves from those attacks. Karate students learn how to defend against attacks from several different directions, even simultaneously. Businesses as well can be attacked on several different fronts at the same time. Threats can come from inside, such as employee thefts, or from outside, such as burglary, or even farther away if foreign politics affect supply chains.

Throughout this book, I have outlined concepts or methods that any organization can implement to better protect its interests and more importantly, its employees—from building awareness about potential, real concerns; to learning how to block; to how to kick and how to recover when knocked down and nearly out. These are all topics covered throughout this book.

Of course, part of learning karate or other martial arts is the periodic testing and the belt levels, including a black belt for the experts of the sport. The same could be said of all organizations. How well protected is it? Does the business have a black belt or does it have a white belt and is early in learning and development? Each chapter concludes with several pointers that help determine your own organization's belt level. There are examples or criteria based on the ideas covered in every chapter for all belt levels from white (beginner) advancing up to black belt. If a business meets all the criteria listed for the black belt and each of the other belt levels, it can consider itself well protected, at least in regard to that specific chapter.

Martial arts come in many different styles and formats. Some, such as a more traditional form of karate, including Shotokan karate or tae kwon do, are more aggressive and meet force with force. Other martial arts, such as aikido, use an opponent's motion and attacks against them by deflecting or redirecting an attack. Every organization must balance its security needs with the right level of protection. What works for a nuclear power plant will be very different from what works at a retail outlet. Many businesses thrive on attracting customers to their premises, not discouraging them or driving them away. Finding the right level of protection is very much like finding the right martial arts class that fits your style or learning objectives.

In addition to the security management benefits, there is one other key benefit: fun. I've loved studying martial arts. It has become a key part of my workouts, keeping them fresh and interesting. It has also helped me deal with tough situations, encountered as a police officer, with confidence and self-assurance. Certainly, as you read this book and take away ideas that will help you create a safer workplace, I hope you also have some fun. Enjoy the process as you work toward your enterprise's black belt!

## WELCOME TO KARATE CLASS

If you've ever taken up a new skill or tried to learn a new way of doing something, you probably remember how awkward and difficult it was at first. As adults, we often do not spend much time learning something new, but think back to a time you did. Maybe it was learning how to swing a baseball bat or developing skills to ride a mountain bike. More recently, think about the last time you got a new cell phone—there was definitely a learning curve.

For someone new to martial arts or a self-defense class, it can be just as demanding. Suddenly, you are in a situation that is unfamiliar with new challenges, struggling to get your body to learn new movements and trying to do something completely foreign.

One of the basic building blocks in the martial arts is stance. The different stances are among the first things taught to new students. The stances help teach a newcomer how to maintain his balance and how to set his body in the right position to perform blocks, kicks, or punches. The stances become the foundation for everything else to be learned.

In karate, different stances are used for different circumstances. One is the front stance. The front stance is very stable, balanced with a slightly lower center of gravity. It is an aggressive stance, one used for several kicks and for punches.

Another stance is the back stance, which is used for quick blocks or fast attacks, generally on a close threat. This is also closest to a traditional fighting stance, ready to move quickly in any direction.

The last stance is a side stance with the feet spread and knees bent, the body ready for a powerful sidekick attack.

Each stance prepares a new student for the attacks and blocks that they will need to learn as they progress. By practicing and learning the basic stances, the student builds awareness of their capabilities, the positioning of their bodies, and the readiness to respond.

So what does this have to do with business? Virtually everything. The new white belt is using the stances to become aware of his foot placement, his balance, and learning how to position himself in new ways. In the workplace, or even in our personal lives, the foundation of organizational self-defense or security is awareness. Awareness is the base needed to develop any program of protection.

A business, school, church, hospital, or any organization interested in implementing a security plan needs to become aware of its footing or posture. By that, I am referring to the understanding of exposure to risk, understanding the possible problems, and developing a focus on security.

Think of it this way. One of the main reasons you or I would sign up for a karate class would be to learn self-defense. There could be other factors as well, such as fitness, but generally protecting one's self is a key interest of new students. New white belts learn about footing and balance, not because those things alone will offer protection but because they provide the foundation for more practical applications as students become proficient and advance. Then the karate students can begin to realize the goal of self-defense, namely to protect their number one asset—themselves.

So, one of the first steps of organizational self-defense is to recognize that security is an integral part of the business and identify what needs to be protected and develop a view of what the current footing is in regards to the security or protection of key areas. At this point, you don't need to conduct an in-depth risk assessment. But think about your critical functions, your key assets—the things that make your workplace tick. For a teacher or school principal, the answer may be very straightforward. The goal of the program would first be to protect students and teachers, and second, to protect the school property, both the building and the contents. With a closer look, you might think of the school's reputation; what would be the media and parental response to a critical incident, especially for private or charter schools?

For other managers, the identification of key assets may not be as easy. If you are a manufacturer, your business may depend on a wide variety of processes, each of which could be a key asset that needs some level of protection. For example, you produce the infamous widget, each of which is made with 10 parts that you order from different suppliers. An event at a supplier location could stop you in your tracks. Perhaps part number four of your widget is shipped from overseas and the dockworkers at the port where your parts are exported go on strike. Can you continue to operate and produce widgets minus one part?

Maybe you run a small office. You might have typical office equipment, computer, important information, or client lists. From my experience in law enforcement, I knew that every night or weekend I could park my patrol car in an office park or group of buildings and find unlocked doors within a few minutes. Would you want to hassle with replacing computers or printers or re-creating missing data or files because no one locked the door?

No matter what type of organization you work for, there are common functions. Each area has potential ties to security, and just being aware of some of the associated risks can help manage and reduce those risks (Figure 1.1).

Every company will vary to some degree. You may have a legal department, for example, something that could be considered part of the overall leadership and management in this model. The idea here is to reinforce that security is, or should be, a vital element of the overall organization and its functions (Table 1.1).

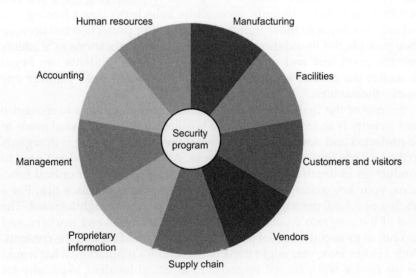

FIGURE 1.1   The security program plays a vital role throughout an entire organization.

**TABLE 1.1**   These are All Simple Examples to Get You to Think with a Security Filter or Mind-set

| Process | Security Connection |
| --- | --- |
| Human resources | People are credited as the most valuable assets by most decent companies. People truly make the difference between failure and success. Before or during hiring, background screening should be done to protect the organization's interests. When things go wrong, investigations into threats or other wrongdoing are vital to that continuing protection. |
| Manufacturing | All the equipment and goods that are used to create your product are valuable assets that need protection in order to protect the overall business. |
| Facilities | Obviously, each site and building will have specific issues, from neighborhood crime patterns, to video surveillance, alarms, lighting, and hours of operation. |
| Customers and visitors | The safety of everyone on the premises is crucial, as is the protection even if their presence is "virtual" such as an online shopper. While it is not typically a conscious concern, if customers do not feel safe at your site, they will go somewhere else. |
| Vendors | Like employees, vendors and contractors have access to facilities and often with less in the way of training, screening, or other checks and balances. |
| Supply chain | Any interruption in critical supplies can have a huge negative impact on the business. A well-rounded risk assessment can help identify potential problems, even from foreign suppliers. |
| Proprietary information | It is hard to imagine any organization that does not have valuable information on hand, whether customer files, credit card information, or precious trade secrets. Information comes in both physical as well as electronic formats, and this is an area in which physical and IT security need to coordinate to best protect that information. |
| Management | Leadership is responsible for the normal daily decisions but also must be able to evaluate risks created by security events and make strategic decisions on how to best manage and reduce those risks and the exposure to issues such as liability. |
| Accounting | Accounting or finance is responsible for the overall funding of the firm. There may be cash on hand to protect, as well as financial assets. This is also an area with a higher risk of internal embezzlement. |

## INCREASING AWARENESS

The main point of awareness is to develop an understanding of the impact of lax security. Once you or your organization has that basic understanding, you can begin to take the right steps to create a safe workplace.

Awareness alone, however, is not quite enough. To become an effective foundation, awareness needs to be converted into action—an ongoing state of alertness. For the new karate student, the instructor would not just say, "Balance and footing are important." No. The student actually practices so it becomes a routine matter to be aware of balance and stance in order to acquire the building blocks for later, more advanced, moves.

In business, security concerns should be taken into account and risks considered as a regular part of any decision-making processes. Ideally, this would become an automatic thought process or consideration whether expanding, contracting, or implementing new processes or operations, including changing hiring practices.

In reality, this does not always happen. For example, one hospital was planning to add a day care service for employees. Staff retention is important in any organization and can be very competitive in health care. Older hospitals in urban areas may be competing for clinical staff against new hospitals with the latest medical equipment, located in suburban areas with lower crime and other perks, such as easy or free parking. So staff satisfaction is very important. From a strictly business perspective, the idea looked attractive. The impact on staff morale was considered as was the potential usage, locations were discussed, and budget issues were reviewed. However, the security department was overlooked and potential safety issues were not taken into account. There was no discussion of any security concerns. Family custody disputes, physical security of the premise, policies, and procedures to ensure against abductions or screening out sexual predators from the hiring process are all some basic issues to address. Any failure in one of these key security areas could have resulted in loss of life or serious injury, plus a huge impact on the hospital's reputation. A serious incident would also undo any improvement to employee satisfaction.

This is an example of how security awareness was not even a part of the business process or decision. There was no underlying foundation or level of alertness even in an environment where there are security compliance issues and in a high-crime locale where there had been past crime concerns.

Think of your own organization. When was the last time that security concerns were discussed in depth? Or even considered at all? For that matter, who in your organization is responsible for security issues? For many companies, there is no one in the role of security director.

Many organizations are not large enough to have a full-time security director on staff. However, there should still be one person who is responsible for security issues, even if it is part of the overall job description. Has someone been assigned that role or responsibility? Have they received any training regarding security matters?

There have been studies by the United States Chamber of Commerce that show nearly one-third of businesses declare bankruptcy due to employee theft. One out of every three business bankruptcies! As a former police officer, I've had business owners explain how an employee embezzled or stole money, in some cases, taking enough so the owner could not meet payroll obligations. If a business cannot pay staff then there is no one to handle customers, and without customers, there is no more income. You can see how this becomes a vicious cycle in a worst-case scenario.

Larger businesses or organizations may be able to survive without declaring bankruptcy. Losses can have a very real impact on a company, such as lower salary increases, reduced capital for reinvestment, or delayed purchase of equipment.

What is the real cost of loss? Imagine that a $1000 laptop is stolen. What is the real cost to replace that computer? The answer will depend on your profit margin, which varies widely from industry to industry. Say you operate on a tight margin of 2%. That $1000 laptop would require additional gross revenue of $50,000 to make up the replacement cost. The value of the loss divided by your profit margin gives you the gross sales needed to recoup that loss. Looking at it this way, you can see what an impact unbudgeted losses can have on a business. Remember that losses due to theft also don't bring any value to your business where other expenses do, or should. Buying textbooks for students may be a necessary and planned expense, budgeted into the financial planning process. Ideally, the purchase will show a return, in terms of better education for students. Or take the case of a business that purchases $50,000 in advertising. Advertising expenses bring back a greater return that increases sales. Replacing stolen property does nothing to advance or help your business.

## Making It Happen

We have discussed many reasons why security should be important to a business from a basic operating perspective. So far, we have not looked at the impact of violent crime on victims, coworkers, public relations, staff retention, or the related liability. Violence in the workplace will be covered more in depth in Chapter 8. Hopefully, without dredging up that kind of fear mongering, you can already see the benefit of integrating security into the workplace to make it safer for employees and even protect the very survival of the organization.

## EXAMPLES OF SECURITY CONSIDERATIONS

Checklist of security considerations for operational decisions:

1. Will the proposal change access to the facility? Will there be new hours of operation, open doors, or changes in staff hours?
2. Will the proposal move, add, or impact any critical operations? Don't forget to include the impact of outsourcing.
3. Will the staff, visitors, vendors, or customers have the same expectation of safety, and will the organization be able to maintain that level? For example, for a new building or addition, will the same type of burglar alarm or access control system, video surveillance, etc. be in place?
4. Will there be additional risks in terms of valuables as a result of a change? Cash handling, for example, could lead to a higher risk of robbery.
5. Will critical information, such as customer lists or physical documents, be exposed?
6. Are there changes in the surrounding environment or neighborhood that could change the risk posture? Are there increased crime reports by the local police? For this information, check and see who in your business looks into matters or concerns with the local police department.

There are many, many variations of the types of questions that could be asked. However, there are two critical items to remember: (1) that security and safety could be changed or affected by operational decisions, and (2) any changes must be evaluated in order to maintain a safe workplace.

As an organizational leader, there are a number of ways that you can change corporate culture to make security a key business process. Perhaps the most important step is for leaders to set an example, demonstrating the importance of security practices. Managers should follow basic steps themselves, such as locking doors, safeguarding important documents, and protecting property, such as laptops. Imagine a school or company that has all visitors check in and wear a visitor badge on the premises. If a CEO or a school principal is not willing to stop and talk to a person wandering the halls without a visitor badge, will other employees or teachers do it? Who will then? If you, as a leader, do not practice fundamental security safeguards, then you cannot expect your employees to do any better.

Part of building organizational awareness will be through staff training and education. Key policies should be reviewed by employees and contractors on an annual basis, and new employee orientation should include security topics to introduce important elements of the protection plan to all incoming employees.

Another key component will be to assign security responsibilities to one individual or dedicated group. Official job responsibilities and duties should be listed to ensure that someone in the organization is taking responsibility or acting as the security representative for the organization. The individual should attend training specific to security and keep up to date in the industry, as any employee would do in other disciplines or areas of expertise.

So you may or may not be in a role to authorize or make operational decisions related to security. Then how do you get the powers that be to integrate security and safety concerns?

---

## IDEAS TO CREATE SECURITY AWARENESS

1. Newsletter:
   a. Monthly or even weekly
   b. Beware, this takes time and commitment
2. Security training during new employee orientation
3. Process to report and document crimes on the premises
4. Annual refresher on security-related policies and procedures
5. Speaking of, have policies on security topics in place:
   a. Weapons and contraband
   b. Access control
   c. Visitor management
   d. Cash handling
   e. Robbery prevention
   f. Background screening for new employees
   g. Lockdown process
   h. Security guard force management
   i. Crime reporting
   j. Workplace violence and employees involved in domestic violence (DV) situations
   k. Travel security
   l. Security risk assessment (annual)
   m. Security management plan and annual review
   n. Video and alarm management
   o. Alarm response
   p. Crime response
   q. Threat assessment
   r. Bomb threat
   s. Active shooter

*(Continued)*

---

### IDEAS TO CREATE
### SECURITY AWARENESS *(cont'd)*

    **t.** Facility security orders (for security officers)
    **u.** Employee ID badges
    **v.** Drug and alcohol abuse
    **w.** Protection of proprietary information and IT devices
**6.** Monthly security metrics, such as crime on campus, for senior leaders
**7.** Quarterly reports to C-level and board of directors on security risks and potential impact on business operations
**8.** Conduct security drills, such as access penetration, or have a "suspicious" person on premises to test reporting and response of staff

---

You may not be a decision maker, but you can definitely be an influencer and use persuasion to build focus on security and safety. Many organizations have employee groups or councils that meet to review and address any concerns with management. This could be a great forum to start bringing up issues or questions. Once a complaint has been aired, there are several benefits. One is that it serves as notice of a problem, meaning that there is now foreseeability. This could create liability for a company if the problem is not addressed through reasonable steps. Think of your workplace—who tracks or monitors potential safety issues? Does the company have a way to easily pass on information about defective locks or malfunctioning lights? One simple suggestion would be to set up an e-mail account, such as safey@yourcompany.com for employees to pass on potential problems, whether about lights out or known crime in the area (Figure 1.2).

Another benefit is that once an issue is raised, you'll find that others have noticed the same problem and had not brought it up. Or better yet, those others have more information. If you bring up that you've noticed empty liquor bottles near the back door, you will probably hear from someone who works late or comes in early about a group of transients who have been camping out in the area. You've found more information and another witness to a potential problem and can better coordinate with the police to take appropriate enforcement action.

Perhaps the most important benefit of raising security issues is simply that security issues are being raised—that is to say, concerns are evaluated, discussed, and action items addressed. By bringing up issues, you are raising the awareness of security and safety issues within your organization. The National Institute of Standards and Technology (NIST) defines IT security awareness as the focusing of attention on security. That is exactly what has been accomplished by raising issues, questions, and concerns.

FIGURE 1.2 A corporate newsletter on security topics is a great way to keep key stake-holders and employees informed about the risks.

## CONCLUSION

When it comes to creating a safer workplace, whether it is a church, small business, large corporation, school, hospital, or factory, the first step is to increase your security stance. There are many ways to do that, but the main point is to increase awareness of security issues by giving it proper support, importance, and considering security a regular part of the business function. Only then will your company really be safer and ready to move to the ideas in the following chapters.

## BUSINESS KARATE BELT LEVELS

Each chapter will include a chart to test your business karate skill level. When a karate student obtains a black belt, he has passed all the requirements for each previous belt level. To get your business black belt, follow the recommendations for each color or belt level all the way up to the black belt.

Test your company's karate belt level in the discipline of awareness/stance. If your organization meets each belt level in Figure 1.3 and all the standards of the lower belts, you have then achieved that color level.

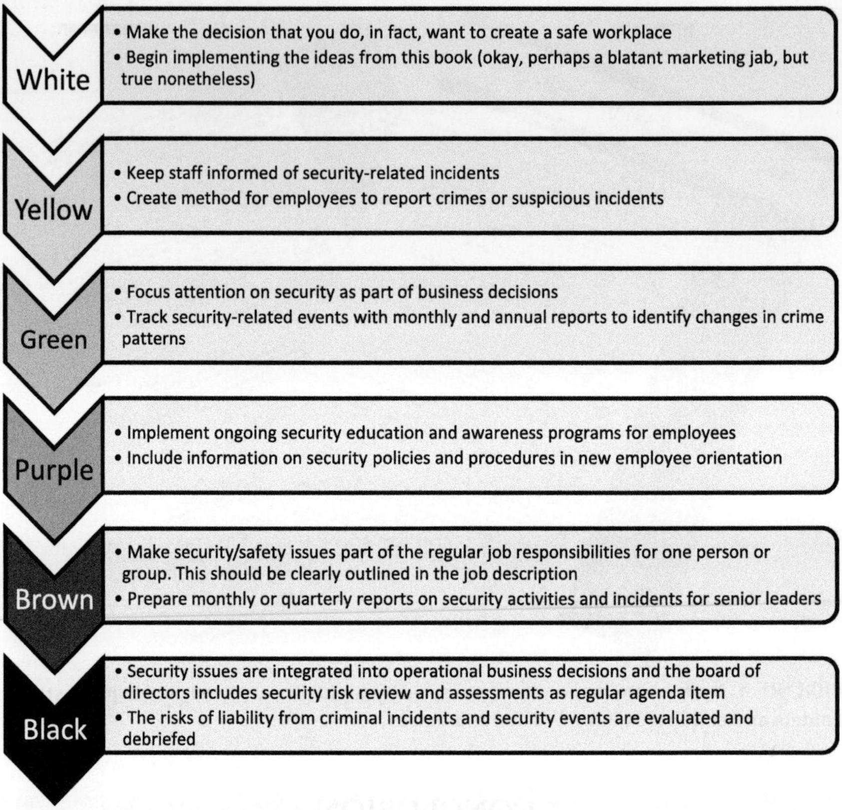

**White**
- Make the decision that you do, in fact, want to create a safe workplace
- Begin implementing the ideas from this book (okay, perhaps a blatant marketing jab, but true nonetheless)

**Yellow**
- Keep staff informed of security-related incidents
- Create method for employees to report crimes or suspicious incidents

**Green**
- Focus attention on security as part of business decisions
- Track security-related events with monthly and annual reports to identify changes in crime patterns

**Purple**
- Implement ongoing security education and awareness programs for employees
- Include information on security policies and procedures in new employee orientation

**Brown**
- Make security/safety issues part of the regular job responsibilities for one person or group. This should be clearly outlined in the job description
- Prepare monthly or quarterly reports on security activities and incidents for senior leaders

**Black**
- Security issues are integrated into operational business decisions and the board of directors includes security risk review and assessments as regular agenda item
- The risks of liability from criminal incidents and security events are evaluated and debriefed

FIGURE 1.3    What is your belt level?

# Further Reading

Employee Theft Still Costing Business, May 15, 1999. Inc.com. Retrieved from www.inc.com/articles/1999/05/13731.html (accessed 17.06.06.).

Wilson, M., Hash, J. National Institute of Standards and Technology, October 2003. Building an Information Technology Security Awareness and Training Program. NIST Special Publication 800-50, Gaithersburg, MD.

# 2

# Developing a Security Focus: Identifying Critical Assets

## BREAKING STICKS AND BRICKS

We've all seen it. Maybe on TV or at a live demonstration. But at some point, you've seen a karate expert square off against a stack of boards or blocks of concrete. She will get set in position, take a couple of slow motion practice swings, and then with a look of grim determination and one swift movement, the object is broken by her hand, foot, or maybe even head. Ouch! How did she do that? The answer is focus. The black belt is able to channel or focus his or her entire body's energy into one point. Delivering that power, with speed, requires focus. Failure to use that focus could mean injury. Hesitation or lack of confidence could mess up or distract the martial artist's focus, causing failure in delivering the necessary power to the right point, and then he or she could injure themself by striking a hard and now immovable object. Done correctly, you get broken boards and smashed bricks. Done incorrectly, you get broken hands and smashed body parts. Karate students practice focus on objects to build confidence and to understand the kind of power and strength they can summon against an adversary should they be forced to defend themselves. The same focus and power can be applied to blocks that will stop an attack cold. These demonstrations and exercises are obviously not designed to ward off attacks by wayward boards and misbehaving blocks but are about building confidence in the ability to focus all that power to one spot.

Organizations or businesses need to develop their security focus in order to channel or focus their protection or security resources to the right location(s). This focus will limit the resources (okay, money), that are invested in security programs or efforts that don't really protect what is important to the business.

The first step to building a security focus is to identify critical assets. Only then can a business learn how to shift their focus into preserving its vital functions. To help identify critical assets, assets will be classified into one of five categories or levels. This helps break down the process so it is not so overwhelming and will help focus on key areas.

Once the organization's assets have been identified and prioritized, you can look at the threats that put those assets at risk. The last step is to combine the assets and threats to those assets and calculate the vulnerability or damage that could impact the business. Think of the acronym A-T-V to remember the process: Assets – Threats – Vulnerabilities.

## BREAKING UP YOUR ASSETS

So that brings us back to assets. Where to begin? How do you start? Everything that goes into your organization is presumably important, or more likely, critical, especially in tough economic times. If it weren't, it would have been cut or eliminated, right?

In order to prioritize and sort all the assets in your company, we will sort critical assets into one of the following five groups (Figure 2.1).

### Level I Assets

The first level of assets is probably the most obvious, but then maybe not. Picture yourself walking into the CEO's office and asking him which is more important, people or things. He will say people, of course. If not,

## Enterprise asset classifications

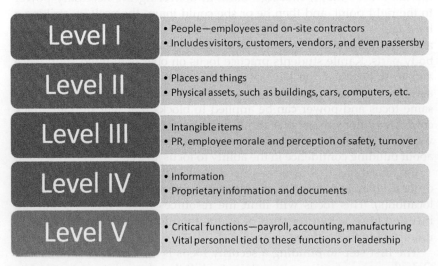

| Level I | • People—employees and on-site contractors<br>• Includes visitors, customers, vendors, and even passersby |
| Level II | • Places and things<br>• Physical assets, such as buildings, cars, computers, etc. |
| Level III | • Intangible items<br>• PR, employee morale and perception of safety, turnover |
| Level IV | • Information<br>• Proprietary information and documents |
| Level V | • Critical functions—payroll, accounting, manufacturing<br>• Vital personnel tied to these functions or leadership |

FIGURE 2.1   This figure demonstrates the breakdown of assets to help with the security risk assessment.

you might want to consider looking for another employer. So, your fol-low-up question will be: Why do we spend so much more time, money, and effort on information technology security than on physical or person-nel security? The answer to that question will tell you a lot about the vul-nerability of IT assets compared to the risks to people or physical property. It may be due to the number of IT attacks or the critical role that IT plays in your business. It could be because everyone talks about IT security a lot more than about staff security. This type of analysis will be covered more in depth in the next two chapters.

Hopefully, your organization values its employees. The cost of turn-over, finding a replacement, advertising openings, time spent interview-ing candidates after reviewing professional resumes, and then, of course, training time and loss of productivity can be very high. The United States Department of Labor estimates that the cost is one-third of the employee's annual salary!

So the organization's people will go into the Level I assets. Level I includes everyone, every person who is directly connected to the organi-zation. This should include the employees, of course, but also any ven-dors or contractors who come onto the property. Certainly, the security of visitors and customers is vital as well. Some organizations, such as schools, hospitals, or retail stores, will have more visitors and customers on site than employees. Even someone passing by the physical location might be considered when thinking of people assets. That person could be a potential customer, depending on your operations, or could become a potential plaintiff in litigation if you do not maintain a safe environ-ment. For example, ignoring burned-out lights or signs of someone hid-ing in bushes on your property could be what prompts a robber or rapist to use your site as the scene of their crime. The victim may decide that the business ignored the warning signs, causing them harm. Some states even allow unauthorized trespassers, including burglars, to sue property owners in premise liability cases. Right or wrong, fair or unfair, that is the environment in which you do business. So it is important to consider anyone who may touch your business or property as a potential asset.

## Level II Assets

People need to have a place to work and the tools to do their jobs. So that leads to the next level of asset classification—buildings, computers, manufacturing equipment, telephones, desks—all the basic property of the business. Think of all the nouns, except people, that make up a business: places and things. These assets make up the Level II category. Many of these may even be listed on the company's balance sheet. However, this list should take a deeper look. Even areas such as parking lots are something of an asset and certainly one of the locations where employees or customers are present. And their property, their cars, are present and should be considered an asset of the organization. If an employee's car is broken into or stolen, there will be a definite loss of productivity as focus shifts from normal work to worry about safety issues. A customer dealing with the same loss will likely never return. In that sense customers are an asset beyond the obvious human factor.

## Level III Assets

Level III assets are less obvious ones. These are often intangible assets—they are not seen or even going to show up on a balance sheet, but they are extremely important to the organization. This is the company's image in the eyes of the public and more specifically in the eyes of your customers. This is your public relations and defines your company's brand and how it is seen in the marketplace.

Unfortunately, it is not difficult to think of firms that have found themselves in a situation, often avoidable, that has severely damaged the firm's reputation. In 2010 British Petroleum (BP) was operating an off-shore oil drill. There was an explosion that killed 11 employees and the oil well was compromised, leaking millions of gallons of oil into the Gulf of Mexico. Due to the widespread damage caused by the spill and the delays in stopping the spill, the extensive media coverage severely damaged BP's public image. The company faced fines and will likely face lawsuits for years to come.

As you can see, it is not only security risks that may affect an organization and its reputation. Throughout history, some names have been associated with a tragedy or disaster and will forever be linked to it. I doubt another ship will be named the Titanic. In terms of security, Columbine High School is synonymous with active shooters in schools.

## Level IV Assets

The fourth level of assets to consider is information. Information technology or IT security gets a lot of attention. Everywhere you turn, someone is waiting to sell you the latest service to protect you from identity theft. Estimates for losses caused by identity theft vary depending on what crimes are included, but by some accounts were as high as $21 billion in 2012. As far as organizations go, we've all heard the stories of large companies, often financial firms or banks, that have lost millions of people's identifying info at a time. In many cases, the information losses could have been avoided with very simple, but effective, security measures. Laptops left in plain view in parked cars or unlocked offices are a great temptation to thieves and are often not well protected. Numerous data losses have come about through these easy-to-avoid mistakes.

The *New York Times* ran an interesting story about a laptop stolen from a car in Washington, DC. The laptop belonged to a NASA employee and was password protected, however, the files were not encrypted and the Social Security numbers, dates of birth, and, in some cases, background investigation information for about 10,000 employees were on the laptop's hard drive. The NASA website claims that the laptop was hidden in the car, but does not go into further details about the vehicle break-in. NASA arranged for credit monitoring from a private firm for the impacted employees, certainly at a cost to the agency (and, ultimately, taxpayers).

Not just large corporations have this risk. Enterprises of any size have information that can be used by ID thieves. Some modern burglars no longer seek out jewelry hidden in underwear drawers or cash but rather look for financial or ID information that can be used to access far more.

It is now less common, but still surprising, to see businesses that include the entire customer credit card number on receipts. A common burglary into a cash register provides not only whatever cash is there, but also personal checks and credit card numbers. That slip of paper could lead to an online shopping expedition. For online merchants, it is equally surprising that there are still some that do not have buyers confirm the billing address or security numbers on the back of the card.

Think of the information available on your customer's checks: full name, address, signatures, bank name, routing number, and account number. Often the ID and phone numbers are written on checks as well. A thief can acid wash the original ink off the check and change whom to pay it to as well as the amount. Or the information can be used to create new blank checks to be passed at other locations. The checks in the cash register are another form of jackpot for thieves.

Beyond the cash register, a thief could find more information that is useful. Some offices, such as those of physicians, have files with names, addresses, billing information, as well as Social Security numbers. There is also the risk of compromising private medical information, creating a violation of the Health Insurance Portability and Accountability Act (HIPAA). The fines for a HIPAA violation can vary, but in one case, a hospital received a civil penalty of $4.3 million! Certainly, with potential fines like that, any organization that handles any type of patient health information should be extremely cautious in how that information is handled and stored.

During a security review, one health care organization had boxes of perfect information (from a criminal perspective), including credit card numbers, sitting in an unsecured area that was accessible to anyone looking.

Some states are considering laws that require companies to provide information on how customers can protect themselves from ID theft after a data loss. The Federal Trade Commission website provides a sample letter that can be used by firms as well. However, these after-incident responses do not necessarily help a company retain customers or protect the company's public reputation. The loss of current and potential customers could be devastating to a firm, one from which it may never recover.

Information can be in two formats: hard copy (printouts, paperwork, etc.) or soft copy (electronic or digital files). The soft copies may be the easiest to overlook despite the efforts of IT departments to protect networks and databases. Many companies not only allow, but expect, employees to use their own computing devices: bring your own device. Tablets or laptops, even smart phones, brought from home become storage sites for valuable business intelligence. These devices may not have the same encryption that a company-owned computer might have. In fact, there has been an increase in identity theft related to information garnered from cell phones. Often, they are not protected with passwords and are connected to online banking accounts, e-mail, documents, and online merchants, making them an easy target for identity thieves or even corporate competitors.

Often, people will leave valuables, including laptop computers, in plain view in parked cars, making attractive targets. Not only do you lose the computer but also the data on the PC if it is not properly protected. You may think that your information is not important, not like a bank that could lose hundreds of thousands of names, Social Security numbers, and addresses at one time. Right? What if you are a small businessman, like an accountant? Your clients' records may be easily accessible to the thief. Sometimes, a suspect who steals a laptop will even contact the manufacturer in an attempt to get the password reset. What is on your laptop or flash drive? Is the laptop or drive password protected or encrypted to keep the data secure in case it is lost or stolen? You can begin to see how physical security and IT security become intertwined.

Think of the other information you keep handy for work, either paper copies or digital versions. What would a copy of a business contract mean to a competitor? Could that be used in a competitive bid process? Pricing strategies could be invaluable in the wrong hands. Contracts or contact lists could identify suppliers or vendors, and any of those things could be used against your company.

## Level V Assets

Level V assets are the business-critical functions necessary to thrive. These are the processes needed for the organization to continue to operate and survive. One example would be payroll for any organization with paid employees. Like it or not, we all need our paychecks. One business owner told me how an employee had embezzled from him and cleaned out his bank account. He then couldn't pay his employees for their work. His business was auto repair, and without employees he could not provide service to all of his customers. So in addition to losing his funds (a level II asset), the theft cost him a key business process, loss of employees, and loss or dissatisfaction of customers—all of which have associated costs as well. Employee turnover costs money, to advertise or post job openings, time to interview and select employees, and advertising to bring back or replace customers, etc.

When you think of the business-critical functions, it is easy to get caught up in thinking of level I and II assets, for instance, the buildings we depend on to carry out those functions or the building that houses manufacturing equipment. But many of these functions could be carried out elsewhere, in another location. This really gets into the topic of business continuity, which is covered in Chapter 10.

This level of asset identification also includes your critical personnel. Again, this ties into continuity of operations. However, it must be identified at this stage in order to build your mitigation plans down the road.

Every role or position should have a backup person—someone who has been cross-trained, knows where the necessary information is located, and knows what needs to be done. This isn't just about good security, but is a good business practice. What if your top employee—the one who handles everything—takes a new job, is incapacitated, or becomes ill? Who can fill those shoes?

Your organization should have a succession plan for leadership in case they are not available or are incapacitated. Start by looking at the top down. If you are an incorporated organization, what do the bylaws state about replacing the board? That possibility is often overlooked but certainly not impossible. You should have a documented succession plan to maintain the appropriate leadership during unexpected interim vacancies.

When talking about board positions, it is easy to think of only large, publically traded companies. However, this level of leadership can be found at many smaller organizations or nonprofit groups. Think of a school board or a church board, or even the board of a homeowner's association (HOA). I was involved in a situation where the entire board for a small HOA resigned following a dispute with homeowners. The story was featured on local and national news. The bylaws did not address the entire board quitting or resigning, leading to confusion and further arguments about how the positions would be filled until the next election.

The board is not the only leadership asset to consider. All levels of leadership need to be considered and the responsibilities held by each. This should be done in conjunction with the critical functions listed as level V assets. The people who make those operations possible need to be considered as leadership assets. They should develop backups who can handle operations in case they are out of commission.

Most of us want to feel valued at our jobs and would like to think that we play a key role. Be tactful in your approach to identifying the roles that are essential versus nonessential, and be clear about how you came to that decision. For example, the business could not exist past the first employee pay date without someone with authority to access bank accounts and make sure that payroll is met. Developing those backup personnel could be part of a program to develop new leaders and help employees develop and move up through an organization. Leadership development is much more than a security function or an exercise in business continuity. It can be beneficial in improving skills among more employees. It may help when a key leader is on vacation or leaves for another role and there is a trained individual who can step in during the interim, one who knows where key information is stored and understands what needs to be done and when.

In the TV game show "Who Wants to Be a Millionaire" contestants could use one of several help options to answer correctly. One way was to ask the audience, which often resulted in the correct answer. The same type of approach can be used to identify and rank your key assets. One method that can be used to capture or funnel the knowledge of your audience or work group is by using the Delphi technique.

A facilitator can use the Delphi technique to get feedback from different individuals in an organization to build a ranking of critical assets. Although the name sounds old, reminiscent of ancient Greece, the Delphi technique is a relatively new concept developed by the U.S. military and is often used to build consensus.

Now, a word of warning: the larger the organization is, the more complex and time consuming this exercise could become. To keep it manageable, break down the process. Use the five levels of assets identified here and set up a diverse group for each category level. You will want to keep the groups relatively small, say about 10 people at most, from a broad range of areas of the organization.

The first step will be to list the assets in the assigned category. Members of the group should all be encouraged to create their list and share with the group. The facilitator can help narrow down or focus the group. Once the list is complete, the group will need to rank the impact that the loss of that asset would have on the business. This ranking by impact of loss will be important later when factoring in threats and vulnerabilities. It is okay if the group ties two assets in terms of impact or value. You can rank by any means you want, such as scoring 1–5 with 5 being the most critical or

| Evaluating and assessing critical assets | | | | | | | | | |
|---|---|---|---|---|---|---|---|---|---|
| Impact scoring criteria - 1–5 | | | | | | | | | |

1 - Minimal level of disruption or impact
2 - Low impact, low risk of loss
3 - Medium level of $ loss, short-term disruption of services, risk to ongoing operations

4 - High cost due to loss, serious or long-term disruption of business operations, high risk of losing revenue
5 - Imminent risk of harm to human life

| Level 1 | | Level 2 | | Level 3 | | Level 4 | | Level 5 | |
|---|---|---|---|---|---|---|---|---|---|
| People | Impact | Property | Impact | Intangible | Impact | Information | Impact | Critical functions | Impact |
| Employees | 5 | Buildings | | Company reputation | | Customer lists | | Corporate leadership | |
| Hours worked? | | Cash | | Public relations | | Pricing information | | Payroll | |
| Locations? | | Goods | | Marketing position/brand | | Supplier Infor | | Accounting | |
| Customers | 5 | Equipment | | Staff perception | | | Contracts | Supply chain | |
| Vendors | 5 | | Manufacturing | Morale | | | Pricing | IT access | |
| Contractors | 5 | | School | Employee productivity | | Business partner contracts | | Critical incident command | |
| Visitors | 5 | | Construction | Turnover | | Leases | | Contract management | |
| Students | 5 | | Medical | | | Patents | | Communications | |
| Patients | 5 | | Pharmacy supplies | | | Trademarks | | | |
| Delivery personnel | 5 | Parking lots | | | | Marketing plans | | | |
| | | Company vehicles | | | | Strategic plans | | | |
| | | Personal computers | | | | Financial statements | | | |
| | | Servers — physical database | | | | | | | |
| | | Furniture | | | | | | | |
| | | Chemicals | | | | | | | |
| | | Labs | | | | | | | |

© Eric Smith 2013

FIGURE 2.2 A chart showing different categories of assets, along with the potential impact of damage or loss to the asset, can be a very useful starting tool for a risk assessment.

having the most impact. Or you could rank on a scale of 1–100 and think of the score as a percentage. For example, the network server might be scored high at 95%, as in there is a 95% likelihood that the business will fail without the server within 5 days. The length of time without an asset is an important consideration. It could even be the scoring measure—the less time that a company can do without a process, the higher the score (Figure 2.2).

## CHOOSING A SCORING METHOD

We've all come across many different types of surveys and rankings at one point or another. Sometimes, a survey may rank results between 1 and 10 or up to 100. Some scales run from 1 to 7. Each has advantages and disadvantages. In terms of scoring for a security risk assessment, I like using a 1–5 scale. With a 1–10 or 1–100 scale, I've noticed that people have different ideas. Some think of 70 as a near-failing "grade," whereas others see a 5 or 50 as average. This creates a situation where people use vastly different numbers for the same criteria. The 1–7 scale helps with some of that outlook, but is easy for people to use a middle-of-the-road score. If something is high, it may get a 7 or a 6, or vice versa, if scoring low. This can still create some variation in the results. A 1–5 scale takes away some of the middle ground and can help narrow down exactly how the group rates an element. No matter which scoring system you choose, it is important to clearly define the scoring criteria to help keep everyone in the group on the same page.

Obviously, the more complex an organization the more involved this process will become. However, when facilitated well, it can be a great tool in providing qualitative data to use in protecting your business.

# CONCLUSION

No one likes to think that her unit or work is not valuable or important. It is critical to remember that this process is for identifying security risks and to help an organization survive or avoid a major loss or emergency. It is something like a snowy day. During a snowstorm, businesses and emergency services often tell everyone that nonessential personnel should stay home. That doesn't mean that your work doesn't need you, but you just might not be needed that day in those circumstances. It is the same here. What loss of a key asset will hurt the business the most in a short time frame? Presumably, all the functions and people contribute to the day-to-day operations, but some are needed immediately for the business to survive.

This process of identifying and classifying the organization's assets, even before coming up with a score, can be eye opening. Certain critical functions, people, or items will become a focal point where the value and potential impact was overlooked in the past. Even the company's brand or marketing position is examined in a different light. This exercise is a great opportunity to look at the organization afresh and gain new perspective into what makes the business tick. And it is absolutely vital to creating a safe workplace and laying the groundwork for the next steps in the security risk assessment model.

# BUSINESS KARATE BELT LEVEL

Test your company's karate belt level in the discipline of awareness/stance. If your organization meets each belt level and all the standards of the lower belts as seen in Figure 2.3, you have then achieved that color level.

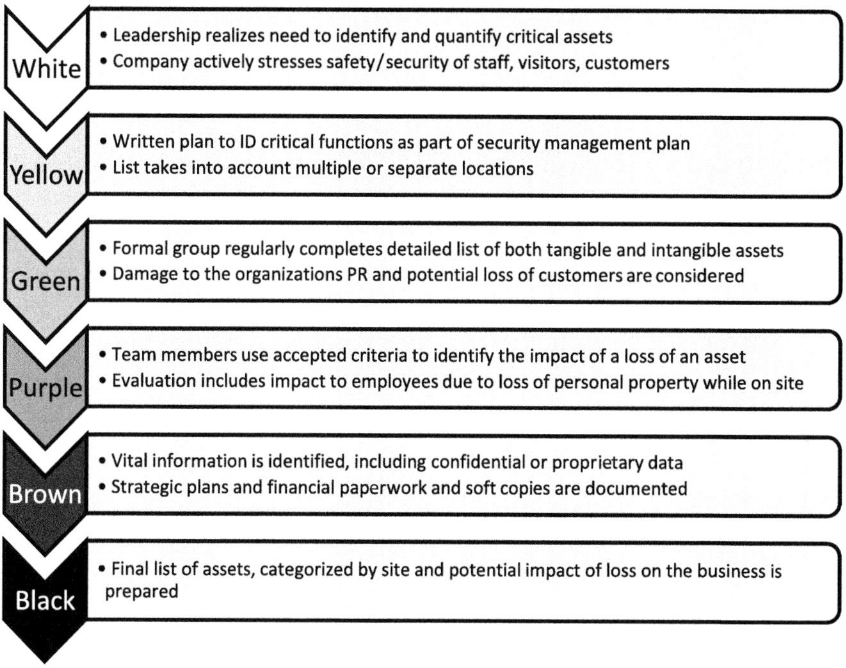

**White**
- Leadership realizes need to identify and quantify critical assets
- Company actively stresses safety/security of staff, visitors, customers

**Yellow**
- Written plan to ID critical functions as part of security management plan
- List takes into account multiple or separate locations

**Green**
- Formal group regularly completes detailed list of both tangible and intangible assets
- Damage to the organizations PR and potential loss of customers are considered

**Purple**
- Team members use accepted criteria to identify the impact of a loss of an asset
- Evaluation includes impact to employees due to loss of personal property while on site

**Brown**
- Vital information is identified, including confidential or proprietary data
- Strategic plans and financial paperwork and soft copies are documented

**Black**
- Final list of assets, categorized by site and potential impact of loss on the business is prepared

FIGURE 2.3   What is your belt level?

## Further Reading

Health and Human Services, February 22, 2011. HHS Imposes a $4.3 Million Civil Money Penalty for Violations of the HIPAA Privacy Rule. HHS Press Office, Washington, DC. Retrieved from: http://www.hhs.gov/news/press/2011pres/02/20110222a.html (accessed 28.11.12.).

Javelin Strategy and Research, February 20, 2013. More than 12 Million Identity Fraud Victims in 2012 According to Latest Javelin Strategy & Research Report. Pleasanton, CA. Retrieved from: https://www.javelinstrategy.com/news/1387/92/1 (accessed 21.11.13.).

Singer, N., November 28, 2012. Losing in Court, and to Laptop Thieves, in a Battle with NASA over Private Data. NY Times. Retrieved from: http://www.nytimes.com/2012/11/29/technology/ex-nasa-scientists-data-fears-come-true.html?ref=business&_r=0 (accessed 28.11.12.).

# Building Skills with Basics: Learning to Identify Threats

## KARATE SCHOOL

Imagine a karate student who only learns one move. Maybe he learns to block a right straight punch. What would happen if he were to face an opponent who was much better rounded? Unless the opponent happened to do nothing but throw a right punch, our one-trick wonder would certainly lose—badly. Not only that, but the practice sessions would become very boring.

The successful karate student needs to train and prepare for a variety of attacks. One of the fundamental ways to build skills is through practice and repetition of the basics: blocks, punches, and kicks. A good instructor should prepare a student to protect himself from the most likely attacks. If the goal is real-life self-defense, then the student will learn to respond to attacks from any direction. He will continually train on the right way to defend and block various attack—not just one, but many, as well as counterattacks.

The martial art learning regime is built on constant practice against different attacks: strikes, grabs, punches, holds, and kicks. These attacks can be from different directions and even multiple opponents. Practice also means throwing lots of punches and kicks as a counterattack and not just in one in direction. Karate students learn to defend against threats from many directions: to the sides, front, back, or a combination. Through karate forms, or kata, students learn how to protect themselves from threats coming from any direction; it's a 360-degree approach to defense.

## THE BUSINESS CONNECTION

Organizations are no different from self-defense students. An organization needs to be prepared to face a wide range of hazards. I once read of a study in which one-third of businesses that close due to an emergency or disaster will never reopen. Larger businesses are not immune either. Pan American Airlines, one of the first passenger airlines in history, went bankrupt after more than 60 years of service, in large part due to the terrorist bombing of Flight 103, which crashed in Lockerbie, Scotland.

Emergencies or disasters can come from almost any direction, influence the business in a multiple of ways, and may be something completely unpredictable. Just as a self-defense fighter cannot predict every variation of every possible attack, an organization cannot predict every event and detail every single item that can be damaging. The fighter will practice and train for different attacks, including multiple opponents. However, it is impossible to predict exactly where each opponent will stand and position themselves or that the attack will always start with a right punch from the attacker on the left, for example, followed by a left sidekick from the center opponent.

Instead, the training focuses on the basic skills of protecting oneself from common attacks and developing the ability to defend more-advanced attacks or combinations. To take it a step further, if you are learning to defend yourself, you need to know what to protect. Obviously, certain parts of your body are more vulnerable or exposed to harm than others, and different types of attacks may pose different risks. A finger poking you in the chest may be annoying, make you angry, and signal escalating violence, but is not really harmful in and of itself. However, the same finger strike to an eye could be debilitating, taking you out of the fight.

Martial arts teach how to block any kick or punch that is going to cause harm and also how to block just that and not overdo it. Blocking a punch by knocking the fist away from your face is sufficient, but to overblock and knock the punch a foot away will leave you more exposed to a follow-up strike. The point is that each threat must be understood, including to the extent of what damage could be done. An organization needs to prevent the damage or impact (as in blocking the punch aside) but does not need to go in excess in terms of protection (i.e., overblocking an attack). That creates higher than necessary expenses and dilutes attention from the real and imminent attacks.

Organizations need to develop responses to common or most-likely scenarios. It will become apparent that many problems will have similar or even the same responses. Imagine an office space. What would happen if a sprinkler head broke? That could mean that a portion of the building may be evacuated and business will have to continue without those affected sections. The same could happen if a nearby spill of a hazardous material forces the same office to evacuate.

## WHAT IS THE RISK?

Naturally, one of the first steps of self-defense is to identify those things that can go wrong. The critical piece here is to clearly identify what those things are—the threats or hazards that can jeopardize or harm your enterprise.

As you prepare to list the threats facing you, it is important to keep in mind that what is considered a threat must be able to harm your operations. If you run a company in Colorado, then hurricanes may not be of much concern, unless you depend on parts shipped through a port in the path of a hurricane. If this were the case, hurricanes could have an impact on your operations and process.

To help with threat identification, focus on the assets you identified in Chapter 2. Those are the areas and items that could most impact your business, and the hazards that threaten those critical elements should get most of your focus and attention.

## BREAKING DOWN THREATS

Hazards or threats can come in many shapes and sizes. To start the process of breaking down or identifying threats, you must understand the types and sources of potential problems.

Threats typically fall into three categories: natural, accidents, and deliberate or criminal. Natural events are those "acts of God" such as hurricanes, tornadoes, blizzards, storms, earthquakes, avalanches, mudslides, and wildfires (not including arson, of course). Accidents are just that—accidents. These unplanned incidents occur through negligence, faulty equipment, random events, or just plain bad luck. These could include truck or train accidents that result in chemical spills. A bridge collapse or hazardous material leakage at a factory are other possible accidents. The last main category is deliberate or criminal acts, such as crime or terrorism.

Deliberate or criminal acts (sometimes referred to as man-made events) can be broken down further. Violent crime is obviously a serious threat, one that could have a huge impact on an organization. The loss of a single employee could have an impact that lasts for years. Aside from the loss of a coworker, friend, or colleague, there is the damage to morale and employee stress. This could lead to increased turnover of valuable team members, as well as directly affect productivity. Lawsuits and bad publicity are additional risks.

Property crime is actually much more prevalent in our society (Figure 3.1). Depending on the industry, crime such as theft can directly reduce your profit

FIGURE 3.1    **Graffiti threatens how customers and employees see the business.** It may also indicate deeper threats, such as gang activity or drug dealing in the area.

margin. A retail store with an 8% profit margin effectively drops to 6% if there is a 2% loss rate. Identifying those crime threats is critical to an organization interested in self-defense.

The last subcategory of deliberate acts is terrorism. After September 2001, terrorism moved to the center of the threat stage and received more attention than most other hazards. Is terrorism a real concern? Without a doubt it has become a very large industry in and of itself with more than one trillion dollars spent on homeland security, according to a study cited in the *Economist*. Certainly, it is a hazard, and a major terror attack could have an impact on your business even if not directly targeted. For example, banks were affected after September 11 when airplane traffic was grounded. Checks could not be sent to the bank holding the account, delaying payments and transfers around the world, which led to reform within the industry. Banks passed the Check 21 act, allowing banks to use digitized check images in lieu of the paper copies. This is one of the reasons that you no longer get paper copies of checks with your statements but are able to view the digital versions online at many banks and credit unions.

## YOUR THREATS

Threats can come in any shape or size. The significant ones are those that affect your business, even forcing it to shut down. The first challenge is to identify those hazards. All organizations should do some form of a hazard vulnerability assessment (HVA) or a security risk assessment—or both ideally as the two overlap but do not cover exactly the same threats. Deciding on the scope of the HVA is the first step. If your company operates across several locations, are you going to include all sites or break it down by locations? How in depth will you evaluate the enterprise?

This is where the prioritized list of critical assets will be helpful. The more critical or necessary the asset or process, then the HVA should be more in depth to be effective.

## ARE YOU A TARGET? USE THE 3 V'S TO FIND OUT

What do crooks look for? Why do burglars pick one house over another? What does a terrorist look for in a target? What do ordinary criminals and terrorists have in common for that matter?

Crooks and terrorists may not be so different after all. No matter how evil their intent, he must still select a target in order to carry out their plan. Robbery suspects first look for the loot before planning their heists. Burglars look for evidence that no one is home, and terrorists want a big bang (literally) for their buck – high publicity.

One well-known bank robber is credited with the statement that he robbed banks because "that is where the money is." A robber wants to gain something – that is the whole point of the crime. They want to make sure that the quick win is on hand. Many are feeding drug habits, gambling addiction, or alcohol. With these kinds of cravings or obsessions, there is no time to waste. They are looking for something of value that can be turned around quickly for cash or traded for drugs.

1. **Value** – The goal is some kind of gain or value. For a terrorist, the value may be high publicity, such as a famous building or critical infrastructure or large number of potential victims. For crooks, it may just be something worth stealing.

Favorite targets of robbers are convenience stores and taxi drivers. It is not too hard to figure out why – both are easy to find and convenient to the crook. In fact, two recent suspects in Denver have called the taxis to their location in order to rob the driver. It doesn't get much more convenient than that – the victim comes to the crook. These are examples of highly visible targets. Terrorists like visibility too, but in a slightly different way. They want a target that will generate a lot of publicity and garner their group the visibility and attention. Blowing up a bomb in the middle of the desert will not get that attention, as compared to blowing up a crowded nightclub or embassy.

2. **Visible** – The target must be visible; crooks have to know it is there and an attack must generate the kind of visibility a terrorist wants. Schools, landmarks, or crowded venues will offer that kind of media attention and visibility.

*(Continued)*

---

### ARE YOU A TARGET? USE THE 3 V'S TO FIND OUT *(cont'd)*

Of course, the crook must be able to achieve their nefarious goal or at least have a hope of it. The famous gold depository at Fort Knox would be an example of something that is highly visible, of high value, but with little chance of success. A terrorist might love to steal a missile from the military, but the chances of getting to it are nil. There is virtually no vulnerability.

3. **Vulnerable** – The victim must be susceptible to attack to be a worthwhile target. That is why burglars look for homes with unlocked doors or muggers wait for victims in areas of poor lighting. There is easy access and the element of surprise to help the attacker. Terrorists also need targets that are open to attack. On 9-11, it was relatively easy for terrorists to hijack planes and fly them into the WTC. Today, many of the vulnerabilities that the terrorists exploited have been eliminated.

As an individual responsible for protecting your business, keep the 3 V's in mind – Value, Visible, and Vulnerable. Evaluate the value that criminals may see in your business. Maintain low visibility when possible to minimize the chance of becoming a target. Last, use appropriate steps to reduce your risk or vulnerability to avoid being a victim.

*Reprinted from Business Karate Blog at www.businesskarate.blogspot.com.*

---

The good news is that you are not in this alone. Most cities have an office of emergency management (OEM) or a similar position. If so, the OEM is a good place to start and find out if there has been a community-wide HVA and to learn more about the hazards you face strictly based on your location. Some will be obvious. As mentioned earlier, a business in Denver will not have to worry about hurricanes but may instead have to consider tornadoes and certainly blizzards instead.

You may be surprised about some of the hazards. You may learn that a utility failure is a risk due to aging infrastructure. Being aware of this and understanding the impact can help determine the correct emergency plan. If a power feed is a potential weak link, more effort may be turned to running your business without power. That could mean installing generators or taking steps to transfer certain functions to another location or letting employees work from home (see, it's not all bad).

The Federal Emergency Management Agency (FEMA) is another resource. There are online classes geared to training individuals and organizations on how to respond to emergencies. Local FEMA representatives, as well as the local OEM, can help identify the most likely natural threats and many of the external accidental hazards, such as hazmat spills.

The local police department is another resource. A security risk assessment that does not look at local crime rates would be a waste. Most departments can provide crime analysis or a crime map of the community. Some even make crime maps available online and they can be customized by address, how big an area to search, time frame, and even types of crimes. It is important to keep in mind that police departments only track crime reported to them. Many crimes go unreported to police. Some estimates are that as much as 80% of crimes are never reported to the police. How often have you or has someone you know been involved in a minor crime and no one notified the police? Remember to take that into account when looking at your local crime statistics.

Your threat analysis should also include a bit of research. Pay attention to stories in the news about problems encountered across the industry to similar organizations as well as local news stories. You may learn that a nearby river is likely to flood due to heavy rains and then evaluate the impact. An example within the industry would be health care. If hospitals around the country are reporting high levels of assaults on nursing staff, then the local hospital is facing the same challenges.

After you look at the industry, community, and news, there is still one key area to look at for threats. What kinds of problems go on at your location or within the facilities across the organization? Organizations that don't have a regular security leader probably don't have a process for tracking or documenting incidents.

Employees may not even report crimes to management. If there is no tracking or documenting crimes on or around the facility, then it may be a challenge to get an accurate picture of the security threats. If one employee's car is broken into in the parking lot, the story may be passed around the facility and quickly become grossly exaggerated. One break-in quickly becomes 5 or 10 as people hear the story multiple times from different people. The details change with each telling, so it sounds like a completely separate crime. It is something like the game of telephone played by children. Someone starts a sentence whispering to the child next to him. He, in turn, whispers to the next person in line, until it gets to the end. The last person repeats what he heard, and it is generally completely different from the original line.

If there is no process in place, set up a way for reporting and tracking events. Three things are necessary to make this effective. One is the process itself: how are incidents reported? It could be as simple as having a

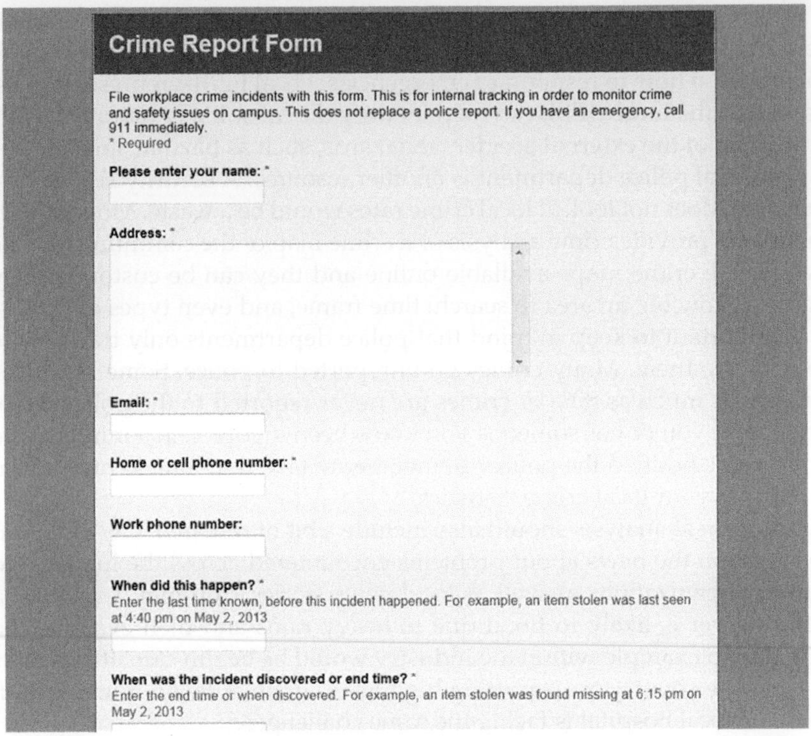

## Crime Report Form

File workplace crime incidents with this form. This is for internal tracking in order to monitor crime and safety issues on campus. This does not replace a police report. If you have an emergency, call 911 immediately.
* Required

**Please enter your name:** *

**Address:** *

**Email:** *

**Home or cell phone number:** *

**Work phone number:**

**When did this happen?** *
Enter the last time known, before this incident happened. For example, an item stolen was last seen at 4:40 pm on May 2, 2013

**When was the incident discovered or end time?** *
Enter the end time or when discovered. For example, an item stolen was found missing at 6:15 pm on May 2, 2013

FIGURE 3.2   **Setting up an online crime reporting form for internal use is a relatively easy process.** The screenshot above shows a form created with Google Drive.

dedicated e-mail to send issues, i.e., security@yourcompany.com. Perhaps online forms created internally will work for your organization, as in the example shown in Figure 3.2. There are also commercially available occurrence reporting software solutions.

Second, you will have to educate staff members about how and when to use the process. Reminders should be sent out periodically about how to report incidents. All levels of management should follow up with any employee involved in a crime to make sure it was reported.

Third, someone needs to be responsible for reviewing, tracking, and following up on reported issues. This should be clearly defined and included in the job description; otherwise, it could slip through the cracks and no one will follow through. It may be a passion for one individual, but if he leaves, or is promoted, is there someone replacing him in his role who understands that security is part of that position? The tracking of security incidents should include creating some simple tables noting the number of incidents each month.

It is a simple process to set up a self-reporting form for employees to report crimes or suspicious incidents. If necessary, your company's IT department may be able to set up the form in a way that allows you to track incidents with spreadsheets and sort data with pivot tables. Below is a sample report with the type of information that should be included. You can customize the form as needed. For example, add a drop down menu with a list of company locations to identify where the incident occurred. This will be helpful for tracking any patterns or identifying problems.

**Crime Report Form**

File workplace crime incidents with this form. This is for internal tracking in order to monitor crime and safety issues at work. This does not replace a police report. If you have an emergency, call 911 immediately.

*\* Required information*

**Please enter your name:\***

**Please enter your street address:\***

**E-mail:\***

**Home or cell phone number:\***

**Work phone number:\***

**When did this happen?\***

*Enter the last time known, before this incident happened. For example, a stolen item was last seen at 4:40 p.m. on May 2, 2013.*

**When was the incident discovered or end time?\***

*Enter the end time or when discovered. For example, a stolen item was found missing at 6:15 p.m. on May 2, 2013.*

**What type of crime or incident are you reporting?\***

*Check only one (most serious) from the list below.*

- Aggravated assault (deadly weapon or serious injury, i.e., broken bones)
- Simple assault
- Sexual assault (all types including groping or fondling)
- Homicide
- Suicide
- Kidnapping/custody violation
- Disturbance
- Threat/menacing
- Weapon violation
- Drug or alcohol abuse
- Robbery (threat or use of force used)

*(Continued)*

- Burglary (to building, safe, or vending machine)
- Theft
- Fraud
- Vehicle break-in
- Auto theft
- Vandalism (including graffiti)
- Trespassing
- Loitering
- Suspicious person/activity
- Other:

**What happened?***
*Please explain what happened, in a clear and concise way.*
**Where did this occur?***
*Provide an exact location where the incident took place.*
**List all witnesses.**
*Be sure to include the full name, address (if known), phone numbers, e-mails, or any other contact information of all witnesses.*
**Do you know who the suspect(s) is in this incident? Enter "no" if unknown.***
*If you know the suspect(s), provide all known information, including name(s), description(s), and how you know they are the suspect(s).*
**What property was involved or is missing?***
*Include a description and approximate value of any damaged or missing property. Be sure to indicate who owned it.*
**Were the police notified?***
- Yes
- No

*If police were called and a report taken, enter the police report number below:*
**I declare that all information provided is true and factual.**

If your business does not have a dedicated full-time security leader, it is still critical to assign that job function. Organizations include security in a wide variety of areas. Sometimes it is found within the HR department or within facilities. Some businesses include security within the legal or compliance department. One important aspect is to make sure that the security function has at least loose ties to the CEO so major security concerns can be addressed at the highest levels.

Typical crimes against persons:

- Assaults
  - Aggravated assaults: attacks involving a deadly weapon or serious bodily injury (permanent scars, broken bones)
  - Simple assaults: any injury, sometimes legally defined as causing pain
- Robbery: stealing something directly from a person by force or by threat involving a weapon
- Homicide: any murder, manslaughter (hopefully a category rarely used)
- Suicide
- Kidnapping or abduction
- Disturbances: any disruption or disorderly conduct that disrupts normal or peaceful operations; includes shouting, yelling, profanity
- Threats: any statement or action that creates fear of imminent harm (may be verbal, written, or a gesture, and would include items such as bomb threats)

Crimes involving property:

- Weapon violations: no threats made, but could include violations of company policy or illegal concealed carry
- Drug/alcohol abuse: any illegal use of substances or impairment
- Burglary: unlawful entry onto a premise in order to commit a crime such as theft
- Theft: stealing something of value
- Vehicle break-in: unlawful entry into a car to commit a crime inside (again, usually theft)
- Auto theft: stealing of the entire car
- Vandalism: damage to property, including graffiti
- Trespassing: unauthorized entry or presence on property
- Loitering: hanging about for no legitimate purpose (not a crime anymore in most states, but a good measure of potential problems on the premises)
- Suspicious person or activity: any person or situation that seems out of place

The responsible individual should be able to attend training in security management or at least on risk assessments. Professional groups such as ASIS International offer webinars and seminars to help develop those skill sets.

Another option is to use security consultants. A consultant can come in on a one-time basis and conduct an in-depth analysis. The recommendations may include a prioritized list of steps to help reduce that risk.

| | Incident | January | February | March | April | May | June | July | August | September | October | November | December | Average |
|---|---|---|---|---|---|---|---|---|---|---|---|---|---|---|
| | **20XX Your Organization Name** Security Incidents | | | | | | | | | | | | | |
| Crimes Against Persons | Aggravated Assault | 0 | 0 | 0 | 0 | 1 | 0 | 0 | 1 | 0 | 0 | 0 | 0 | 0.2 |
| | Simple Assault | 1 | 0 | 1 | 0 | 0 | 1 | 0 | 2 | 0 | 1 | 1 | 2 | 0.8 |
| | Sexual Assault | 0 | 0 | 0 | 0 | 0 | 1 | 0 | 0 | 1 | 1 | 0 | 0 | 0.3 |
| | Assault | 1 | 0 | 1 | 0 | 1 | 2 | 0 | 3 | 1 | 2 | 1 | 2 | 1.2 |
| | Robbery | 0 | 0 | 0 | 1 | 0 | 0 | 0 | 0 | 0 | 0 | 0 | 0 | 0.1 |
| | Homicide | 0 | 0 | 0 | 0 | 0 | 0 | 0 | 0 | 0 | 0 | 0 | 0 | 0.0 |
| | Suicide | 0 | 0 | 0 | 0 | 0 | 0 | 0 | 0 | 0 | 1 | 0 | 0 | 0.1 |
| | Kidnapping / Custody Issues | 1 | 0 | 0 | 1 | 0 | 0 | 0 | 0 | 0 | 0 | 0 | 0 | 0.2 |
| | Disturbance | 2 | 3 | 1 | 4 | 7 | 2 | 2 | 1 | 4 | 5 | 3 | 6 | 3.3 |
| | Threat / Menacing | 3 | 2 | 1 | 6 | 4 | 1 | 1 | 3 | 5 | 1 | 2 | 0 | 2.4 |
| Property Crimes | Weapon Violation | 1 | 0 | 2 | 0 | 0 | 1 | 1 | 0 | 3 | 2 | 0 | 0 | 0.8 |
| | Drug / Alcohol Abuse | 6 | 8 | 4 | 2 | 2 | 4 | 0 | 1 | 3 | 2 | 4 | 6 | 3.5 |
| | Burglary | 0 | 0 | 1 | 0 | 0 | 1 | 0 | 0 | 1 | 0 | 0 | 0 | 0.3 |
| | Felony Theft (> $1,000) | 1 | 0 | 0 | 1 | 0 | 0 | 0 | 2 | 0 | 3 | 0 | 0 | 0.6 |
| | Larceny (< $1,000) | 4 | 5 | 3 | 5 | 6 | 8 | 9 | 4 | 2 | 3 | 4 | 2 | 4.6 |
| | Fraud | 0 | 1 | 0 | 0 | 2 | 0 | 0 | 1 | 0 | 0 | 4 | 3 | 0.9 |
| | Vehicle Break-in | 1 | 0 | 1 | 0 | 0 | 3 | 2 | 2 | 0 | 1 | 0 | 0 | 0.8 |
| | Auto Theft | 1 | 2 | 4 | 1 | 0 | 0 | 0 | 0 | 0 | 0 | 0 | 0 | 0.7 |
| | Vandalism | 0 | 0 | 0 | 3 | 3 | 4 | 6 | 2 | 5 | 1 | 2 | 1 | 2.3 |
| | Trespassing | 10 | 12 | 13 | 9 | 4 | 6 | 11 | 10 | 2 | 8 | 5 | 14 | 8.7 |
| | Loitering | 3 | 2 | 2 | 3 | 4 | 2 | 1 | 2 | 3 | 2 | 1 | 2 | 2.3 |
| | Suspicious Person/Activity | 4 | 4 | 2 | 8 | 5 | 3 | 3 | 2 | 1 | 2 | 1 | 4 | 3.3 |
| | Other | 14 | 15 | 12 | 11 | 13 | 14 | 17 | 10 | 9 | 4 | 8 | 6 | 11.1 |
| | **Total Person Crimes** | 7 | 5 | 11 | 11 | 12 | 5 | 4 | 7 | 10 | 9 | 6 | 8 | 7.9 |
| | **Total Property Crimes** | 45 | 49 | 44 | 43 | 39 | 46 | 50 | 36 | 29 | 28 | 29 | 38 | 39.7 |
| | **Total Incidents** | 52 | 54 | 55 | 54 | 51 | 51 | 54 | 43 | 39 | 37 | 35 | 46 | 47.6 |

Business Karate (www.businesskarate.com)                                          Form prepared by Eric Smith

**FIGURE 3.3** An example of a table that can be easily used to track common criminal events and is split into two primary categories: personal crimes and property crimes. The table automatically calculates the average in order to help identify trends out of the normal range.

A different choice is the use of business coaching. Businesses may have coaches to help with a variety of concerns, and the growing field of security coaching may be the best choice. A coach can help guide the risk assessment project and provide valuable insight and suggestions. A coach can build a long-term relationship with the business and be an ongoing resource, whereas a consultant may be around for a few days as part of one project.

# CRIME TRACKING

Now that you've set up a process for employees to report criminal events, the next step is to track crimes and look for any trends that could indicate a problem.

A common method is to simply tally the totals for the month and create a chart for a visual reference. The various crimes that were listed in the sidebar can be used as the backbone for the table. Of course, some of the ones listed, such as homicide, will be very rare, and hopefully never occur at all. Even though these categories create additional rows or data on the tables, it is good to keep them there as a reminder of the more serious, but less frequent, events that can affect the organization (Figures 3.3 and 3.4).

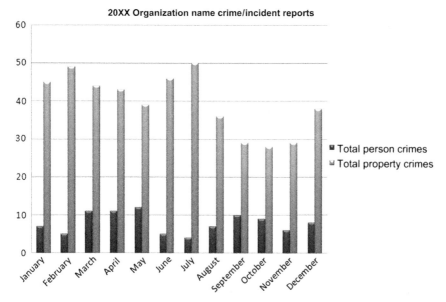

FIGURE 3.4 **Creating a chart from the data in Figure 3.3 provides a great visual reference that helps identify trends.** A chart can be easily incorporated into a monthly newsletter or report to senior leadership and helps focus attention where needed.

## PROBABILITY

Once you've listed out the hazards your organization faces, you need to develop a way to prioritize your focus. To do that, you need to look at the likelihood of each hazard and estimate the probability that it will occur.

In Chapter 2, we looked at the Delphi technique and how that could be used to rate the criticality of various assets. The same, or a similar group, can go through the same process to estimate the probability or how likely that particular threat will actually occur. Earlier, when rating the value or criticality of each asset, a rating scale was used. Be sure to use the same rating scale for probability. For example, if you used a 1 to 5 scale, with 5 having the most impact, use the same 1 to 5 scale. Five should indicate the highest probability of the event happening.

As the group works through the list of hazards or threats it is possible to break it down further into security risks versus all-hazards risks. This is helpful to focus on security-related problems and separate those from business continuity risks or general emergency management. Crime or security risks are more frequent and more likely to be faced by an enterprise than a major disaster, and crime can have an impact on a business on a day-to-day basis.

## GOING BEYOND

When looking at threats, it is important to take a deeper look. As with assets, there are those potential problems that are obvious and then those that are much less apparent.

Supply chain problems are a huge potential challenge, no matter the type of business. If any piece of that supply chain dries up or disappears, there could be a direct impact even if the supplies seem like they would be easy to get elsewhere.

A security guard force company issued uniforms to their employees, including winter jackets. The vendor that supplied the uniforms in turn ordered uniform parts from various other suppliers, acting as the middleman. When the Chinese company that made the jackets went bankrupt and closed due to a global recession, there was no one else able to supply the same jackets. While replacements were being sought, the security officers responsible for conducting patrols were entering the winter months without jackets. Newer officers had never received them and senior officers needed replacements. When a replacement jacket was found, the style was different, detracting from the "uniform" appearance. The new jackets were not as popular with staff, generating "jacket envy" and some staff dissatisfaction.

This was a relatively minor bump but is a good real-life example of the impact supply chain disruptions can have. Hazards that are more serious could include weather, such as a hurricane delaying shipments or damaging a warehouse in another country. There could be risks from political changes, social unrest, labor strikes, as well as internal crime and fraud.

The headlines are full of potential problems and challenges. In January 2013, Al-Qaida terrorists took over a gas energy plant in northern Africa, holding numerous hostages until Algerian forces liberated the plant. Across northern Africa, there have been numerous threats of Al-Qaida activity, including the attack on the U.S. embassy in Benghazi, Libya, in 2012. Any company relying on that region for supplies or operations should be on alert to the potential threats and interruption to business as well as to the company's PR.

Not all threats are deliberate or involve terrorism. Bangladesh is home to over 4000 garment factories, providing clothing to businesses around the world. In November 2012, a fire broke out in one factory that supplied clothes to Walmart and Sears. The fire killed 112 people and sparked investigations into the cause, as well as the working conditions. Again, this is just another example of how businesses may be in jeopardy from various threats across the globe.

In some cases, companies are legally obligated to monitor their suppliers for certain violations. California has proposed a new law that requires businesses to investigate the staffing of their suppliers. A business could be held in violation if any of its suppliers are involved in human trafficking as a source of labor. The intent is great, but one has to wonder how many businesses will be ready to take on that task and truly conduct that kind of investigation into all suppliers and even their suppliers' suppliers.

This brings us to compliance. Compliance and regulations are often created out of good intentions, but remember the old saying "The road to hell is paved with good intentions." In one survey, business professionals were asked about threats to their business and many responded that they were worried about excessive regulation or compliance. Regulatory compliance can translate into a real drain on productivity. Employees or departments focused on traditional functions may have to split their attention with compliance issues. Typically, this means completing forms or reports in a specific manner and tracking measures or data differently. Often there are specific requirements on how tasks are done or what is done.

Hospitals are one industry that faces a lot of regulation and compliance. The majority of hospitals in the United States have chosen to be accredited through The Joint Commission (TJC). TJC sets a long set of standards that cover a wide range of hospital operations from clinical to nonclinical, including security and facility operations. A large percentage of effort is placed on meeting TJC standards and the required reporting formats. Hospitals are surveyed at least every three years, and as that window gets closer, more and more effort goes into documentation and making sure that everything is in order.

It is interesting to note that TJC accreditation guidebook has grown much thicker over the years. This is typical of regulatory bodies and even governments. More and more rules are created while previous ones stay in place as well, making it more difficult to stay caught up, no matter how well intentioned the organization is.

So regulation is another set of potential threats. The impact on productivity and staff time may definitely take away from primary business goals. In addition to those risks, there is the risk of fines or penalties if compliance is not achieved. Keep in mind that while intentions may be good, there may be unintended consequences.

A complete look at the threats to your business should include the traditional concerns, such as crime and disasters. Remember also to give careful consideration to the other types of risks you may face. Often these are hidden beneath the surface but could be just as destructive to your organization and livelihood.

## CONCLUSION

Self-defense is fundamentally built around defending oneself from attack, multiple types of attacks, whether kicks, punches, or grabs. Protecting an organization involves the same concept protecting from attacks or threats of all different kinds. Threats can be man-made, including crimes, or natural disasters. Hazards include disruptions to supply chains or even excessive regulation resulting in loss of productivity. Understanding those hazards, and how likely or possible they are to occur, is the first step toward a solid security plan.

# BUSINESS KARATE BELT LEVELS

Test your company's karate belt level in the discipline of awareness/ stance. If your organization meets each belt level and all the standards of the lower belts as seen in Figure 3.5, you have then achieved that color level.

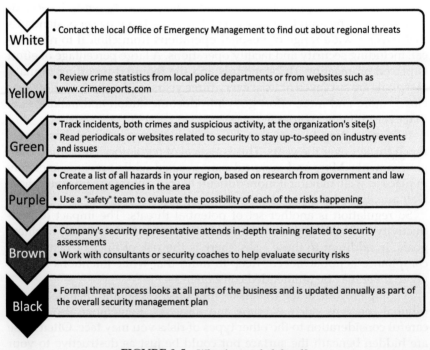

**White**
• Contact the local Office of Emergency Management to find out about regional threats

**Yellow**
• Review crime statistics from local police departments or from websites such as www.crimereports.com

**Green**
• Track incidents, both crimes and suspicious activity, at the organization's site(s)
• Read periodicals or websites related to security to stay up-to-speed on industry events and issues

**Purple**
• Create a list of all hazards in your region, based on research from government and law enforcement agencies in the area
• Use a "safety" team to evaluate the possibility of each of the risks happening

**Brown**
• Company's security representative attends in-depth training related to security assessments
• Work with consultants or security coaches to help evaluate security risks

**Black**
• Formal threat process looks at all parts of the business and is updated annually as part of the overall security management plan

FIGURE 3.5    What is your belt level?

# Further Reading

Deterring terrorism - Is America spending too much on homeland security? (2011, April 30). The Economist. Washington D.C. Retrieved from: http://www.economist.com/blogs/gulliver/2011/04/01deterring_terrorism. (accessed 09.02.2013).

# 4

# Playing with Blocks: Vulnerabilities and Protecting What's Important

## IN KARATE CLASS

Karate students learn many new physical moves and techniques. Often, the focus is on attacks and combinations of punches or kicks designed to stop an assailant. In movies, kicks and punches get the attention—a flying sidekick or a wide "haymaker" punch makes for exciting-looking fight scenes. However, one of the most important, if underrated, techniques is the block.

If you are faced with a situation in which you have to defend yourself, one of the first things that you will likely have to do is block an attack of some type. Society teaches us that "good" people do not strike first. A person should wait until another person attacks before reacting. Of course, this can be very dangerous as real-life fights are often determined with the first punch and may not last much beyond that.

Whether sparring as a sporting event or fighting for self-defense, blocking is critical. Failure to block an attack could result in a point being scored against you. On the street, failure to block an attack could be disastrous. A good practice session includes practice on how to block and what to block.

Being able to block an attack, whether the first one or one in the middle of a fight, is critical—and not only blocking but also blocking correctly. That is to say, not over- or underblocking as well as protecting the right targets.

New martial artists often overextend their blocks, which actually exposes them to follow-up blows. Imagine blocking a punch headed straight at your nose. You could block it aside with a quick swing of your forearm. However, if you overblock or overextend your blocking arm to push the punch away, you could leave your nose open to a follow-up punch. In the moment, with adrenaline flowing, your block could push the incoming punch far out to the side when really a slight slap will deflect the punch a few inches—all that is needed to keep the punch away from your face. It also leaves your blocking hand still in position for another quick block.

To be effective, a block also has to be strong enough to actually deflect or stop the attack. A half-hearted or weak block will not be enough to stop a committed attack. Along those lines, the block has to have enough force to actually protect yourself combined with the focus to deflect an attack.

Go back to that punch to the face. A half-hearted block, weakly thrown, will not change the direction of that incoming punch. Likewise, blocking full force, but stopping short of the point that deflects the punch, leaves you just as vulnerable and exposed to that attack.

The last error has to do with knowing what to block. Obviously, some parts of the body are more sensitive or more exposed. Blocks should be focused on those areas that are most vulnerable where an attack could cause real harm or take away your ability to protect yourself.

Putting effort into blocking a glancing blow to your thigh may be unnecessary, where completely blocking a kick to the groin is vital. Martial art students learn the differences through drills and repeated practice.

## THE BUSINESS CONNECTION

There are many parallels between karate blocks and how businesses protect themselves. Organizations have to know what to protect—the critical assets that keep them going, as we looked at in Chapter 2. They need to know what to protect themselves from, as in the threats identified in Chapter 3. And last, they need to know how to block or how to mitigate and manage those risks.

To fully complete the security risk assessment, it is crucial to understand the concept of vulnerability. I like to think of vulnerability as the harm done. Going back to the karate example, a punch to the nose would be far more harmful than the exact same punch to the leg or arm.

In business terms, your nose is a critical asset. It helps you breathe, smell the air around you, and, hopefully, adds to your appearance. The threats could be punches, kicks, head butts, and so on. Now we have to look at the likelihood or possibility of each of these threats actually happening. For someone to kick your nose, they would have to be very flexible and a kick has to travel farther, going from the ground all the way to the head. A head butt can only be delivered at very close range. In this example, a punch would be the most likely, or probable, threat. So we have a high-impact, high-probability event.

However, we have not taken into account anything that may lessen the impact or reduce the probability. The most obvious way to mitigate is to keep your guard up and practice blocking to reduce the likelihood that the punch to the nose will connect. Of course, the probability of a kick or head butt could change. If you are knocked down or slip, a kick could become much more likely being closer to the ground. Failing to keep an attacker at arm's length could increase the risk of a head butt landing. As we prepare our security risk assessment, the probability might be lower, but the impact remains high. The steps to mitigate any blow to the nose should be considered and evaluated even when the probability is lower, when the impact is high.

This is a simple example, but it helps illustrate the final component of the security risk assessment: vulnerability or exposure to harm.

## THE ASSESSMENT MODEL

When it comes to risk assessments there are many models used to come up with a way to identify the most pressing risks. I like to keep it straightforward and fairly simple. So far, the method shown here lists the hazards (or crime) as a column on the left side. The next columns indicate which classes of assets are potentially affected by that threat, then the probability followed by the impact. The last section is mitigation or prevention. If an event is likely to happen and could be very negative, but steps have been taken to reduce the risk or likelihood, then the severity or harm will be much less and may be removed entirely.

Imagine that your organization includes a retail store and one of the identified threats is a robbery. After reviewing industry data and local crime reports, you realize that your store has a high probability of experiencing a robbery. Your probability would be a 5, if you choose a 1 to 5 scale. The impact is the next item to calculate. Let's say that one day's worth of receipts being lost or stolen could actually jeopardize the ability to pay both employees and key suppliers. On top of that, the top salesperson has said that if she is robbed she will quit. You might decide that the impact is a 4.

Of course, we have not taken into account any steps to mitigate a robbery. This could include anything that will lessen the impact or prevent it from even happening. In our situation, the store has video cameras, including one by the door where everyone entering can see that they are on video. Signs announcing that money on hand is limited can help reduce the loss and deter a would-be robber. Adding an armed security officer is another deterrent. The store has moved signage and shelves away from windows so there is a clear view of the parking lot and a set of mantrap double doors is added. Hiding spots near potential escape routes have been eliminated. Let's say that a lot has been done to mitigate a robbery, including staff training on how to respond and recognize suspicious activity, so we will score our mitigation at a 1, meaning we've taken all reasonable steps.

So to come up with a vulnerability score, we can find the sum of the probability, impact, and mitigation scores. Using the case above, probability was 5, as was the impact. The mitigation score was 1. The total score was 11. The highest score, with high impact, probability, and no mitigation would be 15. The best score would be a 3, if the probability was 1, the impact also low or 1, and the maxim mitigation steps were in place, also a 1.

Of course, scoring mitigation is dependent on understanding what steps can be taken to reduce the likelihood or impact of a crime. In upcoming chapters, we will look in depth at steps and methods to fight crime and reduce the risks.

## BLOCKS AND MITIGATION

In order to score an organization's prevention or mitigation to various threats, there must be an understanding of the security measures that can help limit damage or reduce the likelihood of a threat from occurring.

Police officers are trained on the idea of minimize-maximize during a gun battle. Officers need to minimize themselves as a target as in shelter behind cover or drop to a kneeling position. They are also taught to maximize their distance from the shooter. The farther away you are, the less likely you are going to be hit. The same general concept applies here. A business needs to minimize the critical assets to a threat and also maximize the distance to the threat to keep it at arm's length.

Another example of a way to reduce the harm or impact is through insurance. Insurance transfers a share of the loss away from your company, or minimizes your exposure (at an expense, though). This is just one example of mitigation or reducing the impact of an event or preventing it from happening in the first place.

Imagine that you work for any organization with a large amount of cash on hand. Banks or retailers come to mind. A church, though, can have large cash donations every week. I know of one case in which the manager of an apartment complex had large amounts of cash each month when the rent came due. In this complex, the tenants all tended to pay in cash as many were unable or did not get bank accounts, due to many being in the country illegally. As it turned out, some unsavory individuals realized that the cash on hand at the beginning of the month was a very attractive target. Fortunately, the police were notified as the details of the would-be robbery leaked out. The plan was broken up and never carried out.

If this were your problem (and I can think of worse than having lots of cash on hand), what are some of the measures that come to mind?

A drop safe is one possibility. Immediately putting large amounts of cash in a safe that is not accessible can be one way to maximize the distance between the cash and the crook—the safe keeps the thief away. It is common to see this kind of prevention at convenience stores where signs let would-be criminals know that the clerk has access only to $20. However, that may not work in every case. For example, with our church example and a large amount of cash at once, what steps could be taken?

A safe to keep it locked until it is counted may still work. Often, church members volunteer to help count the money, at which point it is vulnerable. Other security measures may include locking the facility during the counting as well as walking the exterior, and checking for suspicious activity or people, before, during, and after the money is counted.

## PRACTICAL EXAMPLES OF SECURITY MITIGATION

There are a large number of security measures that can be used to mitigate risk, and throughout this book we will go into more detail on many of them. Keep in mind that creativity is the only limit you have when dealing with security protection. One police department parked patrol cars in bank parking lots in response to an increase in robberies. Another organization changed its security coverage routinely to keep the bad guys guessing. One day an entrance was closed, or all bags being carried in were searched, or an extra security officer was posted on the main drive up to the building.

For the sake of the security risk assessment, you can refer to a list of possible mitigating factors and use the list with your Delphi group as a reference or checklist to help with scoring. Later, we will go into more detail about prevention from both internal and external threats.

Some examples to keep in mind are:

1. Video surveillance system (VSS), also called closed circuit television (CCTV): pro—great tool for after the event; useful for investigations; con—does not necessarily deter crooks; after all, that is why we can watch TV shows, such as World's Dumbest Criminals
2. Burglar or forced entry alarms
3. Tip lines: anonymous callers can be the best source for identifying and finding internal embezzlement
4. Audits: not as effective as tip lines per some studies, but the threat alone has deterrent value
5. Access control limiting unauthorized access can limit theft or robbery and even assaults
6. Open views: a parking lot situated in front of an office building with windows overlooking the area is more secure than an isolated lot at the back with no one to see what is going on
7. Duress or panic alarms can help staff feel safer and, when used properly, help alert others during a robbery

8. Training is often overlooked among many high-tech solutions but is the fundamental way to build awareness and support for security measures
9. Policies are another way to build organizational support and help deter and prevent a wide variety of crimes
10. Lighting is another way to mitigate crime
11. Security staff can be a visible deterrent and responder, as well as help check and maintain security equipment
12. Drills, especially following training, help staff respond in the best manner to deal with unexpected emergencies and security events
13. Continuity planning
14. Threat assessment team to help investigate and address violent or escalating behavior
15. Insurance is a way to limit the size of a loss
16. Personal safety/self-defense helps build staff confidence and perception of safety
17. Key control and inventory

## SPECIAL CONSIDERATIONS

So far, our focus has been on a general security risk assessment, something that should be done every year. There are other situations that come up that may change the risk picture, even if temporarily.

Short-term planning can be based on a single event that affects the organization or some planned, albeit temporary, change.

A single event could be a bike race that runs by your organization. A race could involve street closures as well as crowds in the area. Another example would be if your city hosts a national political convention, either Democrat or Republican. Both will involve many security issues, traffic blockades, and protests. If your organization is involved in an industry that could be impacted by politics, you could find yourselves a target of protests.

When the Democratic National Convention (DNC) came to Denver in 2008, there were widespread concerns. Hospitals were worried about protesters, as health care was a hot topic during the election. There were also concerns about crowds as some planned protests would be camping and marching by some of the hospitals. The campuses in the area were worried that protesters or campers would overwhelm the facilities just through use of the restrooms alone. In addition, there was the possibility of high-profile patients. With politicians and media figures in town, especially with Denver's higher elevations above sea level, there were certainly concerns about security in case a high-profile individual had to be admitted for medical care.

Other planned incidents may include construction projects or upgrades. For example, replacing transformers or electrical equipment could mean power outages, which in turn could affect duress alarms or access control devices. Many locked doors are required to fail to an unlocked mode in case of fires and sometimes even power outages. These types of projects need special security focus.

Another aspect of assessing security risks is long-range planning. Business goals cannot be overlooked, so a review of strategic goals or plans should be part of the security assessment. Growth can mean additional hiring as well as adding buildings or expanding facilities. The obvious security changes would include the screening of new employees, as well as physical security of the buildings. Parking lot safety is a common concern of employees. Any growth or expansion should include a review of parking areas and the impact on safety. Growth can also mean new risks in the form of the supply chain if new suppliers will be needed or added.

On the other hand, strategic planning may mean downsizing to reduce expenses. That could mean lower employee morale and a higher risk of internal fraud or theft. Worries about layoffs and job security can easily translate into workplace violence. Security goals in that case should include training on identification of risky behaviors as well as how to de-escalate situations. Another risk of downsizing and layoffs is access control. Do any of the laid-off employees have master keys or access to the facility, including access to IT databases or servers?

## PUTTING IT ALL TOGETHER

The last piece of the security assessment process is to put all the work done so far together in order to rate the risks and identify those areas that are most vulnerable.

Our Delphi group has one last task, which is to score the mitigation steps currently in place for each of the threats identified earlier. As mentioned, the same scoring scale should be used. If a 1 to 5 scale has been used, then use the same scale where 5 is the least prepared and 1 is the most prepared (Figure 4.1).

Of course, to help minimize subjectivity some basic guides should be given to the group. Explain that highly prepared should include all mitigation factors, such as training or drills, current policies, and applicable security measures. It really would be the perfect example. If an element is not currently in place, the score should be less for that threat (Figure 4.2).

Once the group's results are in, all the data can be combined and scored in a spreadsheet. In our example, using a 1 to 5 scale, a high-impact, high-probability event with no mitigation would score $5+5+5$ for a total of 15. On the other extreme, a low-impact, low-probability

Security risk assessment scoring matrix

| | Threat | Impact on | Probability | Mitigation | Security risk |
|---|---|---|---|---|---|
| **Personal crimes** | Aggravated assault | | | | |
| | Simple assault | | | | |
| | Sexual assault | | | | |
| | Robbery | | | | |
| | Homicide | | | | |
| | Suicide | | | | |
| | Kidnapping/custody issue | | | | |
| | Disturbance | | | | |
| | Threat/menacing | | | | |
| **Property crimes** | Weapon violation | | | | |
| | Drug/alcohol abuse | | | | |
| | Burglary | | | | |
| | Theft ($1000 or over) | | | | |
| | Misdemeanor theft (<$1000) | | | | |
| | Fraud | | | | |
| | Vehicle break-in | | | | |
| | Auto theft | | | | |
| | Vandalism | | | | |
| | Trespassing | | | | |
| | Loitering | | | | |
| | Suspicious person/activity | | | | |
| **Natural events** | Avalanche | | | | |
| | Drought | | | | |
| | Earthquake | | | | |
| | Flood | | | | |
| | Hail | | | | |
| | Landslide | | | | |
| | Tornado | | | | |
| | Winter storm | | | | |
| | Wildfire | | | | |
| **Other man-made events** | Accident | | | | |
| | Chemical spill | | | | |
| | Fire | | | | |
| | Gas leak | | | | |
| | Hostage situation | | | | |
| | Intruder on grounds | | | | |
| | Civil disturbance | | | | |
| | Power failure | | | | |
| | Terrorism | | | | |

FIGURE 4.1  A spreadsheet can be used to create a security risk scoring matrix.

## CALCULATING A SECURITY VULNERABILITY SCORE

There are various tools and methods to calculate vulnerability in order to quantify risks. For our purposes, we will use a simple formula: Probability, scored between 1 and 5, with 5 being the most likely; add the impact score, again a 1 to 5 scale, with 5 being the most severe impact; add the mitigation score, where 1 is the most prepared and 5 is the least prepared for the event. Take the sum of the three scores and divide by the maximum score (15, using this scale) and multiply by 100 for a percentage score.

$$[(Probability + Impact + Mitigation)/Maximum\ Score] \times 100 = Security\ Vulnerability\ Score$$

event with strong mitigation would be $1 + 1 + 1 = 3$. Using this model, vulnerability scores will range from 3 up to 15. This allows you to sort through all the risks or threats and focus on the ones that are most likely to harm your organization. You can easily convert this to a percentage by dividing the sum by the total maximum score, or 15. At the low end, a score of 3 would be a 20% on the matrix, where a high-impact, probable, and poorly mitigated event would be 100%. Either way, the point of the scores is to serve as a tool to compare one risk to another and should not be interpreted as a form of probability.

As you review the list, you may find that some of the scores do not make sense. A particular crime scores higher than you think it should, for example. In those cases, you may want to review the scoring and look at the impact, probability, and mitigation scores. Sometimes, in hindsight, you may realize that something was overlooked or needs to be re-evaluated. That is okay. Your risk assessment is a tool to help guide you, and making adjustments is part of that assessment process.

Once you have your risk assessment you can use this to develop a plan to address any gaps in your security program. Those areas that scored highest should become the focus as you move forward. Often, you cannot change the impact, or even the probability, but you do control mitigation. Your assessment becomes the tool to help focus on those security measures that are most needed and also serves as a tool to present that need and value to the company's leaders.

| | | Scoring criteria | | |
| Impact on organization | Probability | Mitigation | Security risk |
| --- | --- | --- | --- |
| 5 - Very high (Risk of serious injury or death) | 5 - Very high (Very likely, imminent or happens on a regular basis) | 1 - Very high (Maximum use of security mitigation measures) | Score based on impact, probability, and mitigation |
| 4 - High (Severe long-term disruption or high cost, risk of injury) | 4 - High (Fairly probable or likely event will occur) | 2 - High (Resonable security measures in place) | The higher the score, the greater the risk - address higher scores first |
| 3 - Medium (Short-term impact or disruption) | 3 - Medium (Event is possible) | 3 - Medium (Some security measures currently in use) | |
| 2 - Medium low (Some impact on operations) | 2 - Medium low (Not very likely to happen) | 4 - Medium low (Protection measures need improvement) | |
| 1 - Low (Little impact on business operations) | 1 - Low (Little likelihood or possibility of event occurring; extremely rare) | 5 - Low (No steps or measures in place for protection) | |

FIGURE 4.2  Well-defined criteria will help the group come up with the most accurate scores and make the matrix more useful.

Put the security score model to the test. Think of a crime, such as petty or misdemeanor theft, that is common, so probability might be scored high, say a 5. The impact on the business is likely fairly low, for example, a 2. It could be scored lower or higher depending on your corporate culture. Victims of minor theft may see the impact much higher and leave—they could be customers going to another store or employees working somewhere else that seems safer to them. The next element is mitigation: how much is in place that should be? If there is visitor management to enhance access control and video surveillance in place, but unattended areas or no security personnel or no personal lockers for items, the mitigation score might be mixed. For this instance, we will score mitigation as a 4 (rather lacking in security measures). The next step in calculating the security score is to sum probability + impact + mitigation, or $5 + 2 + 4 = 11$. Take the sum, divide by the maximum points (15 in our example), and multiply by 100 to get a percentage score. Using our results, theft scores a 73%.

## CONCLUSION

Over the last three chapters, we have identified critical assets and threats to those assets, and then reviewed the steps in place to protect those same assets. By multiplying the probability, impact on the organization, and mitigation score, we came up with a security risk score. The higher the score, the greater the risk. This allows your organization to focus on the greatest risks and is a tool to help quantify those risks. In turn, that helps explain the reason for capital requests or for new security measures to alleviate or minimize the dangers.

Your security risk assessment is a vital piece of the security management process and is the backbone of future improvements and focus of security efforts.

## BUSINESS KARATE BELT LEVELS

Test your company's karate belt level in the discipline of awareness/ stance. If your organization meets each belt level and all the standards of the lower belts as seen in Figure 4.3, you have then achieved that color level.

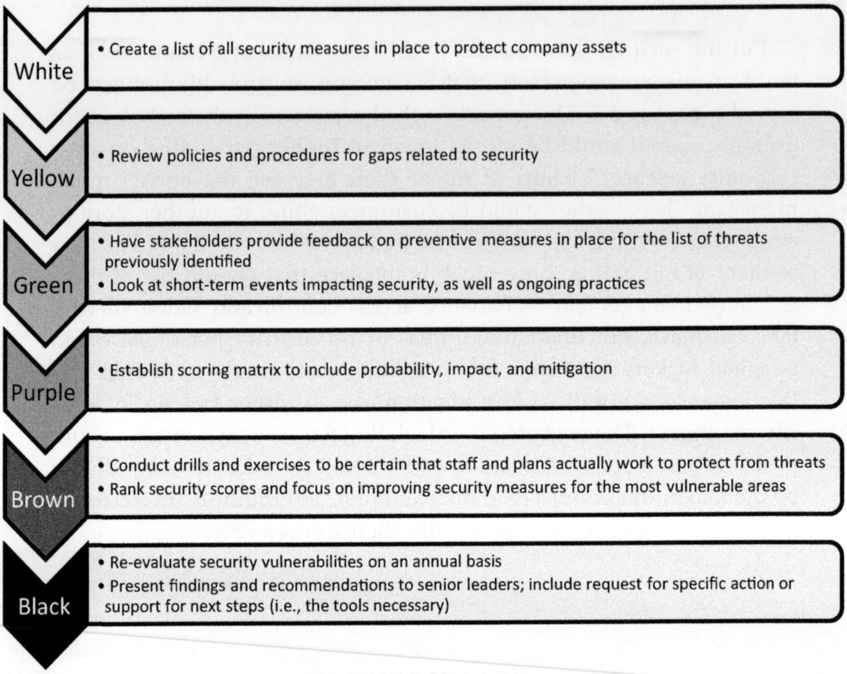

**White**
- Create a list of all security measures in place to protect company assets

**Yellow**
- Review policies and procedures for gaps related to security

**Green**
- Have stakeholders provide feedback on preventive measures in place for the list of threats previously identified
- Look at short-term events impacting security, as well as ongoing practices

**Purple**
- Establish scoring matrix to include probability, impact, and mitigation

**Brown**
- Conduct drills and exercises to be certain that staff and plans actually work to protect from threats
- Rank security scores and focus on improving security measures for the most vulnerable areas

**Black**
- Re-evaluate security vulnerabilities on an annual basis
- Present findings and recommendations to senior leaders; include request for specific action or support for next steps (i.e., the tools necessary)

FIGURE 4.3    What is your belt level?

# 5

# Practice Makes Perfect: Karate Forms and Organizational Memory

## KARATE BACKGROUND

Have you ever watched a group of karate students working out and noticed that they would perform a series of movements in unison, almost like dance moves? Martial arts are centered on these forms or katas. Every belt level will have specific forms that students must learn before advancing to the next belt level.

Why do martial art students learn forms? It is not as if you can predict the exact sequence that opponents will follow during an attack. The reason is to build muscle memory. Practicing forms is one way for new, and advanced, students to learn combinations of attacks and blocks and be able to flow from one to another quickly and easily. The responses become second nature, instinct. That means martial artists can react to an attack without the delay of thinking first. All that comes from muscle memory— the body's ability to react instinctively or automatically.

Through practice (translate as lots of repetition done correctly) each move becomes natural. The correct foot placement for balance, the proper motion in a block, and the smooth follow-up attack are all examples of motor skills that can be done quickly, without thinking to slow the movement.

Of course, there is bad muscle memory as well. Repeatedly practicing a skill using the wrong technique is not effective or helpful. Throwing a punch a thousand times in practice, but doing it incorrectly, such as keeping the wrist bent, could be disastrous in a real situation. The wrist held at a bent angle during a punch will quickly become a broken wrist. The correct practice develops good muscle memory so there is no, or at least little, risk of a broken hand when throwing a punch.

## BUSINESS APPLICATION

Just as a body builds muscle memory and instinctive responses, organizations have built-in or programmed memory as well. This organizational memory can show itself in many different ways. In general, there are those things we do at work, or at least the way they are done, simply because that is what a previous leader wanted. The "why" may be forgotten, but the task lives on, sometimes long past the original reason.

With focus and training, organizational memory of the good kind can be built as well. A well-developed organizational memory builds an instinctive, almost automatic, approach to handling challenges, even potential disasters of all kinds.

There is bad organizational memory too. This can be seen when the proper procedure is skipped or not followed and bad habits develop. Eventually those practices become the way new employees are trained and how everyone does some task, while the original purpose is overlooked. A common example would be remote door opening. Many organizations have locked doors and sometimes visitors or deliveries may need access. A buzzer may be set up to alert employees who are supposed to check with the person at the door via an audio or video intercom before releasing the door lock. Over time, employees get in the habit of opening the door when it buzzes and soon skip the intercom check—they just reach back and hit the release switch without checking on who is entering. A step in the process is skipped, and in short order a bad habit develops. New employees will likely be told just to hit the release and may not even learn how to use the intercom or camera to check who is entering.

The good type of enterprise-wide memory is a vital way to get everyone in the business to respond the correct way to emergency or security issues. The ultimate goal is to build a natural, intuitive response.

## HOW TO BUILD ORGANIZATIONAL MEMORY

Dwight Eisenhower was faced with one of the biggest challenges in history. He had to plan the invasion of Europe that would begin the downfall of Nazi Germany. He is often quoted as saying, "Plans are nothing; planning is everything." The plan was simple: invade Europe and defeat Germany. Of course, the devil is in the details—the planning. Eisenhower had to stay a step ahead of the Nazis by picking a location that was suitable for an invasion, but unexpected. That involved gathering and reviewing intelligence, aerial photos, and reports from spies and resistance fighters.

Then there were the logistics—feeding and supplying the armed forces from different countries, and gathering ships and conducting training while trying to keep the Germans in the dark. In addition, he had to deal with the political wrangling of different leaders, each focused on their own agendas or their military branch. In the end, the final decision was his alone and largely came down to sketchy weather reports. Of course, as we know, the plan was successful, and the invasion established a foothold in France from where the Nazis were slowly beaten back until Germany surrendered the following year. Planning *was* everything.

Organizational memory means a plan, and a good plan means careful planning. A plan for employees to use generally means a policy, and its twin, procedure. Policies and procedures are, or should be, the best way to build the response a business is looking for. Policies and procedures should also be the basis for staff training.

Unfortunately, there is a lot of confusion about policies and procedures. First, many people don't differentiate between the two. Second, some companies do not bother and either have none, or they are so poorly written as to be useless.

Policies and procedures are not the same thing at all. Going back to our previous example, the policy is the plan. The procedure is based on the planning. Policy is the "what," as in what is the goal? The procedure is the "how."

Policies reflect the business's goals for protection and security. In a very broad sense, that could be business continuity during or following an emergency, or how to minimize the impact of a security breach or a criminal event, or how to maximize the ability to deal with an incident.

Procedures need to outline exactly how those goals should be accomplished. What steps do employees need to follow? The steps need to match specific security goals. Procedures also need to be regularly reviewed to evaluate the steps followed and assess how well goals are being met; then one can adapt and adjust as needed. The review should include debriefing of incidents, analysis of drills or events at other locations. Procedures involve the actual "doing," and that means detailed preparations.

When I am giving a talk or training on security procedures and am explaining the difference between the plan and planning, I like to use a cooking analogy. I am not a cook by any stretch of the imagination. My kids do not even trust me to make toast and seem to believe that I would manage to burn down the house; my wife will not let me in the kitchen. Fortunately, my wife is a great cook. One of her many good dishes is chicken marsala. She doesn't make it very often, pointing out that it is very complicated and has 14 distinct steps to cook it. Since it is more complex, when she does make it, she uses her recipe.

In fact, most of us (or you, since I am not allowed in the kitchen) will use a cookbook. The recipe is the policy and procedure. Since we want to cook chicken marsala for dinner (or tacos, an omelet, or whatever you want), the policy statement is "how to make chicken marsala." The policy states the goal we want to achieve. The recipe is the procedure that outlines each step and explains exactly what to do—what temperature to set the oven at and how long to cook the chicken or how to mix the sauce.

You have the desire, you have the recipe, so are you ready to go? No! There is still something missing: the ingredients! The policy and procedure will only get you so far. They are the plan. You still have to gather everything needed. The preparation work is missing. If our recipe was a true detailed procedure it would tell our cook how to get to the grocery store, with directions and details on what to do (get a shopping cart, go to aisle five, pick out mushrooms, then proceed to aisle seven for cooking wine, etc.).

## DEVELOPING PROCEDURES

As you can see, the "how" or procedure is often much more difficult to create. Procedures have to be a realistic set of steps that can be followed. To be realistic, keep in mind the target audience. Will employees have the tools and abilities to carry out the procedure? You also have to think of the type of policy and procedure. Some, such as responding to an active shooter, have to be designed so that employees or faculty will be able to remember and follow it under extreme stress. In other words, keep it simple.

When I was a police officer, there were policies (and procedures) for almost everything. Obviously, many were for high-stress situations that could arise without warning. Examples were pursuits, use of force, hostage—these were called "red" policies. An officer had to know these as there would be no chance to read them and clarify details, such as when a pursuit was justified and when it was not.

There were also "yellow" policies—those that might not involve imminent danger but were still extremely important. The policy on when to make an arrest is a good example. In the field, an officer might have to make that decision without the chance to peruse the policy and fully contemplate the decision.

The last group consists of the policies that impact operations but are not time sensitive. The uniform policy or guidelines on bidding for shifts are those that can be reviewed as needed when a question arises.

Keep in mind the red factor. The higher the level of stress or danger involved, the simpler and more direct the procedure should be. An emergency policy and procedure should be built around a simple concept such as the Department of Homeland Security's message "Run, Hide, Fight," three words that sum up what the initial response should be during an encounter with an active shooter. More details may be added to the emergency response plan, such as notification, liaison with police, accounting for staff, media management, recovery, and so on. Those particulars fall under the yellow category, after the scene is secured or under police control.

# CHALLENGES AND PITFALLS

Even the most well-thought-out plan can hit unexpected snags and could even turn out to be completely ineffective. Snags come in different shapes and sizes, from lack of buy-in to lack of training and lack of authority. The largest hang-up is probably that the policy is just plain bad.

One of the first potential challenges is lack of support or buy-in. The policy may be the "what" and the procedure may be the "how," which could lead to staff wondering "why?" Why are we doing this? Why this way? Why has it changed—we've always done it differently before.

Whether introducing a new policy or reminding everyone of an existing one, be sure to communicate the "why." For example, "We have to practice evacuations twice a year due to local fire code and could be fined for noncompliance. That would mean smaller raises or tighter department budgets."

The policy cannot be draconian or overly burdensome either. People will find work-arounds. It also has to make sense. Information security is one of my favorite targets for this topic. In one case, physical security was involved in a difficult termination. As happens much too often, it was the end of the day on a Friday. The one person normally responsible for the department employees' access to the corporate network had left. The information technology department refused to suspend the terminated employee's network access without that one individual filling out the appropriate forms and submitting them to the IT security team. As a result, the terminated employee had access for longer than he should have. He was actually seen in and out of the facility, including using computers made available to the public. If that ex-employee had wanted to, he could have easily installed malware or created backdoor access to the network and done extensive damage to the corporation. Even without that knowledge, it would have been easy to copy any materials that could have been used to violate various privacy rules and put the corporation at risk of liability.

Other examples include changing passwords too frequently or making the combinations of capital letters, numbers, and symbols so tricky that most people write the password on a sticky note that they post on the monitor at their desk.

Encryption programs for laptops are another challenge. It is necessary, as we saw with the stolen NASA laptop, but also has to be software that reflects job responsibilities. One program that I dislike is Credant. To move files from a laptop to a flash drive, the flash drive must be encrypted with a password, which is fine. However, to use those files, it is necessary to run an .exe (executable) file, enter the password, and finally copy the file to the new computer. I often give presentations or talks at different locations and quickly found that bringing my PowerPoint on a flash drive created problems. On the presentation computer, I needed permission to run the .exe file, which is a file type that can sometimes contain viruses, and as such, is not always allowed without having administrator rights to that computer. If that does not stop me, I am forced to copy the entire file or presentation to the computer; potentially others could use my work or redistribute it without permission. So in essence, it creates less protection for those files simply by the way the software is set up. This is an example of unintended consequences. By the way, the easiest work-around is to use a desktop computer to save the file to a flash drive. Another unintended consequence is that the Credant software has partially encrypted my laptop hard drive on several occasions, destroying data and creating loss of files and work.

Another source of failure when it comes to policies and procedures is lack of training. We've already looked at a couple of examples where it is necessary to know an emergency procedure immediately. There are times, though, when staff may know the text of the procedure but not how to implement it.

During drills testing the response to an infant abduction, gaps in implementing the procedure were identified. Staff took the right actions responding to doors and exits and checking people who could be concealing an infant. But when the abductor (simulated, of course) was confronted, the training fell apart as the stress level increased. In one case, an employee knew that she needed to call security but could not remember the number to call on her cell phone. In another incident, employees grabbed the suspect, causing her to drop the infant—fortunately, just a doll used for the drill.

The main lesson learned was that the normal training was not enough for stressful situations. However, this lesson would have been missed completely if drills had not been done. Testing the plan thoroughly is a necessity for completion. Without training and testing, you might think that you have good processes in place to the point of creating a false sense of security.

Another consideration is the authority of employees to carry out the procedure. Are you asking the custodian to decide if the public Wi-Fi is deactivated during a hostage crisis? The responsibilities have to be outlined in the procedure. A well-written policy will include specific information on who is responsible for each specific procedure. Remember to list the responsible individual or group by title or role, not by name, in case that individual leaves or transfers to another position.

## BAD POLICIES INCREASE RISK

Another unanticipated problem is that policies can create liability by creating a duty to act that exceeds normal standards or requirements. The accompanying sidebar outlines some of the liability risks.

## ARE BAD POLICIES MAKING YOU A LIABILITY TARGET?

Risks come in all shapes and sizes—and more importantly from any direction. Typically, we think of risks as those dangers or hazards that are coming at us from others, maybe employees, but usually from outside our organizations. Sometimes, however, we may be our own worst enemy.

One way we cause ourselves to stumble is through poorly written policies. Policies and procedures are the backbone of many organizations and embraced by HR departments. Policies should be guides or even educational tools letting employees know what the company expects for a given situation. The procedures should outline how the staff will do that.

However, there are times when a policy causes more harm than good. In fact, it can put an organization in a dangerous situation, exposing it to more loss than is necessary. Bad policies can increase the risk of liability at the worst end of the spectrum. At best, a bad policy can create inefficiencies, be unproductive, or simply be misguided. Somewhere in the middle could be employee dissatisfaction when a policy attempts to solve a problem that doesn't exist.

A poorly written or thought-out policy is an unnecessary risk and creates increased liability. This may sound dramatic, but is not as infrequent as you might think. When an organization faces a lawsuit, the courts will quickly look to policy manuals and whether or not the company followed their own policy. This means that if a policy is more restrictive or requires acts above and beyond typical case law, you increase the risk of losing a lawsuit.

As a police officer, we were expected to know the law as well as policies for a wide variety of situations and had to be able to act in seconds. I was surprised at one point in my career to find that our department's policy for use of force was more restrictive than state law. One example had to do with the use of deadly force to defend yourself or someone else. Under state law, an officer would be justified to use deadly force to stop an attack that could cause death or serious bodily injury. Per policy, an officer could not respond to an imminent attack involving serious bodily injury with deadly force. That would mean that a suspect wielding a baseball bat swinging at your knees threatening to cripple you or a victim would not justify a deadly response per policy. If an officer did face that situation and shot an attacker to stop harm to themselves or another, the department could be sued for failure to follow its own policy.

*(Continued)*

## ARE BAD POLICIES MAKING YOU A LIABILITY TARGET? *(cont'd)*

Police pursuit policies are another potential hot topic. An overly restrictive policy, as compared to local laws, could increase the risk of liability if it is not followed. On the other hand, limiting pursuits may reduce accidents and injuries to innocent bystanders and presumably reduce the chance of a situation that would generate a lawsuit.

You might be thinking that these examples have nothing to do with your own situation. However, you might be in a position increasing liability inadvertently through other, more mundane, policies. For example, suppose you have a policy of doing a background check on all new hires and the policy states that it is supposed to include a reference check. The screening includes a criminal history check or a verification of past work history, but no one ever calls a reference. In the event that an employee commits a crime and it is discovered that the company was not following its own policy, there could be an increased possibility of failing to act as promised.

There is also the correlation to compliance issues. For many different industries, there are compliance or accreditation concerns. In health care, for example, most hospitals choose to be accredited through The Joint Commission (TJC). One TJC requirement is that an organization follows its own policies. It follows, then, that the policies need to be realistic to ensure that employees do, and are, following the policy. If a policy is overly cumbersome or not practical, then the hospital could be out of line and be found to be out of compliance during an audit or survey even though the policy exceeds TJC standards.

Policies and procedures are necessary, and when well written, help employees perform their jobs more effectively and to understand what is expected. Good policies also help organizations protect themselves from mistakes and avoid legal pitfalls. The wrong or poorly written policy can do the exact opposite. Each policy should be carefully thought out, with the goals identified and any potential legal risks evaluated.

## Testing Procedures

Going back to our karate forms, a student practices over and over to build muscle memory. Practice through training and testing is the fundamental way to build organizational memory and develop the automatic or instinctive responses your business needs to function optimally, especially during emergencies or major security incidents.

## ARE BAD POLICIES MAKING YOU A LIABILITY TARGET? *(cont'd)*

Testing can be done in a number of different ways, and most likely, some overlap or combination should be done to be the most effective. The obvious test is a traditional one, a quiz to test how well employees know the policy and procedure. These tests may show how well the basic concept is understood but do not really test the ability to respond in a crisis or time-sensitive situation. That is where scenarios, such as facilitated discussions, are useful. The facilitator can ask a group follow-up questions or what-if questions, even changing key points of the scenario to emphasize learning.

Workplace violence is a good example. Most companies have something in place regarding the response to workplace violence. The policy may be a simple statement that violence and/or harassment will not be tolerated. The procedure may ask employees to report acts of violence and threatening behavior.

It sounds simple enough so far, right? Report acts of violence. The facilitator of a tabletop drill can delve further, though, and really question the group about what they would report. For example, would it be a threat if a new employee said that he was treated badly at his last job and he should have "gone postal"? No one at the new place has been threatened, right? What if he added that he would do just that if he were fired from the new position? Is it threatening if an employee sends long, rambling e-mails complaining about his unjust treatment—daily? What if someone is routinely rude, even flipping off coworkers when challenged on something? When is the right time to report this kind of behavior?

Perhaps the best type of testing is drills, in particular, fully functional drills. Fully functional drills create some of the same stress factors, require staff to respond to a situation, and are a great way to test response plans. Functional drills are planned exercises, albeit not always announced, that simulate some type of security emergency crisis. Everyone involved will be expected to respond as close as possible as they would to a real situation. A bomb threat could be a functional drill. A caller makes a staged threat while observers check to see if the right protocol is followed and that the threat is relayed appropriately. The organization should evaluate the threat, decide whether to evacuate or not, and conduct a search for suspicious items. Evaluators look for specific tasks and provide a critique at the end of the drill during a debriefing session.

All these testing techniques and practice build organizational memory.

*(Continued)*

## ARE BAD POLICIES MAKING YOU A LIABILITY TARGET? *(cont'd)*

### Where to Start

If you do not have any security policies or need to make changes, the thought of all that work can be overwhelming. Where to start? Earlier we mentioned "red" policies, those that address emergency situations. These policies are the most critical to know since the events can happen quickly and there may not be the opportunity for employees to go back and brush up on the details.

It certainly makes sense to start with those critical policies first. The next tier should be the situations that come up more frequently, perhaps even daily. Point of sale could be an example. Retailers have to (or should) have special controls in place at the point of sale to prevent employee theft, including "sweetheart" deals to friends as well as the theft of cash from the register. Working at the cash register could be a daily experience, so the policy on cash-handling procedures should be a high-priority focus.

Once you have decided what training needs to be done, you must figure out the "how." Training can be done in person, with either a classroom session or one on one such as with a training employee or mentor. Classrooms can be good when a group of employees need the same training. One-on-one training works better for developing specialized skills where tasks might need to be demonstrated and then repeated by the student.

Another training option, one growing in popularity, is computer-based training. The advantage is that employees can learn in smaller segments and work around their schedules. Instead of sending employees to a full eight-hour day, and perhaps paying to backfill a position, employees can do the training in smaller sections that fit into daily schedules. For example, 30-minute training can be covered during a slow part of the day. Also, there is no instructor tied up each time an employee wants or needs training. The downside is that there could be upfront costs for learning management software. Of course, it is possible to create your own using Microsoft's PowerPoint or a similar program, recording audio and creating a slide show.

With any form of training, there must be tests. That is the only way to be certain that employees have mastered, or at least grasped, the policy and procedure in question. These tests should not be designed to trick students but should reinforce key points and vital steps.

## ARE BAD POLICIES MAKING YOU A LIABILITY TARGET? *(cont'd)*

The ultimate training is realistic drills to see if employees are able to, and actually do, follow protocols in real-life scenarios, set up with objectives and goals that demonstrate how effective the learning has been. Debriefing should assess any gaps in training or in the policy or procedure.

Drills can be eye opening and expose serious gaps in an employee's understanding of policies. If you've been involved in creating a policy, drafting the procedure, and understand it front and back, it is easy to assume other employees will be just as familiar with it. Do not assume that is the case! Tabletop sessions or even quick discussions can reveal a lack of understanding about the procedure. During a drill on active shooter scenarios in a hospital, I was surprised to find that hospital staff were unsure about how to respond to medical calls while an active shooter was on the loose and randomly shooting victims. I had thought the policy was crystal clear that everyone should shelter in place until police were on the scene and an all clear was given. Clearly, this drill emphasized the need for additional training and a refresher.

### Practical Examples

What security policies or procedures an organization needs depends on a wide variety of factors. What type of business is involved? A retail outlet will have very different security concerns than a school or a nuclear power facility. The number of employees, access by visitors or outsiders, and type of critical assets at the site and the location all play into the security demands. Those needs dictate the individual security policies and procedures that should be in place for a given business or organization. Table 5.1 provides an overview of common procedures, listing each as either emergency, urgent, or administrative. This provides a basic starting place in building your own security measures.

There are some common requirements for any organization, however. Even very different corporations will have some similarities, leading to some basic security procedures that every company should have in place.

*Reprinted with permission from the Business Karate Blog.*

*(Continued)*

## ARE BAD POLICIES MAKING YOU A LIABILITY TARGET? *(cont'd)*

**TABLE 5.1**   Sample Security Policies

| Red (Emergencies) | Yellow (Urgent or Immediate) | Green (Administrative) |
|---|---|---|
| Active shooter[1] | Weapons and contraband[1] | Background screening[1] |
| Hostage[1] | Drug and alcohol abuse[1] | Information security[1] |
| Robbery[1] | Access control[1] | Security management plan[1] |
| Bomb threat response[1] | Visitor management | Video and alarm testing |
| Assessing violent threats[1] | Cash handling | Crime prevention[1] |
| Alarm response | Workplace violence (including domestic violence)[1] | Travel security |
| Emergency lockdown | Crime reporting[1] | Investigations |
| | | Identity theft prevention |

[1] *Must-have security policy.*

Every organization should have a written policy or procedure on active shooters. Even small businesses have been targeted by killers, often former employees. Every staff member should know what the emergency process is. The Department of Homeland Security (DHS) uses a quick reference, originally developed by the Houston Police Department: Run – Hide – Fight. There is a simple reminder supported by videos, posters, and flipcharts on the DHS website. Of course, running should include alerting others to help everyone escape or hide. Practical steps specific to the organization on how to barricade themselves or special needs should be included in the policy and in training.

Along the same lines is a hostage policy. Providing some basic information on how to react during a hostage situation is a necessity. Who will liaison with police? How should employees act? For example, do not try to negotiate or make promises, but do talk about your personal life to make yourself a person, not just a target to the hostage taker. For staff not in the immediate area, stay away, out of danger.

As you go through the list, some points are perhaps more obvious than others. For example, you might wonder what domestic violence has to do with workplace violence. Why should a company policy address something that happens in an employee's personal life? If an employee is a victim of domestic violence and calls the police, the suspect may be arrested and the victim could even be relocated to a safe house or stay with a friend or family member. The suspect may not know where the victim is staying, but the suspect does know where the victim works. Many domestic attacks occur at work, in particular when an employee is arriving or leaving from work. Policies that encourage victims to report problems to their manager, and practical steps to protect them, do become a vital way to protect others in the workplace. Providing photographs or pictures of the suspect to employees at entrances or on the grounds is extremely important. Other employees can be on the lookout for the suspect; copies of any restraining orders can be kept for convenient reference for law enforcement; staggering or shifting the employee's hours and monitoring the parking lot for the suspect or his or her vehicle are a few steps that can be taken to protect a victim while at work.

## CONCLUSION

For a response to become instinctive, lots of practice is necessary. In any sport, the successful athletes are the ones who practice harder, longer, or tougher than the rest. That practice and repetition builds muscle memory, so the response is natural and flows smoothly. Karate students use forms to repeatedly practice combinations of blocks and attacks to build that level of muscle memory.

Building organizational memory requires a certain dedication and determination as well. However, with some effort and careful planning, organizations can develop that same level of instinctive response. Instead of karate forms, the foundation is policy and procedure. Developing well-planned and rehearsed procedures will help protect organizations when things go wrong.

## BUSINESS KARATE BELT LEVEL

Test your company's karate belt level in the discipline of awareness/stance. If your organization meets each belt level and all the standards of the lower belts as seen in Figure 5.1, you have then achieved that color level.

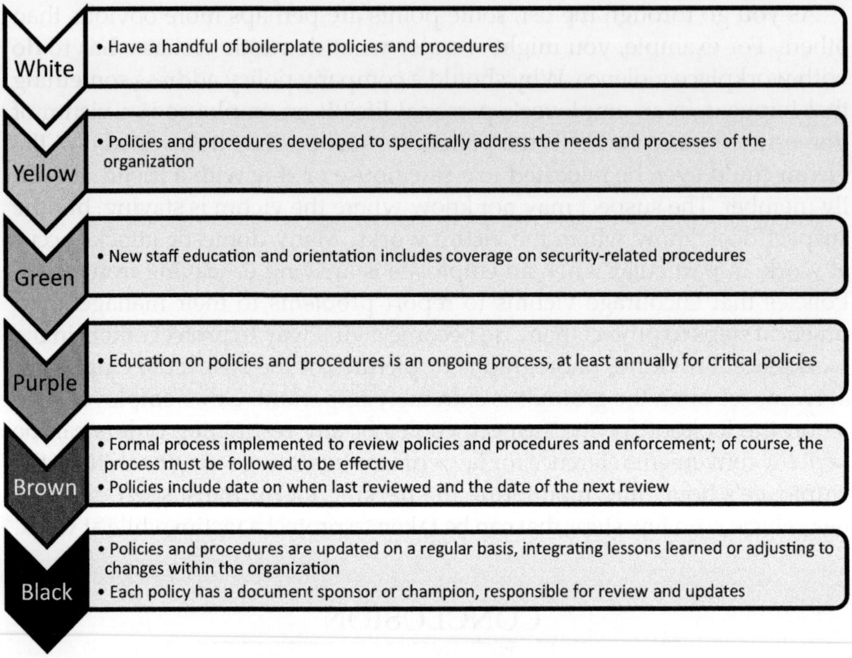

**White**
• Have a handful of boilerplate policies and procedures

**Yellow**
• Policies and procedures developed to specifically address the needs and processes of the organization

**Green**
• New staff education and orientation includes coverage on security-related procedures

**Purple**
• Education on policies and procedures is an ongoing process, at least annually for critical policies

**Brown**
• Formal process implemented to review policies and procedures and enforcement; of course, the process must be followed to be effective
• Policies include date on when last reviewed and the date of the next review

**Black**
• Policies and procedures are updated on a regular basis, integrating lessons learned or adjusting to changes within the organization
• Each policy has a document sponsor or champion, responsible for review and updates

FIGURE 5.1   What is your belt level?

# 6

# Punching: When They Are Close Enough to Kiss— Internal Threats

## WHEN TO PUNCH

Punches, kicks, knife-hand attacks, elbow strikes, sweeps, and joint locks—the list of potential attacks could go on and on. Karate students learn a variety of ways to stop an attacker. Perhaps the most ubiquitous of these attacks is the punch, which is the only attack that has its own sport (boxing) completely dedicated to it. Punches are used in probably every form of martial art and self-defense. Some, like tae kwon do, stress kicks for a majority of attacks, but punches still play an imperative role.

When I studied tae kwon do, I remember one instructor who was fond of saying that punches were best when your opponent was "close enough to kiss." This is not the mental image you want when talking about self-defense. The point, however, is valid. Punches are best for an attacker close to you and "in your space." He is too close for a kick to work. You may not have the right balance for a knee or elbow strike. In close quarters, a punch is a quick and easy way to get back in a position to block or protect yourself from follow-up attacks.

## WORKPLACE PUNCHES

What do punches have to do with workplace security? Think of those who are inside your outer defenses and may be "close enough to kiss." Employees!

Employees may pose a greater risk than the crooks on the outside. Employees have access to large areas of the business, and depending on their role, may have access to some of the most valuable assets your business owns.

Retail outlets have discovered this threat. Shoplifters steal on average $129 per incident, while employees steal $715 per case, according to the 25th Annual Retail Theft Survey (2012). The survey estimated that one out of every 40 employees was actually caught stealing! That number does not include those who were not apprehended.

## START AT THE BEGINNING

So if employees pose such a significant threat, how do you avoid the risks? Option #1 is simple: don't have any. That is not a very realistic approach though. Even many small businesses operating out of a home office have part-time employees or contractors. Contractors pose some of the same risks, so we will consider them as employees.

Preventing employee theft starts at the hiring phase, even with the original posting. The original job post should state that a background check will be conducted and should include some details. For example, if a credit check will be done, as well as a reference check, that information should be included in the posting. A word of caution: I've seen many prospective employees fail the background check, and I can only assume that they think it is a false threat or bluff.

The initial application is the next step in the process. Applications should always be used. Do not skip this stage by accepting only a resume or curriculum vitae. Resumes can be formatted in many different ways and may not include all the necessary information. For example, gaps in employment history are easier to hide in a resume. Other information required in an application may also be missing, such as salary or pay rate, or even reasons for leaving a previous job.

Gaps in employment can be very telling. Some gaps may be easily explained. For example, a layoff during poor economic times is understandable, as is a layoff when a company closes, announces bankruptcy, or has other reasons for cutting costs—something easily confirmed with a quick Internet search for business news. Frequent gaps could mean that the individual has been fired or let go. If that happens you should wonder why. The candidate may not be able to handle the jobs or is unable to get along with managers or coworkers. If fired, it could be for dishonesty, harassment, inappropriate interactions, or other problems. In any case, you need to do some digging in the interview to find out why that is.

If an applicant justifies each termination by blaming his or her manager, that should be a red flag. Again, many people have had personality conflicts with a past boss. But if every job ends the same way, that could spell trouble and you should not expect that things will end any differently.

Another aspect to look at with job history is the time spent at each job. If someone has a history of changing jobs every few months, that could show a lack of focus in their career. Often, employees on the job for less than 90 days cause more problems, such as theft, or threatening behavior.

Besides security risks, high turnover results in extra costs for hiring and training. There is also the impact on customers or clients if they become frustrated dealing with new, inexperienced employees.

## INTERVIEWS

After reviewing the applications and selecting the top tier for the next step, the interview becomes a key component to gauge the applicants for their skills and knowledge as well as honesty and potential violence. Interviews are the point in the hiring process where the rubber meets the road. This is the opportunity to follow up on any questions raised by the application.

I hate to be the bearer of bad news, but there is no magic formula or set of questions that will automatically pinpoint a liar or security threat. If predicting human behavior were an exact science, there would be little need for recruiters or human resource departments.

It is not all dark, though. There is some good news. With the right techniques and questions you can do a better job of weeding out more potential problems.

First and foremost, be consistent in your questioning. You need to ask all applicants the same questions to better demonstrate equality or fairness in the hiring process. If you are ever faced with a discrimination suit, it will be much easier to defend when the same questions are asked of all employees. I do know of successful business leaders who randomly ask questions of applicants and do not keep any notes. The questions still run along a consistent theme, such as describing leadership style, how discipline is handled, or how employees are recognized. Personally, I like to plan the basic questions ahead of time and keep some notes on the responses. My notes are very brief. To keep my focus on the interviewee, I mark a plus or negative depending on if I thought that question was answered adequately. I may add one or two words to help remind me of the answer.

Use open-ended questions for interviews whenever possible. Letting an interviewee sail through your screening with simple "yes" and "no" answers reveals nothing about the candidate. One-word answers do not show his or her true qualities and certainly do not tell you anything about his or her ability to communicate. Perhaps a job requirement is to be able to use Microsoft Excel. You could ask, have you used Excel before? You will probably get an "oh, yes" response. An open-ended question would be, tell me how to create a pie chart in Excel. The answer will tell you much more about the candidate's actual ability as well as a sample of how she communicates or explains ideas to others.

If reviewing work history, you can still use open-ended questions. Compare the following two conversations:

Interviewer (I): "I see you worked for ABC, Inc. for 3 years."

Candidate (C): "Yes, I did."

I: "And you left for the Widget Co. due to a raise?"

C: "That's right. It paid much more."

Or:

Interviewer (I): "I see you worked for ABC, Inc. What did you do there?"

Candidate (C): "I started as a sales representative taking calls from potential customers. They actually promoted me to customer service as I did a good job and the new customers wanted to keep working with me."

I: "What did you like best?"

C: "Definitely, working with the clients."

I: "Why did you leave for the Widget Co.?"

C: "I was hired to be the manager of the customer service department. It was hard leaving ABC, but this was too good of an opportunity to pass up."

As you can see, open-ended questions can reveal much more information during an interview. This approach also helps build a certain rapport, and if an applicant is comfortable you will find out much more about them.

Human Resource directors are very fond of consistency when hiring, or in any practice. Consistency does not mean that you cannot follow the flow of a conversation or ask for clarification during the interview. Even though you want to be consistent, be sure to ask follow-up questions. Digging into answers can be very revealing. If someone says that she left a job due to a personality conflict, do not let that go without further exploration. A simple "What happened?" can open the door to a flood of useful information. Each answer may lead to another question. Do not be shy about asking more questions if you do not understand something.

Interviewer (I): "Why did you leave ABC?"

Candidate (C): "My boss, she didn't like me."

I: "Why not?"

C: "She thought I stole something."

I: "Why would she think that and what was missing?"

C: "Some cash was missing from a secretary's desk. She thought it was me because some of the other coworkers accused me of taking stuff from their lunches out of the cafeteria."

I: "What made the others accuse you of that?"

C: "Well, I thought the lunch stuff had been in the fridge a long time and no one was going to eat it anyway."

Now, this simple exchange has revealed a lot more than a personality conflict and raises several potential red flags. Your candidate may have problems getting along with coworkers, and there could be issues with his or her truthfulness.

Typically, I like to start an interview with questions about the candidate's work history and experience. It can serve as an icebreaker and gives the candidate a chance to start with a topic she knows well—herself. It is also a way to see how she communicates. Someone who starts down a long and uninteresting duplicate of their resume may not have the interpersonal skills necessary for the job. Or they might just be nervous.

This is where a question may actually be too open-ended. Starting with "So, tell me about yourself" is dangerous to you and to the candidate. You may only hear those things the candidate chooses to share. On the other hand, many candidates will just ramble through their life story, especially candidates with less interviewing experience. The point is not to set him or her up for failure, but rather to learn if they have the combination of skills to do the job and can be trusted.

Instead, ask open-ended questions about a specific position or education. If the application or résumé indicates that the candidate led a team through a project, ask questions about her role and what she did. You may discover that instead of leading the team, she was simply a participant. Again, this helps get a more accurate picture of the skills, abilities, and experience of the candidate beyond the inflated version that often appears on resumes or applications.

Next, I move to specific requirements, such as credentials, professional certifications, training, or ability to meet standards.

Even asking questions about education or degrees is an opportunity to be open ended. You can ask about specific classes or coursework and how that would apply to the current opening. It is also one way to avoid hiring someone with a degree from a diploma mill—an unaccredited college or university that sells diplomas that are not backed up with education or course work.

A good tactic is to let applicants know up front that you will be checking references and contacting past employers. Another tactic is to remember the names of previous managers or references and mention them by name when asking the applicant what that individual will say about them. Sometimes applicants seem surprised when the name is mentioned and almost worried that you may actually know them personally.

When checking references, it is always good to confirm how the individuals met, how long they've known each other, and what the working relationship was. It is surprising how much you can learn by just asking some basic questions. If he or she moves forward in the interview process, you can compare the answers with what the reference says as a way to cross-reference the information and, potentially, the integrity of the applicant.

The last element of the interview is scenarios. Asking about past situations or posing "what if" scenarios are useful for looking at how applicants respond to realistic job demands. Scenarios can also be used to gauge honesty or integrity by asking about past situations.

## BACKGROUND CHECKS

The interview is only part of the story. No matter how good you are at interviewing, someone may lie or, at worst, manipulate what she says. Or, at best, you hear her perspective on past work experiences. Even a great police investigator may only get confessions in 80% of their cases. That is a phenomenal success rate, but when it comes to hiring, do you want to take the chance that 20% or more of your applicants have hidden key elements from you during the interview? No? I did not think so. That is why a solid and consistent background check is so vital to the hiring process.

As with any issue related to human resources, there are potential legal issues. It is a good idea to run your hiring process, including how you will conduct background checks, past an attorney who specializes in the HR arena. If you operate in multiple countries, it is critical to check the legal issues in each country or jurisdiction where you hire employees.

### EUROPEAN UNION CERTIFICATE OF GOOD CHARACTER

Multinational companies must comply with laws and regulations of the countries where they operate. Part of the background screening process for countries in the European Union can include a request for the Certificate of Good Character from the applicant or employee. This certificate is one

## EUROPEAN UNION CERTIFICATE OF GOOD CHARACTER *(cont'd)*

way of showing whether or not the individual has a criminal history. The challenge is that each country has a different method for getting that certificate and the certificate may look different, including being printed in the local language. Be sure to know what a genuine certificate looks like and what security features it should have, such as embossed stamps or watermarks—to help prevent making a decision based on a forged document.

The British government provides background screening through the Disclosure and Barring Service (DBS), formerly the Criminal Records Bureau. The DBS website includes guides for employers looking to conduct background checks in countries around the world. The international information can be found at https://www.gov.uk/government/publications/criminal-records-checks-for-overseas-applicants. Beware that some of the links in the various files may change or rules may be updated. However, this is a good resource to use as a starting point.

Background checks come in many different forms and should be customized or suited to the organization as well as the position.

I once met a small business owner who used his own method for a background check. He told me that he would ask each applicant if she were there to steal from him. He would pull out a $100 bill and put it on the table in front of her. "If so," he would tell the candidate, "go ahead and tell me now and you can take the $100 bill and walk away." I'm not sure I would recommend this method—it seems a way to reward dishonest behavior. However, the owner felt that it worked for him.

A good, general background screening should include several elements. One is confirmation of work and employment history. Do the dates and titles match up? Second, check on any applicable education. If a degree is a requirement, do a quick check to confirm that it is from an accredited university or college. Third, contact references and find out how well or how long they have known the applicant. Are there any concerns related to honesty, anger or violent behavior, or ability to work well with others? Forth, a criminal history should be part of the screening. Are there any convictions for crimes that could affect the applicant's ability to perform the job at hand? Fifth, a check of the applicant's credit history is highly recommended, especially if they will have any fiduciary duties (i.e., bookkeeping or cash handling). Last, a verification to check for a valid Social Security number, in the United States. Using E-Verify protects a company from accusations of knowingly hiring anyone in the country illegally.

Before looking at each of these areas, let's take a step back and think about the goals or objectives of the background screening. Is the goal to find the "perfect" candidate? That could be a long search as perfection is a rare quality (especially finding it in others!). When it comes down to it, there are just a few goals to focus on:

1. Is the person honest?
2. Will he or she create a hostile or violent workplace?
3. Do they have the experience and knowledge necessary to perform the job?

The answers to these three questions will indicate whether that person is the best, though maybe not perfect, fit for the opening.

---

## EMPLOYEE BACKGROUND CHECKS, EDUCATION FRAUD, AND DIPLOMA MILLS

Some bad decisions are easy to correct. Many are not. Hiring the wrong person can be a very expensive ordeal and may be very disruptive to your business, coworkers, and, perhaps worse, to your customers. According to the Department of Labor, the cost of turnover is approximately one-third of the employee's annual salary.

When employees steal, the average cost per incident is much higher than the losses due to outsiders, such as shoplifters or burglars. The cost on average is $62,000 for a lower level employee and increases the higher up in management the employee is. There is also the impact on the company reputation if an employee is not properly vetted and causes harm, especially in an event that garners a lot of media attention.

According to a study by the Society of Human Resource Management (SHRM), as many as 53% of resumes contain false information and 78% are misleading. The three most common areas falsified are education, job titles, and dates of employment. In general, a call to past employers will help validate past job titles and dates of employment. Human Resource departments are often allowed by policy to provide that much information, and, hopefully, you have a background screening that includes making those calls.

That leaves education as a "high risk" area that is often falsified. And that leads to the question, how risky is it to hire someone with exaggerated or falsified education? That depends on the position, how critical the education requirements are to succeed, and what is needed to help your organization succeed. In my opinion, the most important aspect is that the candidate is truthful about the information on their resume or application. If they are deceitful at this stage, how could you ever really trust them after they are employed?

## EMPLOYEE BACKGROUND CHECKS, EDUCATION FRAUD, AND DIPLOMA MILLS *(cont'd)*

First, you must clearly identify what education is needed for each job description. That base requirement helps to determine what kind of educational background you need to verify and helps guide the screening process.

Second, confirm that a potential candidate meets the necessary requirements. Sounds obvious, but dig a little deeper. This means that you need to verify that the education meets your requirements. Did the classes teach the basic skills or knowledge necessary? Did your potential new employee pass the curriculum?

Third, the college or university needs to be researched. The education provided must be accepted or, at the least, the school must teach to a level that matches the industry. In short, is the degree in question issued by a recognized or accredited college or university? If not, the degree could be from a diploma mill—an institution that sells degrees without any education or curriculum supporting it.

This all leads to the verification process.

Start with the college or university. Is it accredited? If not, that does not mean that it is not a valid education. Some schools choose not to be accredited as they feel it might conflict with their goals—religious schools are one possible example. For colleges and universities in the United States, accreditation can be confirmed online through the Department of Education.

Search the Internet for information on the school as well. If the university does not have information about the curriculum or education process—beware. Some diploma mills go so far as to offer education credits for work experience and do not require a student to attend any classes, either online or in person. There have also been programs set up that appear to be affiliated with legitimate universities, but have no connection.

Next, verify that the candidate attended and graduated from the program. Many universities will send an official or unofficial copy of the transcript directly to an employer. This is even done for many professional certifications in order to confirm that minimum standards are met. Within the European Union, the comparable transcript of record is used to verify class work and grades. A copy of a degree provided by an applicant could easily be forged on a computer, so rely on verification provided directly by the school.

Education tends to be more of a dominant focus on entry-level positions where there is not a lot of work history to review. However, many

*(Continued)*

## EMPLOYEE BACKGROUND CHECKS, EDUCATION FRAUD, AND DIPLOMA MILLS *(cont'd)*

industries deal with compliance issues and some require verification of education for many positions. Health care is one example. Hospitals that want to be accredited by The Joint Commission or those that want to be eligible for Medicare/Medicaid funds must meet specific standards surrounding verification of licensing and background screening. The Sarbanes-Oxley Act requires that all officers of publically traded companies have background screenings done, including verification of education.

Getting the right people on board is one of the tougher decisions and is not easy. A background screening that includes educational experiences is one piece to help build the right team for long-term success.

*Reprinted with permission from the Business Karate Blog (www.businesskarate.blogspot.com).*

Checking employment and education history is one way, beyond the interview, to look into the applicant's knowledge and experience and see if it matches the requirements of the position.

The reality is that many companies will not provide any information other than dates employed and job title. It is not illegal for companies to provide information, but is seen as a risky practice, presumably for fear of liability if the wrong information is disclosed. That said, the individual answering the phone might be more forthcoming. In one case, I called the previous employer and the woman who answered started out very friendly and happy to help. As soon as I gave the name of the applicant, her demeanor changed, and she said that she would have to transfer me to the legal department. The applicant had told me that there had been issues, but had sugarcoated the situation and tried to put a positive spin on it. I was suspicious, and by calling the previous employer, learned enough to know that the applicant had left under a dark cloud of suspicious circumstances that, combined with other information, led me to choose someone else.

References may provide a bit more insight. Do not assume that because someone is listed as a reference that he or she will always give glowing reviews. Many references are never even asked about whether or not they would give a good review. Some may not know the applicant for any real length of time and may not be able to give more than perfunctory answers about the candidate. On a couple of occasions, I've found that two acquaintances meeting at a job fair have agreed to be references for each other.

**TABLE 6.1**   Reference Checklist

Applicant name:

Reference name:

Date:

Phone:

1. How long have you known the applicant?

2. List three strengths of the applicant:

3. What is their main weakness or area to improve?

4. How would you rate the applicant's trustworthiness on a scale of 1–10, with 1 being the lowest? Examples?

5. If you were me, would you hire the applicant? Why?

When talking to a reference, respect his or her time. Have five or so questions and finish up quickly. You will get more productive responses. Some ideas are listed in Table 6.1. You can customize to match your needs or the position. How long have you known each other? How did you meet? What is a strength? Weakness? Would you have him or her housesit for you? Describe a time you've seen him or her handle a conflict or disagreement with others. Ideally, you want to gauge honesty and integrity while minimizing the risk of bringing on board someone with a negative or hostile personality.

The next step is to check for related criminal history. This step can only be done after a conditional job offer has been extended. There are many different companies that offer this type of service. When selecting one, confirm which court records are included in the database and how far back does the check extend. Some may only look at a local jurisdiction or state and not include other states. If a candidate was charged with a crime elsewhere, it would be missed completely.

In the United States, arrests are generally not allowed to be used as grounds to eliminate a prospective employee. Only convictions may be considered. After all, the law states "innocent until proven guilty," and an arrest is probable cause, not guilt. I have to confess, as a former police officer, that when I made an arrest, I was certain of the individual's guilt and the courts would drop charges, offer pleas to lesser offenses, and so on. It is hard for me to ignore arrest records, if available.

Part of the criminal history is to decide what convictions have an impact on the job or position. For example, multiple convictions related to driving under the influence would have an impact on a position that requires driving. An arrest for assault could be a factor if hiring security personnel and there is a worry of someone being prone to using excessive force. Theft, fraud, or embezzlement charges are a red flag for any position.

It is important to let applicants know that a criminal history will not automatically eliminate them from consideration. However, failure to be truthful during the application and interview process will. If at any point during the screening any discrepancies or lies are uncovered, question the applicant, but if it is not resolved, the process should end. If the individual is not honest at the start, how could you ever trust them in the future?

---

### SECURITY HIRING MAXIM

- Do NOT hire anyone who lies or is dishonest on the application or during the interview!

---

Credit history is another key component of a comprehensive background check. In the world of loss prevention, when it comes to employee theft a serious red flag is someone who is in over his or her head financially. Worries about bankruptcy, paying debts, or saving her home can all be serious motivators.

Credit checks become more critical as the position increases in responsibility. According to a study on workplace fraud published by the Association of Certified Fraud Examiners, the highest losses come from the employees highest in the organization. The median loss by dishonest executives was $573,000 as compared to the employee median loss of $60,000.

In the United States, the Federal Fair Credit Reporting Act has strict guidelines on how credit reports can be used and what has to be disclosed to the applicant. Employers must get permission, in writing, from the applicant and notify them that a credit check is part of the screening process. If a decision not to hire is made based on the credit report, the information used for that decision must be provided to the applicant, along with details on the individual's rights. The applicant must be given the chance to respond and verify its accuracy. Last, the name of the consumer credit agency that supplied the negative information must be given to the applicant. For the latest information, employers should check with the website of the U.S. Federal Trade Commission. Also, some states have strict rules on the use of credit reports, so check with your local states as well.

The last major step in the background screening process for employers in the United States is simply to verify that the applicant is able to work in the United States. Verification of the Social Security number using E-Verify is the easy way for that. If this step is skipped, you could have illegal aliens using forged SSN cards. That puts others at risk of a form of identity theft and tax liability. Your business could be the subject of a raid, and many employees could be detained, creating work stoppages as well as negative PR. E-Verify information can be found on the website from the United States Citizenship and Immigration Services (www.uscis.gov).

## DRUG USE AND PHYSICAL REQUIREMENTS

Now that you've take a thorough look at the conditional hire's background, you should check their present state or condition as well.

A drug screening is a typical process. Bringing on someone who uses illegal drugs or abuses prescription drugs could be a serious problem. Loss of productivity, excessive absences, safety, erratic mood swings, and theft are all problems stemming from drug abuse. The challenge is that so many different drugs are available and stay in the body different lengths of time. The screening should be reviewed periodically to test for the most likely substances used in your region or community. Even legal products can be used for a drug-induced high. In the past, air duster cans contained a chemical in the spray that could be inhaled to create a high. Street chemists are constantly creating new synthetic concoctions, such as bath salts, to get high. New synthetic drugs may not be illegal as the law has to catch up and there may not be any tests yet developed to detect a new synthetic.

In some states, marijuana has posed a special problem. States have legalized or are legalizing marijuana and issue special prescription cards to allow holders to possess specified amounts of the drug. However, court cases have supported employers who terminate individuals on the job under the influence of marijuana. Even in states like Colorado, where a prescription may be granted, it is limited to use at home, not in public. Marijuana is still considered a controlled substance under federal law as well.

Alcohol is a legal product that can generate lots of issues. Any substance abuse policy should address being under the influence of alcohol while at work. Unfortunately, short of someone showing up intoxicated at the job interview, it can be very difficult to detect. Some alcoholics are notoriously good at hiding their drinking.

If a position requires physical actions, such as lifting, the final screening should include some tests to ensure the applicant meets those requirements. If a position, such as security patrol, requires walking, establish a baseline such as walking 300 yards in three minutes. Lifting 25 lbs and carrying it 100 yards could simulate carrying a fire extinguisher during an emergency response. The key is to make sure that all screening tests reflect realistic job expectations. A requirement to do 20 pull-ups does not reflect anything about most jobs and should be left to elite military forces, but walking up two flights of stairs in less than a minute may. One manager liked to meet applicants at the entrance to the company and conduct the interview while walking around the facility at a moderately brisk pace. The position required walking and he could gauge basic fitness and energy by how well the applicant kept up during the walking interview.

## ONBOARDING AND FOLLOW-UPS

Once you've screened your applicants and brought them on board, it is not time to forget about them. There should be a process in place that outlines when an employee will be screened again. Some positions requiring top-secret clearance could involve rescreening every few years. In other cases, there could be a requirement to check criminal histories more often due to local licensing regulations. For example, security officers in certain cities or states are required to be licensed and renewed annually. Checking for criminal history is part of that licensing procedures, as well as drug screening.

Other organizations may choose to reassess when an employee is promoted to a new role. This should be consistent and done for all individuals in that position or department. Promotion to a senior leader may be the time to reevaluate or if the person is moving into a position with financial responsibility. The Sarbanes-Oxley Act requires that publically traded companies conduct background checks, including education verification, on key top leaders and board members. The purpose is to ensure that investors are making decisions based on legitimate financial statements rather than fraudulent or overblown estimates of market value.

Standards specific to certain industries mandate periodic review of an individual's criminal history. For example, the North American Electrical Reliability Corporation (NERC) is a nonprofit group responsible for monitoring the reliability of the power grid. NERC has implemented standards related to critical infrastructure protection (CIP). Standard CIP-oo4-1 requires that any employee with responsibility for critical cyber assets have a "personnel risk assessment" completed initially and then every seven years. This criminal history looks at the past seven years so any convictions would show up at some point.

Orientation and training are the next touch points that, correctly done, can build a base of trust and integrity. If the person doing the training for your new hires is that guy who is negative and "bad mouths" your organization, you are off to a bad start. This person will show the new person all the "tricks" on how to get away with things such as where to hide to slack off, how to abuse the clock-in/out process, and even how to "score" free stuff in the cafeteria. You will build a foundation of abuse, maybe theft, or at best someone so unhappy that they quit immediately to find a job with a more legitimate company.

Instead, orientation should cover the company ethics and value on integrity, but more importantly, share examples where employees demonstrated those ethics and how the company recognized their actions. The trainer should reinforce that and strive toward creating a state of mind or environment of integrity. A positive, professional environment where employees like coming to work will go a long way toward creating a place where dishonesty will not be tolerated (more to follow on this).

## SECURITY EDUCATION AND AWARENESS

Remember how the martial artists develop skills and improve speed through repeated practice? Ongoing practice and training keeps karate students focused, flexible, and fit. Likewise, once employees have been interviewed, screened, oriented, and trained, it is vital to reinforce security skills or awareness over time. This is generally referred to as security education and awareness training or SEAT.

Security education and awareness can come in many different formats or styles and be delivered in a multitude of ways. Newsletters, online or computer-based training, staff debriefings or meetings, and instructor-led classes are all examples of ways to conduct SEAT.

Monthly or quarterly newsletters are one way to provide ongoing security awareness. Newsletters should include tips related to safety at work, as well as personal safety, to help maintain interest. More in-depth training can cover how staff recognize violent warning signs or surveillance by potential terrorists.

SEAT should include information on how thieves operate and how simple carelessness can be so detrimental. How often have we heard that valuables should never be left in plain sight in a parked car? And yet, walk through any parking lot and you will see a wide variety of valuables in plain view, many even with the car unlocked. GPS devices, cell phones, laptops, tablets, purses, or duffel bags are just a few of the common items found, tempting would-be crooks. On rare occasions you can even find firearms. A few straightforward reminders with real-life examples may be enough to change behavior. Better yet, back up the training with rewards. With the parking lot example, randomly select cars in the employee lot that are locked and have no valuables in view, and reinforce that behavior with a small reward for the employees, such as a free lunch in the cafeteria.

The same could apply to passwords. Keeping track of dozens of passwords can be overwhelming. The easy answer is to write down all the passwords somewhere close to the computer for easy access.

Both examples are easily fixed, but may need the occasional reminder. Both could easily result in loss of key proprietary information.

## EMBEZZLEMENT AND EMPLOYEE THEFT

Embezzlement is the greatest form of risk related to employee theft. It is internal fraud, usually on a grand scale. In fact, one study estimates that organizations lose 5% of their revenue to fraud. Embezzlement often goes on for a long period of time, and the losses are far greater than most other forms of theft. The average in 2012 was $140,000 per incident, according to the Report to the Nations on Occupational Fraud and Abuse: 2012 Global Fraud Study published by the Association of Certified Fraud Examiners (ACFE). Moreover, the higher the position of the perpetrator in the organization translates to a greater amount of the loss.

Per the study, one way stood out as the most likely method to bring the crime to light (Table 6.2). It was not audits or even sound bookkeeping. Both help, but the number one way embezzlement was discovered was through tips; see Figure 6.1. Another employee or even customers noticed or suspected a problem and alerted the company, triggering an investigation.

Various studies have shown that a large number of companies, more than half, have lost 4–6% of total revenues to embezzlement. Clearly, embezzlement is a severe threat to any organization, and every business leader should take it very seriously.

One of the methods proven to help unmask embezzlement is the use of tips. Regulatory compliance for different industries frequently requires having an anonymous tip line in place to report fraud. The Sarbanes-Oxley

**TABLE 6.2**    Uncovering Internal Fraud

| Uncovering Fraud | % of Cases |
| --- | --- |
| Tip | 43.3% |
| Management review | 14.6% |
| Internal audit | 14.4% |
| By accident | 7.0% |
| Account reconciliation | 4.8% |
| Document exam | 4.1% |
| External audit | 3.3% |
| Alerted by police | 3.0% |
| Surveillance | 1.9% |
| Confession | 1.5% |
| IT controls | 1.1% |

*Data from 2012 study by the ACFE.*

Act, a law pertaining to publically traded companies on U.S. exchanges, is one such example.

Putting a tip line into place is a great start, but needs to be supported with training and awareness. What should employees report? What does suspicious behavior look like?

The best place to start is with the red flags—common actions or behaviors that could be a sign of fraud (see Table 6.3). The most common red flag

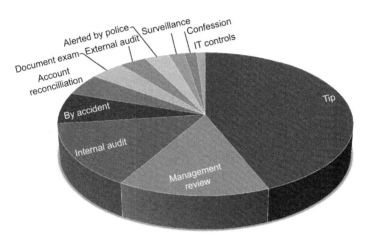

FIGURE 6.1   How fraud is discovered.

TABLE 6.3   Red Flags

| Common Red Flags Indicating Fraud |
| --- |
| Living beyond means |
| Financial troubles |
| Unusually close to vendors or clients |
| Control issues (i.e., refusal to take vacations) |
| Divorce or family problems |
| Defensive or suspicious |
| Addictions or substance abuse problems |
| Past employment issues |
| Complaints about pay or lack of authority |
| Excessive pressure to succeed |

is living beyond his or her means. To be honest, that is sometimes hard to see in our society where so many people have second mortgages or large credit card debts and seem to buy everything under the sun. Still, as you get to know people, there may be signs of extravagant living. Financial difficulties are another flag and almost the opposite of the first. Ongoing worries, beyond the normal, about money or finances could be a problem. Often, this could be tied to divorce, foreclosure, or even alcohol or drug addiction. Child support payments and even restraining orders can also be red flags. Gambling is another frequent cause.

Red flags at work could include unusual control of financial dealing or records. Often this shows up as refusal to take vacation and letting someone else handle accounts while he or she is gone for fear someone else may discover ongoing fraud or embezzlement.

Embezzlement can take several different forms. The most obvious involve the skimming or theft of cash. An employee could accept payment from a client but pocket the money instead of recording it or steal cash prior to depositing it in the bank. There are other, more complex methods as well. One example is a situation where an employee creates invoices for fictitious items or services. The employee could even create another company to send the invoices to and receive payment. Dishonest employees may manipulate payroll as well, such as receiving overtime pay for hours or time never worked. An employee with financial responsibilities can alter financial records to make an organization appear more successful and more valuable, bringing in investors or potential buyers. This can be done by inflating assets or revenues and underreporting expenses.

Aside from some of these embezzlement schemes, employee theft is another concern. Employees may steal cash or inventory. Employees may also give family or friends "sweetheart" deals and discounts at the register. Cash handling is a typical vulnerability. If you have points of sales or registers, individuals should be signed in with their own code to use the register. Drawers should be counted frequently to identify any losses. Point of sale software can alert managers to unusual activity at the register as well. Too many refunds, discounts, or voided transactions may indicate that someone is stealing from the register.

## PREVENTION

No matter what type of organization or business you are responsible for, there are some common ways to help create an environment of honesty and integrity. You may never completely eliminate the risk but should focus on minimizing the risk. Basically, this means creating a workplace where employees feel valued and appreciated (and in turn appreciate their job), understand the expectations, and feel comfortable bringing concerns forward.

How to show employees are valued or appreciated? That probably means something different to each of us. Recognition of good work is certainly one way. Perhaps less obvious is getting rid of coworkers who create a negative environment or leave the brunt of work for others. Those employees can have a very negative impact on everyone else. Often, other employees will not complain but could search for work elsewhere. Terminating the few problem individuals can bring everyone else up and boost morale.

Pay is another way to show real value. HR folks often point to studies that show employees do not leave jobs for pay but rather because of their immediate supervisor. Pay and compensation may not be the only factors, but do play a critical role, not just for retention, but also in regards to employee theft. Security Director's Report outlined a study tying pay with employee theft. Organizations that paid employees even a bit higher than market wages were less likely to have employee theft. According to the study, that difference caused employees to value their jobs more, and they were less likely to tolerate thefts by coworkers and less likely to steal themselves.

Employee morale may not seem like an obvious security issue or as having ties to loss prevention. However, companies that foster or tolerate disgruntled employees will run greater risks. Disgruntled employees create a sense of lack of caring about customers, coworkers, and the company. They may justify stealing by thinking that what they take is owed to them.

Morale is also affected when employees see others "get away" with serious offenses. If someone steals or threatens others and is allowed to continue that behavior, other employees will stop trying or give up good practices. After all, if there are no repercussions, why strive harder to be honest in company business?

In another study, researchers found that ethical leadership had less impact on those within a work group than the ethics of the peers. The researchers placed test individuals in groups assigned to work on a specific task and instructed not to use the Internet to find the solution. Finding the right solution meant each group member would earn an extra $300. One individual planted in the group would suggest "cheating" and offer to use the Internet with a smart phone. The other group members, also acting on previous instructions, would either agree with the cheater or not. In most cases, the test individual went along with whatever the group wanted to do. In the sample groups where the members agreed to use the Internet anyway, the individual was less likely to report the activity later to the researchers. When the group members disagreed with the Internet usage, the test individual was more likely to report the incident afterwards.

The bottom line is that employees are more likely to work ethically if coworkers are also ethical. Of course, that does not relieve leaders from the responsibility of setting a good, positive example. Many employees will pick up on how they should act by the actions of their department manager or director. That good example alone can help build a higher level of ethics and integrity in employees.

## LEADERSHIP ROLE

Setting an example and being a positive role model is only part of the leader's role. It is important to build a sense of "organizational justice." In the workplace, leaders, and the companies they represent, are being evaluated and judged by employees. Employees need to feel that everyone is treated fairly. The same standards apply to all employees. If some are treated with favoritism, that creates a standard of inequality. This perception of fairness and equality goes a long way toward creating an ethical work environment.

Leaders have to be certain that their actions match what they say. In other words, lead by example.

As a leader, you need to create an open door policy—a real open door policy. I haven't met a leader yet who doesn't claim to have an open door policy. However, I've noticed that all too often anyone who attempts to use that open door gets quickly shut down. The not-so-open door leader may belittle the messenger, not take it seriously, or act uninterested. Sometimes, the reaction comes across as a threat. I have found that expressing any concerns is often met with a reply that ends with, "I have an open door policy if you want to continue this discussion," generally after a belittling reply. That invitation to meet feels more like an invite to step into a lion's den. No thanks, I'll keep my concerns to myself in the future! This creates leaders who only hear what others think they want to hear regardless of the facts—not a healthy leadership environment for any organization.

## CONCLUSION

As we've seen, your own employees, those closest to you, are often the most damaging and responsible for the greatest risk to your enterprise.

The best protection is a multilayered approach. Careful screening and selection of new employees can help eliminate some risks. Once on board, lay the foundation with high-quality, positive training, maintain employee morale, and be a role model of the expectations and behavior everyone should demonstrate. Provide training to identify suspicious activity, and create an atmosphere to support and listen to anyone with concerns.

Changing the workplace will not happen overnight, but with careful planning and some hard work, you can begin making the right changes to build an encouraging and ethical environment.

# BUSINESS KARATE BELT LEVEL

Test your company's karate belt level in the discipline of awareness/ stance. If your organization meets each belt level and all the standards of the lower belts as seen in Figure 6.2, you have then achieved that color level.

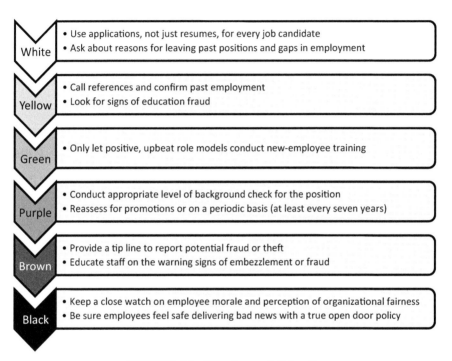

FIGURE 6.2   What is your belt level?

## Further Reading

Association of Certified Fraud Examiners (ACFE), 2012. Report to the Nations on Occupational Fraud and Abuse: 2012 Global Fraud Study. Austin, TX.

Jack L. Hayes International, Inc, June 2013. 25th Annual Retail Theft Survey. Wesley Chapel, FL.

State of Texas, Office of State Auditor, December 2000. An Annual Report on Full-Time Classified State Employee Turnover for Fiscal Year 2000. Retrieved from: http://www.sao.sta te.tx.us/reports/main/01-703.pdf (accessed 21.11.13.).

Statistic Brain Research Institute, publishing as Statistic Brain, July 16, 2012. Resume Falsification Statistics – Statistic Brain 2012. Retrieved from: http://www.statisticbrain.com/ resume-falsification-statistics/ (accessed 21.11.13.).

# 7

# Getting Your Kicks: Responding to External Threats

## KARATE KICKS

Punches may be the most natural or common types of attack, but martial arts are most closely identified with kicks. Flying sidekicks, spin kicks, and kicks extending up above an opponent's head are some of the images that come to mind. All seem to demonstrate power, flexibility, and even grace.

Kicks are a key attack in martial arts. Kicks are extremely powerful. Think how much stronger your legs are than your arms. Your legs are also longer, giving you more reach. A kick can hit an opponent who is out of range of a punch or other strike with an arm or hand.

Martial artists can use kicks to strike or distract an opponent with a weapon, such as a knife. Making both feet a potential weapon gives a karate student more choices in his arsenal. If a punch misses or is ineffective, he may be able to continue the attack with a kick.

Some martial arts stress kicks more than others. Tae kwon do is supposed to be 80% kicks, for example. The tradition or story is that the Korean people were overrun and ruled by armed warriors or bandits. The terrain was hilly and rolling. To add to the challenge, the peasants were not allowed to have weapons. The early roots of tae kwon do were developed as a way that the people could fight back and eventually win back their independence. Kicks became an integral part of unarmed combat as a way to use the power and reach of the legs to battle enemy warriors. The steep terrain also played a role, as the ability to use a high kick on an opponent uphill was vital to success. Eventually, this ancient fighting technique was adopted into modern tae kwon do in the mid-twentieth century. At least, that is how I've heard black belt instructors describe the history.

Modern practitioners often use the power of kicks to break several inches of wood with one blow. Sparring techniques are filled with roundhouse kicks, crescent kicks, jump kicks, sidekicks, and spin kicks. Each has its advantages and disadvantages, which can give a skilled black belt a win in a self-defense situation.

## BUSINESS KICKS

Punches are useful for an attacker very close to you, as we've discussed. In contrast, kicks are most beneficial against an opponent just outside your arm span. If punches are for internal threats, kicks are your protection against external threats.

External threats come in many different forms, each with a different degree of danger or risk. This is a good opportunity to review your threats identified in Chapter 3. Some external threats may be actual disasters or widespread events, such as a tornado or hurricane. These kinds of threats will be evaluated and discussed in Chapter 9.

Specifically, we are talking about external crime. Examples include shoplifting, robbery, burglary, vandalism, and sexual assaults. Data loss, hacking, or malware are also external crimes that can damage your business. Each one is a danger of direct loss, damage to your company's reputation, or harm to employees or customers. To protect your business, you must consider each and the best measures to put into, or keep in, place.

## IT GETS PHYSICAL

An Internet search of the word *security* provides over a million results. Many of those are related to information security. Information security, or Infosec, receives a great deal of attention and can be a very real protection from legitimate threats. Malware, spyware, denial of service attacks, or botnets (taking over other computers to assist in a coordinated attack), are some examples of potential problems or risks. Information security, however, often does not include some of the more physical threats.

Valuable information is not always electronic in form. Despite the move to electronic files or copies in place of hard copies, paper copies still exist. After all, what office doesn't have printers, paper, or file cabinets? Paperwork or hard copies are one form of information that can be lost or stolen. Customer files could be invaluable to a competitor or identity thief. Many offices keep detailed customer information on hand for billing, including address, Social Security number, and even salary or work information. There have been cases of burglars breaking into medical offices, not for cash or drugs, but for customer files to be used for identity theft. Crooks can even use online sites to sell information to identity thieves across the globe. Mortgage brokers, accountants, and financial planners all have critical information about customers on hand.

Any business that accepts checks should keep in mind the risks posed. Stolen checks can be acid-washed and reused for fraudulent purposes. Acid washing is a method to remove ink and rewrite the amount and "pay to" items on the check. Employee files are another source of critical information with addresses, credit information, and Social Security numbers.

Even day-to-day paperwork can pose risks. A company or department's profit and loss statements are an example. A competitor would find it very useful to see your expenses, revenues, and budget. Your business rival could compare productivity, related billing information, and overhead to its own practices and use that to advantage during any competitive bids or requests for proposals. Remember that a trash can is not a security measure. Paper copies in the trash can be recovered by others with a bit of "dumpster diving." Use a high-quality shredder that cuts paper in multiple directions, not just long strips, to protect even trash from corporate espionage. Shredder services are a great way to get rid of valuable paperwork that you want to dispose. It is vital to check, though, on the company and make certain that it provides a true security service. Verify that employees have been screened, and review the process they use to destroy critical documents.

Invoices and detailed bills also contain proprietary information. Details on prices and billing practices could be invaluable to competitors. Unfortunately, you do not have complete control as these items are, by nature, shared with customers. However, even as a customer, you may have reasons to keep that type of information confidential. If you have negotiated an excellent deal with a supplier, you may not want others to know and try to negotiate the same deal for themselves.

We have talked about some of the risks of a lost or stolen laptop. Besides the IT solutions, such as encryption or passwords, some basic crime prevention can go a long way. I know of one case where a tax accountant left a laptop and briefcase in his parked car. The laptop was in plain view. Someone broke in and stole it, along with the briefcase. The real loss was to that accountant's customers whose information and tax paperwork were on that laptop and their receipts were in the briefcase. The loss forced some clients to file extensions for their returns and potentially risk paying interest on any amounts owed. And, with the worries of ID theft, the customers had to create credit alerts with the three credit reporting agencies and monitor credit reports for fraudulent activity. All could have been avoided with common sense crime prevention. Do not leave valuables in a vehicle. If you do, put them in the trunk—out of sight.

How many of the affected clients were likely to use that accountant again or recommend him to friends or relatives? I doubt any.

Many businesses are beginning to expect or even require that employees provide their own IT devices, such as laptops or tablets. This is commonly referred to as "bring your own device" or BYOD. The risks in these cases include inconsistency or insufficient protocols to protect company data. Laptops or flash drives may not be password protected or have encryption software on the drives. Laptops and other wireless devices are susceptible to hacking, in which someone can use an exposed wireless connection to install software or malware, track passwords, or even use the device as a tool to attack other cyber targets (botnets).

Public wireless, or Wi-Fi, can be a security nightmare for anyone accessing the Internet at his or her local coffee shop, bookstore, or other public site. If you are using public Wi-Fi, for starters turn on your computer's firewall and disable file sharing. As a business using BYOD, this is one aspect you will not be able to control directly, and you need to educate employees about the uses of public Wi-Fi. Confirm the name of the Wi-Fi connection with employees. Some hackers will create a wireless network that "spoofs" or mimics a real one. If you log into this fake network, the hacker will have access to everything you do and type online.

Typing in passwords or those already stored in your computer could lead to compromise. Some hackers will use public Wi-Fi to detect passwords stored in the computer's registry. Whenever possible, only log onto websites that use an encrypted connection. This is most easily detected if the URL starts with "https" instead of just "http." The letter "s" at the end indicates an encrypted signal and helps protect activity on that site.

Several other steps can be taken but are more technical. One is to create a dedicated virtual private network (VPN) so that you will be hidden from hackers while online. The best method is simply not to do anything confidential while using a public Wi-Fi. Save your banking or online shopping for the safety of your home. Work offline on documents or other projects that could be critical information, such as your strategic plan, and do not access financial files from public hotspots. A good rule of thumb is to assume that anything you do or access on the Internet is not secure. Limit online usage to reading the news or other nonconfidential activities.

Passwords are not the only targets of high-tech theft. With so many different online sites or logins to remember and frequency of changes for some, it is hard for most of us to remember all the numerous and complex passwords. It is natural to write down the latest passwords and keep them some place convenient. That could be a sticky note on a monitor, a piece of paper in an adjacent drawer, or a notebook with a list of current passwords. So many people work in cubicles that the risk of data loss is compounded by the lack of privacy. Anyone walking by or after-hour cleaning crews or even overnight security could quickly find key passwords. Even offices near windows or public areas could be jeopardized.

Conduct a security audit that includes a detailed assessment of all information on hand and the associated risks. Look at measures as well as the actual practices used on a daily basis. How often do employees print critical paperwork and leave it on the printer for anyone to see? Printing a termination notice on a shared printer can be a problem, especially if found by the employee to be terminated or disciplined! The greater the risks, the tighter the security measures that should be in place. And most of all, remember the physical side of information security.

## VANDALISM

Vandalism is particularly challenging as an external threat as there is often no clear motive other than random destruction of property. That said, even without a rational motive, there are warning signs as well as steps to prevent vandalism.

Graffiti is probably the most common form of vandalism. Many jurisdictions even have special laws related to graffiti, or tagging, as it is commonly called. In addition to laws about destruction of property, there are those that cover the defacing of property. Even tagging that is easy to clean up or repair (i.e., soap on a window is defacing) can result in criminal charges against a suspect.

Graffiti can be a real risk to your organization. It is typically highly visible and creates the feeling of an unsafe environment. Imagine that you are choosing between two restaurants for dinner. One's parking lot is surrounded by walls or dumpsters covered in tagging. The other is surrounded by clean dumpsters and graffiti-free walls. All things being equal, most people will feel safer parking in the lot without the graffiti (see Figure 7.1). Preventing graffiti is just one way to make your business more competitive and give yourself the edge.

FIGURE 7.1    Isolated spaces and graffiti create the perception that your business is not safe.

Graffiti is often a warning of other criminal activity in the area. Tagging may be used to mark gang territories or even be a form of advertising. A dollar sign, for example, has been used as a way of showing that there is drug dealing in the area. Signs vary from region to region, gangs involved, and change over time. Check with your local police gang unit for current information in your area.

All this can create negative publicity. Some basic prevention tips will help protect your business and the customers' (and employees') perception of safety.

Lighting is key. Most taggers operate at night so they can work undetected. Lighting is one of the best protections, not just from graffiti but also from many crimes of opportunity. Whenever possible, increase lines of sight around the building to help detect criminals. Motion-activated lighting is a great tool as well. As a police officer, when walking through an area looking for a prowler or trying to set up a perimeter around a suspect, motion-activated lighting was always startling and upsetting. Suddenly, you felt exposed and naked and that everyone around was watching you. I can only think that for crooks the feeling is much worse and more likely to scare them off to find another location to ply their dishonest trade.

Keep bushes trimmed to less than three feet high and all branches of trees removed up to eight feet high. The shorter bushes and loss of low-hanging branches take away hiding spots and give people on the property better lines of sight.

Take away the large smooth surfaces so often used by taggers. Vines or latticework can be used to help cover large blank walls. Chain link or other, more decorative, fencing a few feet out from the surface can make it nearly impossible to tag. Another option is to plant low, thorny bushes around the base of objects to thwart someone trying to stand near the wall. Of course, if you want to look like a fortress, you could use concertina wire—not a look that works well for most businesses.

Almost any surface can be hit by taggers, including company vehicles or trucks, as well as fences or electrical transformers. Focus on the largest surfaces first or areas with a history of vandalism. Most taggers want the graffiti to be seen, so they will focus on highly visible, large areas. When graffiti does show up, clean it immediately. If it is not there, there are no bragging rights, no marking of territory, and no other symbolism. The crook's prestige and "artwork" is gone. On the other hand, if the vandal is successful, he will be back—after all, success breeds success. Check your local hardware store for cleaners specifically designed to remove graffiti.

Glass etching is another form of tagging and can be much more destructive or at least costly. In this case, an acid is used to mar or scratch designs or characters into glass. Other than replacing the glass, there is no real repair. Use the same types of security measures to reduce the risk.

# BURGLARY

Burglary is another challenging threat. By definition, burglary is a crime that happens when no one is supposed to be around. Business break-ins are more likely to happen at night or on weekends. According to FBI statistics, the average loss per business burglary is over $2100.

Burglaries come in several different formats. Many home burglaries occur through unlocked doors or windows. It is also surprising how many businesses are left unlocked. When I was training new police officers and wanted to work with them on building searches, we would go to a business park and begin walking around, checking doors until we found one unlocked.

Most burglars, however, are looking for a "quick win." A common business burglary is a smash and grab where the crook breaks in a window or door, grabs some key valuables, and quickly leaves before police arrive. Liquor stores are common targets for this type of crime, although many small businesses are hit by someone looking for cash in the registers or safes.

Some of the same security measures that protect your business from graffiti work just as well on burglary. Lighting is still a great crime deterrent. In one study by the Department of Justice, suitable lighting was the best crime prevention technique. Clear lines of sight are another helpful way to protect the property. Eliminating hiding spots increases the chance of the suspect being seen or detected. It also removes areas where the burglar may stash or hide stolen goods as he makes multiple trips into the building for stolen goods.

Just as with a car, keep valuables out of sight and out of reach from windows. A laptop or desktop computer or other high-value targets within view and easy reach increase risk of a smashed window combined with sticky fingers.

When assessing burglary risk, another landscape aspect to consider is ground cover. Flower gardens often are covered in mulch, but many businesses have rock gardens around the property. Large river rocks can be great around outer edges of a property. They are harder to walk across and can help reinforce territory and can reduce trespassing. The same rocks near windows or parking lots can be dangerous. You are providing a would-be burglar with conveniently located burglary tools. Large river rocks are great for smashing windows on buildings or vehicles (see Figure 7.2). For any landscaping near windows, replace large rocks with small rocks, less than one inch in size. It is much harder to break through most glass with small rocks or mulch.

Other burglary concerns are the doors and locks themselves. We've all seen some cop or detective show where the investigator quickly opens a locked door with a credit card. It can be that easy, but only if the door does

FIGURE 7.2   Tall bushes and poor lighting are great concealment for burglars, and large landscape rocks make smashing windows easy. Note the plywood over the window where one crook took advantage of just that.

not fit the frame properly. Have doors inspected and maintained at least once a year.

Covering door latches with a metal plate or latch guard also helps prevent forced entry, including limiting prying the door open. Keep in mind that the door is only one vulnerable spot—the entire doorframe supports and protects the door and has to be well built for the door to be secure. Doors with glass panels are only as strong as the glass. If a broken pane allows someone to reach in and open the door, then the glass should be reinforced to minimize the risk of entry.

Burglary alarms are another great deterrent. Glass break alarms, door contacts, or motion detectors are all ways to create an alert of unauthorized access. Alarms should include a loud audible noise that lets crooks know that they have been detected and will prompt them to leave quickly before police arrive. The downside is the risk of false alarms. Even bad weather such as winds can trigger alarm systems. If your business is notorious for false alarms, the police may not respond as quickly. Many jurisdictions start charging for false alarms or may stop responding altogether.

Of course, the best locks, alarms, or video systems will do nothing if they are not used. As noted earlier, many businesses are left unlocked overnight, on holidays, or on weekends. Each organization should set up a method to make sure that all the doors are locked at the close of business. Someone or perhaps some group may be responsible for checking that all is locked and any alarms are set. Do not forget to include backups when that group or individual is on vacation or not there.

When setting up or evaluating your burglary prevention plans, include a review of internal safeguards as well. Once a burglar breaks in through the outer layers, what challenges or obstacles will he or she face? It could be as simple as a safe to secure the day's cash receipts or storerooms with strong doors, frames, and dead bolts. This is the point where the security risk matrix performed earlier can be handy. Critical assets should have been identified earlier, and those that are most important to your organization should be highly protected.

Every organization has something different to protect and will need a customized security plan. For example, veterinarian offices may be targeted for the controlled substance ketamine, or Special K, as it is known on the street. Pharmaceuticals, even those intended for animals, can be abused and become a target for addicts.

Motor vehicle offices have been hit by burglars searching for identification forms and equipment to make fake IDs. Forgers can then create authentic-looking IDs to be used for identity theft.

Neighborhood grocery stores have been burglarized by crooks looking for cash in the office safe, and liquor stores for the alcohol. Pharmacies are targeted for controlled substances. Business offices are burglarized for cash, equipment, computers, or even proprietary information.

## WAR STORIES

When I was a police officer, I responded to one burglary that stands out for several reasons. The reporting party (R/P) called as the building's alarm had been activated the night before. On an antistatic electricity floor mat at the entrance to a clean room where delicate electronics were manufactured there were boot prints that did not belong to any of the employees. An inventory was done and one of the company's products was missing.

The item had been manufactured in the company lab and included minute laser cuts similar to a record album (for those of you who remember them). Each item was customized to the client needs. While I don't remember the product's purpose, I do remember the value—half a million dollars! It would be of no use to someone else as it was specifically created for one client.

I quickly learned that the company had gone through recent ownership changes that had been very contentious with a lot of hard feelings and legal wrangling. The landlord or relative who owned the building was involved and on the losing end of the ownership fight. The victim filing the report believed the landlord's family member had used a master key to enter, triggering the alarm, took the inventory, and left. The suspected motive was sabotage with the possibility of using the stolen piece to learn about the manufacturing process.

As the investigation unfolded, I discovered that the mysterious boot prints actually belonged to other police officers. One of the officers was checking the area and found the door unlocked. The second officer arrived to cover and the two searched the building. As soon as they entered, they triggered the burglary alarm. There were no other footprints, nor forced entry on the internal doors or storage locker. The landlord did not have keys to inner doors. To complicate things further, the company had not done an inventory in over a year and no one could confirm when the missing piece was last seen. The client had changed specifications, so the piece had just been sitting around, unused.

With such a long time since the missing item was last seen, it was impossible to investigate further. Over time, many people had potential access to the area, and there was no evidence, only a vague motive, over a sour legal battle. In this case, an inventory of valuable assets should have been conducted on a more frequent basis. Access to the storage area in the lab should have been tightly restricted (most employees did not need access). A video surveillance system would have provided details about access as well and would have cost less than the one missing item.

## ROBBERY

People frequently use the words *robbery* and *burglary* for the same crimes. In fact, legally, the two are very different. Robbery refers to stealing something from the victim with the use of force or by threats. Burglary involves unauthorized entry (i.e., breaking and entering) and then a crime committed within the area, usually theft. If you are out for the evening and someone breaks into your home and steals your TV, it is a burglary. Most people will still say their "house was robbed"—only people can be robbed! A house or place cannot be threatened or held at gunpoint.

Why do people commit robberies? First, as with burglaries, the crook wants something of value. Willie Sutton, a well-known bank robber from the late 1920's into the 1950's, was asked why he robbed banks and is credited with replying, "That's where the money is." (He later denied saying that.) As with many crimes, the robber wants something of value (see Figure 7.3). The typical robber is looking for a quick win to pay for illicit activities or other bad habits. Many want to feed a drug or alcohol addiction. Others need money for prostitutes or to pay gambling debts.

There is another common factor for many robbery suspects. The idea of holding someone up via weapons or by threats adds to his street credentials or reputation. It is seen as a "cool" crime to commit. Many suspects later admitted in prison interviews that there was more esteem connected to committing a robbery as compared to other nonviolent crimes.

**Robbery locations**

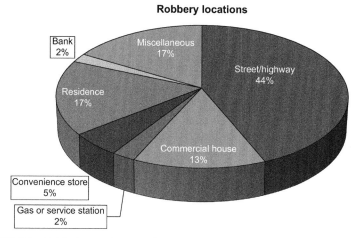

FIGURE 7.3 Robberies can happen almost anywhere, but risks are higher for certain targets that are usually isolated or where employees work alone with cash on hand and open access to the public.

We often like to idolize some criminals, such as Slick Willie Sutton, Jessie James, or John Dillinger, and turn them into modern versions of Robin Hood. However, the truth is that robberies are very dangerous. In fact, roughly 1 out of 10 homicides occurs during a robbery. In prison interviews, convicted robbery suspects admitted that although they did not plan to use violence, they were willing to hurt their victims in order to escape or avoid arrest. Often the suspect was nervous or jumpy and in need of a fix of drugs and on edge, making them prone to react with violence.

These suspects also gave some insight into how they planned their robberies. First, robbers conducted surveillance beforehand in order to case the location. They were looking for escape routes as well as potential problems. The suspects identified where the cash (or other target) was stored or kept and would note how many people were around. The suspects also looked for hiding places where they could wait for their moment out of sight or looked for areas where they could blend in. Most of the robbery suspects preferred to work with a minimal number of other people around. However, a handful preferred crowds as that helped hide their escape and provide a chance to blend in (Table 7.1).

## PARKING LOT SECURITY

Where do you feel safest while at work? How about where you feel the most worried? For many people, they feel the most at risk in parking lots. That is not surprising. Parking lots are more exposed to the exterior environment with less access control, are often isolated, and employees may be alone.

It is easy to imagine all sorts of evil lurking in parking lots. Kidnappers, rapists, and muggers seem to have all sorts of opportunity to carry out their nefarious activities. Parked cars and dim lighting offer various hiding spots and quick getaways. Dealing with the elevated risks is critical to creating a safe environment.

Once again lighting and visibility top the list of ways to make parking garages safer. A general guideline for lighting is that it should be bright enough to read a watch dial or newsprint in the lot. The lighting should be consistent throughout the parking area with no dim or dark areas.

Whenever possible, parking should be located near the front or main entrance with windows overlooking the area. This creates a clear line of sight. If the parking lot is remote or out of sight, such as at the back of the building, encourage employees to walk in or out in groups. Educate everyone on who to contact if there is a suspicious car or person in the lot. Visibility can be increased with video surveillance cameras or extra

**TABLE 7.1**   Preventing Robberies

| Tips to Prevent Robbery |
| --- |
| Watch for signs of surveillance—robbers will case the business watching for the right opportunity |
| • Be alert to individuals or groups out of place or loitering or dressed inappropriately (baggy or cold-weather clothes in the summer to hide firearms or a change of clothes) |
| Minimize hiding spots that crooks could use for surveillance while maximizing your view of the surrounding areas. For example, convenience stores realized that large posters in the windows made it hard to see out and kept an in-progress robbery from the view of passersby. Removing the signs reduced the number of robberies. |
| Limit the valuables that a robber could get during the crime |
| • Drop safes that cannot be opened along with signs warning that the cashier only has a small amount of cash available reduce the risks |
| Minimize escape routes |
| • Sets of double doors that open inward and not in a straight line act as a "man trap" and make escape slower<br>• Limit entry and exit points available to the public<br>• Look at property boundaries—bushes or fences around the exterior that limit escape to one direction such as the main street help prevent robberies |
| Armed guards |
| • Per one FBI study of bank robberies, 96% of all robberies occurred where there was no armed security presence (Federal Bureau of Investigation, 2012) |

security patrols. Signs that let would-be crooks know the area is under video surveillance can be a deterrent. If video is used, be certain to have live shots displayed on screens at the areas where employees would most likely see something out of the normal. A video screen at the front desk is one example where an administrative assistant or gatekeeper can watch it.

## SHOPLIFTING

For many businesses, theft by outsiders is rare. Unlike burglary, theft involves someone who is allowed to be on the property. For other businesses, such as retailers and various shops, theft is much more of a problem, generally in the form of shoplifting.

The National Retail Federation reports that shoplifting accounts for more than one-third of all losses, at nearly 36%. Furthermore, total retail losses are $34.5 billion. That means that shoplifters cost retailers more than $12 billion a year! That is billion with a "b."

So what is a retail leader to do to prevent shoplifting? For once, lighting is not the best solution. Customer service and staff training are the most effective ways to deal with shoplifting.

Shoplifters, like most criminals, want to work undetected. Greeting people as they enter is a great way to create customer service but also create a sense that a criminal is being observed. This is also the first step or place where employees can assess individuals and start to note potentially suspicious behavior. To do that, employees must be trained.

Complete loss prevention training covers how to identify shoplifters and what to do. You cannot spot shoplifters based on gender, age, or race. Instead, focus on behaviors.

A shopper who spends more time watching employees than looking at merchandise could be scoping or casing the business. He or she may be trying to spot plainclothes loss prevention agents or looking for security cameras. Or if employees are seen leaving the area, it could mean the coast is clear for a five-finger discount.

Along these lines, a shoplifter may avoid employees entirely. If an employee approaches a shopper and offers to help and the shopper immediately walks away to look at something in a different area, then that could be suspicious. Often the first instinct is to turn down an offer of assistance, although we may keep looking at the same items. I find that I often decline assistance and then immediately follow up with a question about where an item is located.

Shoplifters often work with others. If individuals seem to have quick conversations with other shoppers it could mean they are working together to shoplift and are comparing notes or conniving to steal something. Shoplifters may coordinate ways to distract employees. One may ask an employee for help away from his or her partner. If alone, a shoplifter may ask an employee to get something from the back as a quick distraction technique.

Pay attention to shoppers who are dressed inappropriately, such as heavy clothes in warm weather or a raincoat on a sunny day. Loose clothing could be another tactic. Both offer ways to hide stolen goods. Another "tell" is frequent touching of the clothes or adjusting sleeves or socks. A shoplifter could be hiding items or checking that stolen goods are not moving. There are some cases where incredible amounts of stolen clothes were found hidden down socks, in pant legs, or in sleeves.

Another tactic is to move items around the store. A shoplifter may move items to a blind spot where the merchandise could be hidden without being observed. Items may also be moved closer to the door to create an escape path. A shoplifter also may move things around and try to conceal valuables or hide them under coats, in newspapers, or even in baby strollers. Sadly, it is common for shoplifters to bring their kids and use strollers or baby bags as hiding spots—an especially evil way to shoplift.

When you are shopping, you will likely pick up the item you are interested in and examine it. You may be looking at quality, price tags, or features. Shoplifters, by comparison, are more likely to keep hands low and out of sight, often behind displays. It is easier to conceal something to steal that way.

## Shoplifter Behaviors

Another common method is to carry "bad bags." Bad bags are shopping bags or even backpacks that can be used to carry stolen goods (Table 7.2).

**TABLE 7.2**  Shoplifter Behaviors

| Red Flags or Behaviors of Shoplifters |
| --- |
| Carrying bags or other items that could be used to conceal stolen goods when entering |
| Shopper's clothing is out of place or inappropriate for the weather, such as a raincoat on a sunny day |
| Watching employees more than looking at merchandise |
| May attempt to distract or avoid employees |
| Moving items to other areas within the store, especially to areas out of sight, isolated, or near the door |
| Brief, furtive conversations with other shoppers |
| Hands low and out of sight rather than lifting merchandise to eye level to examine |

Some bags can be very elaborate. I've seen some very complex ones. One shoplifter used a cloth shopping bag that was lined with cardboard and foil. The cardboard made it studier for carrying heavy stolen merchandise. The foil can shield "screamer tags" or exciters. These devices sound the alarms near many store exits when tagged merchandise is removed. In this one case, the bag had a hinged lid. The lid had the top half of grocery items glued to the lid. It appeared that the bag was full of groceries and not useful for concealing goods. However, the suspect had only to lift the hinged lid and could conceal stolen items inside in an instant, as can be seen in Figures 7.4 and 7.5.

## When to Challenge a Shoplifter

One of the biggest mistakes you could make in regard to shoplifting is to falsely accuse an innocent shopper of theft. At best, it is embarrassing

**FIGURE 7.4**   A shoplifter may make a customized "bad bag" to conceal stolen goods. This one was reinforced with a box topped with a hinged lid designed to look like groceries.

**FIGURE 7.5**    The hinged top on this bag left plenty of room to conceal stolen merchandise.

for both the shopper and employee. You will almost certainly lose a customer. After all, who would return to a place that accused them of being a thief? The worst case is a lawsuit. Lawsuits are generally related to inappropriate searches, such as a male employee searching a female suspect or accusations of discrimination, such as race. This comes back to looking at behaviors, not demographics such as race, gender, age, etc.

In addition to behaviors, which are more of a warning sign, employees must make a few other observations before contacting a shoplifter. The suspicious behaviors should attract attention and focus but are not proof that someone is shoplifting.

Store associates must actually see the shoplifter get the item. This is where greeting people as they enter is great—employees can see then if the shopper is carrying anything, including an item that could be purchased in the store or items to return. If they are carrying an item as they enter, then when seen later it could not have been stolen from inside.

Once a shopper or shoplifter is seen retrieving the item from a store shelf, employees have to see him conceal the goods and notice where it is hidden. An employee has to be specific and be able to say that a GPS device, for example, was taken and hidden in the top of the suspect's socks. Next, the shoplifter must be watched as he moves through the store. If the line of sight is broken, the crook could dump the stolen goods somewhere else, possibly because he thinks he is being watched. Last, the shoplifter passes the point of sale or registers and exits the store, a clear indicator that he is not going to pay for the item.

If associates are trained and follow each of these criteria, the chance of falsely accusing an innocent shopper is nearly nil. Some local laws do favor merchants and might make contacts easier, from a legal perspective. For example, in the state of Colorado, it is considered prima facie evidence of theft if someone conceals merchandise on or about his or her person. That means a shoplifter who picks up an item and places it in a bag or pocket could be immediately contacted and subsequently charged with theft. Still it is good practice to follow all the previous steps. It is not hard to imagine an innocent shopper, with hands full, putting something in a pocket momentarily to answer a cell phone or deal with a rowdy or upset child. However, once he passes the registers to the doors without paying, it becomes theft. The shoplifter will certainly claim that he forgot about the item then. I've heard that line from many shoplifters caught in stores only to check and find a criminal history for similar offenses.

Another challenge is the trend to encourage shoppers to bring their own shopping bags. In fact, in some areas it is the law. Boulder, Colorado, recently passed a city ordinance that requires merchants to charge 10 cents per bag for a shopper's groceries or other items. Many are now entering the stores carrying bags bought previously. There is no way to know if any items are in the bag or not when they enter. This makes it that much more critical to actually see a shoplifter retrieve merchandise from within the store, conceal it, and then leave without paying.

## Confronting a Shoplifter

Confronting or challenging someone who just committed a crime is not an everyday experience for most people. It can be very uncomfortable, nerve wracking, and just plain scary for some. When the adrenaline is flowing and the nerves are flying, it is easy for things to go wrong. Training is vital to help associates deal with these situations and remain professional and calm.

As soon as associates see something suspicious or suspect shoplifting, he or she should notify another employee or manager. Never approach a suspect alone. If someone does work alone, calling police may be the only option to get help. In these cases, the individual will have to make a judgment call about whether or not to confront the shoplifter on his or her own.

For stores with a manager on site, the manager should take the lead contacting a shoplifter, or specifically designate who will. Never force an employee who is not comfortable into that position. Identify yourself as an employee and ask them to come back to the office. Have another employee call police. Some police departments will not charge shoplifters if the amount stolen is small. For example, Dallas, Texas, police will not respond if the amount is less than $50. However, if a suspect causes a disturbance or is threatening, the police should be called immediately.

Once in the office, ask for the merchandise back. Do not be specific as the shoplifter may have other items that you do not know about. Ask for identification as well and write down the information for a store report (your local police may have a form that you can use). Confirm current address and phone numbers.

Suspects will often be very cooperative. Others may be argumentative. Some will insult and taunt employees, even possibly make accusations of racism or other insults. Employees must remain calm and ignore the taunts and be professional. If the suspect does run or tries to fight, let them go. The safety of shoppers and employees is worth more than any merchandise. Get a good description and direction of travel to let police know, but do not pursue or follow them outside the store.

## Store Policy

To be most effective, retailers need a written policy on shoplifting. The policy should reinforce prevention by stressing customer service—greeting them promptly. Also, keep merchandise organized and neat. That makes it easier to see when something is out of place or missing. The policy and procedure should also be very clear on the steps an employee must see before contacting a shoplifter as well as who will contact the shoplifter (preferably a manager). The policy should state that shoplifters will be prosecuted. The store will back employees acting in good faith and any court time will be paid for. Also, the policy should include information that suspects should not be chased. Chases can become dangerous as someone may run out in traffic, for example, and get hurt. An injured suspect could sue the store, so it is best to let them go if he or she flees. If you disagree, and I do, be sure to thank lawsuit-happy attorneys that protect crooks.

There are stores that have policies that restrict employees from intervening in known shoplifting incidents. In one case, a customer saw three males stealing from a large department store and she informed employees, who, due to policy, did nothing. The customer confronted the suspects on her own, which put her in a dangerous situation but did lead to the arrest of the suspects. I understand that a hands-off policy may be the safe route in terms of liability, but employees should be allowed to intervene once customers are involved or at risk. A laissez-faire approach to crime only encourages more crime and ultimately increases risks to customers and employees, and even of liability if known criminal threats are not addressed.

## ORGANIZED RETAIL CRIME

Retail losses come in another format as well—organized retail crime or ORC. The words *organized crime* conjure up images of *The Godfather* movie, hit men, contract killings, and the mafia. That is not necessarily the case, but organized retail crime usually does involve a gang or group of individuals working together as professional thieves.

One ORC group was recently arrested in Florida. There were about 18 people involved, and the structure had a hierarchy and levels within the organization. The group was suspected of stealing over $100 million in goods. At the bottom end, shoplifters would enter stores and steal various merchandise, often targeting health and beauty supplies. The shoplifters would be paid cash for the stolen goods, which were then stored in warehouses and later resold at flea markets or even online. One of the suspects had an ebay store that advertised getting items at cost to explain why the goods could be sold cheaper than other sources. The entire operation finally fell apart when two of the shoplifters were caught and arrested, followed by a tip to police letting them know that this was part of a bigger operation.

## CONCLUSION

Businesses face security risks from outside the organization. Losses caused by outsiders can come in many different forms including vandalism, burglaries, robberies, as well as shoplifting. Basic crime prevention steps can help prevent and minimize the risks of becoming a victim. Good exterior lighting, solid door locks and alarms, maintenance, awareness, customer service, and training are all vital parts of a protection plan.

## BUSINESS KARATE BELT LEVEL

Test your company's karate belt level in the discipline of awareness/ stance. If your organization meets each belt level and all the standards of the lower belts as seen in Figure 7.6, you have then achieved that color level.

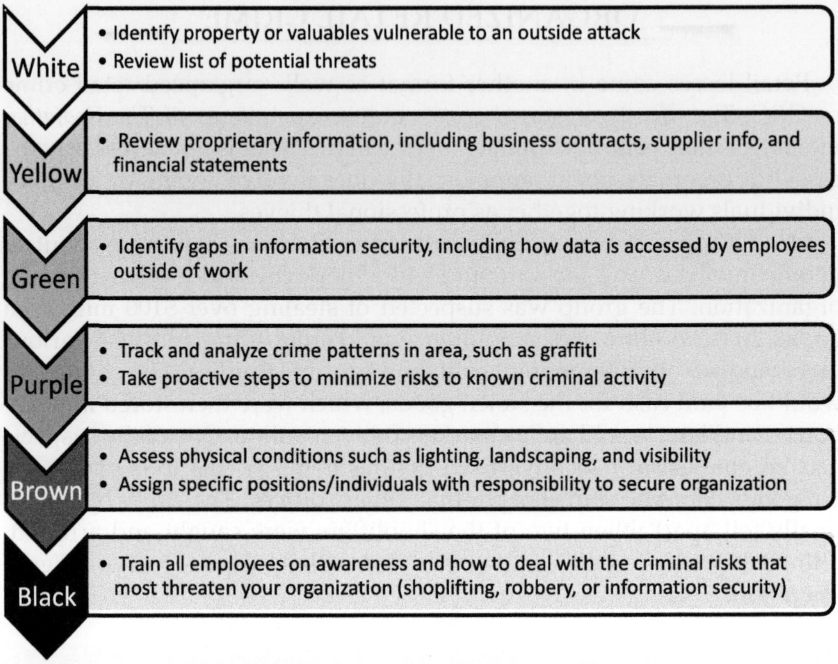

**White**
- Identify property or valuables vulnerable to an outside attack
- Review list of potential threats

**Yellow**
- Review proprietary information, including business contracts, supplier info, and financial statements

**Green**
- Identify gaps in information security, including how data is accessed by employees outside of work

**Purple**
- Track and analyze crime patterns in area, such as graffiti
- Take proactive steps to minimize risks to known criminal activity

**Brown**
- Assess physical conditions such as lighting, landscaping, and visibility
- Assign specific positions/individuals with responsibility to secure organization

**Black**
- Train all employees on awareness and how to deal with the criminal risks that most threaten your organization (shoplifting, robbery, or information security)

FIGURE 7.6    What is your belt level?

# Reference

Federal Bureau of Investigation, April 2012. Bank Crime Statistics. Criminal Justice Information Services, Clarksburg, VW. Retrieved from: http://www.fbi.gov/stats-services/publications/bank-crime-statistics-2011/bank-crime-statistics-2011 (accessed 24.07.13.).

# Further Reading

Federal Bureau of Investigation, October 2012. Crime in the U.S. 2011: Table 23: Offense Analysis. Criminal Justice Information Services, Clarksburg, WV. Retrieved from: http://www.fbi.gov/about-us/cjis/ucr/crime-in-the-u.s/2011/crime-in-the-u.s.-2011/tables/table-23 (accessed 24.07.13.).

Federal Bureau of Investigation, October 2012. Crime in the U.S. 2011: Expanded Homicide Data Table 13: Murder Circumstances. Criminal Justice Information Services, Clarksburg, WV. Retrieved from: http://www.fbi.gov/about-us/cjis/ucr/crime-in-the-u.s/2011/crime-in-the-u.s.-2011/tables/expanded-homicide-data-table-13 (accessed 22.11.13.).

Harrell, E., March 2011. Workplace Violence, 1993–2009 (NCJ 233231). United States Department of Justice, Washington, DC.

Hollinger, R.C., September/October 2012. 2011 NRSS overview. Loss Prevention Magazine 11.5.

Smith, E., March 2011. How to Survive a Robbery. Retrieved from: http://businesskarate.blogspot.com/2011/03/how-to-survive-robbery.html (accessed 25.03.11.).

Smith, M.S., April 1996. Crime Prevention through Environmental Design in Parking Facilities (NCJ 157310). United States Department of Justice, Washington, DC.

# 8

# When Things Get Down and Dirty: Workplace Violence

## KARATE AND GROUND FIGHTING

Traditional martial arts are very focused on balance, footing, blocking, and striking. Many put little emphasis on how to fight from the ground. Some spend a little bit of effort on escaping various holds or grabs. A proficient karate expert is expected to move or block attacks while maintaining balance and remaining standing.

In reality, it is not always possible to stay on your feet. In the heat of battle, fighters stumble or get tripped, struck, pushed, or otherwise lose balance and fall. When gravity takes over, at least one of the fighters will end up on the ground.

Even an experienced karate student may feel like a fish out of water if suddenly defending herself from the ground. This is where a situation can get down and dirty very quickly.

Most martial artists will try to get back on their feet as quickly as possible. Law enforcement and military training, as well as martial arts, teach individuals how to fall the right way and turn the fall into a roll in order to get back up immediately.

A fight may start with opponents standing but often becomes a grappling match where one of the fighters is caught off guard and on the ground. Otherwise, the situation would have been avoided. The goal of savvy self-defense fighters is to break away from the fight on the ground, get back to their feet, and escape.

## VIOLENCE AT WORK

Violence at work is much like ground fighting. It is usually unexpected, often because warning signs were ignored. No one is prepared as it is outside the normal circumstances we are used to dealing with. And, most of all, it is down and dirty, ugly violence, and it is imperative to respond and react to the situation and get back up on your feet, returning to normal functions.

For a business, the best way to deal with violence is to avoid it altogether. Just as karate students try to prevent ground fighting through balance and footing exercises, an organization needs to take steps to prevent workplace violence entirely.

In order to prevent workplace violence, it is important to understand where violence comes from. What are the sources of violence?

In many cases, violence is tied to the industry or type of work. The job with the highest rates of assaults at work is law enforcement. Teachers and retailers are high on the list as well. Health care workers in emergency departments or those who deal with mental health patients are also jobs very high on the list. Other jobs that are high risk include convenience store clerks and taxi drivers. According to data from the U.S. Department of Justice (DOJ) report on workplace violence, the greatest risks are associated with robberies and other assailants, resulting in 70% of the workplace homicides.

Domestic violence (DV) is a very real threat for every organization. Business leaders may wonder why the home life is, or should be, a factor at work. Following a domestic dispute, one partner may move out and the suspect could be uncertain about where he or she is. But the suspect knows where and when the other person works so it is quite common to harass, stalk, and even attack a victim while at work. Like it or not, violence on the home front is an issue that affects workplace safety.

Another common source of workplace violence is from disgruntled or former employees. We've all heard news stories about this type of violence. An employee, usually one with disciplinary issues, or one recently fired, returns to the workplace and "goes postal." In fact, the expression "going postal" came from a couple of high-publicity events where employees showed up at work, at a post office, well armed and hunted down and killed coworkers or managers.

Unhappy customers are another potential source of workplace violence. This may seem less likely on the surface. However, it is not unheard of, as we will see. There have been cases of former patients, frustrated clients, upset constituents, or obsessed individuals who target a business or government agency for a variety of reasons.

## ROOTS OF VIOLENCE

What prompts acts of violence? Why are some individuals prone to act with violence, whereas others never would? I would like to say that I can answer these questions definitively and succinctly. But I cannot. Entire books have been written and college courses taught on the topic, as well as numerous media discussions and politicians politicking on the subject, and we are probably no closer to understanding the true reasons.

As we look at the causes listed herein, there are some common themes, such as deep emotional involvement. In the each case, there is some kind of strong attachment, whether a domestic relationship, employee, or even disgruntled third party. The emotional triggers could be love, anger, fear, or jealousy. Typically, the offender feels like he is running out of alternatives. Perhaps more dangerous is the offender who feels no one listened to his concerns.

Last, for a violent attack to take place, a suspect must have the means and some knowledge of how to carry out an attack or experience to complete it. Too often, in U.S. politics, this is a discussion of gun control. The means or ability is much more than that. In some countries, attacks are carried out with machetes, knives, or homemade explosives. Often, a potential attacker's abilities are not fully understood or clear. The real question when looking at the capability of committing violence is to look at the mental capability. Does the individual have the capacity to commit violence? Namely, is there a history of known violent acts?

## THREAT ASSESSMENT TEAM

Organizations should create a threat assessment team. A threat assessment team includes a cross section of the organization, including a member from human resources, security, corporate compliance or the legal department, a customer service leader, and a local law enforcement officer as well. A senior executive or the business owner should also be involved due to the risks and for support. If an employee is involved, ad hoc members may include that individual's or affected department's manager.

Anytime there is a perceived or potential threat, the threat assessment team should be involved immediately. The threat could be internal or external. The primary role of the threat assessment team is to analyze acts of violence, or potential threats, and take appropriate steps to reduce or eliminate the risk.

Part of the team's role is information gathering and investigation. When emotions start to run high, separating gossip from fact can be tricky. The team needs to find who is involved, exactly what each witness heard or saw, and what background information each knows. The best information comes directly from the original source, avoiding hearsay or secondhand information whenever possible.

The threat assessment team is responsible for analyzing any violent behavior or risk and determining what steps or measures should be taken to protect employees. Unfortunately, understanding what is going on in someone's head is not an exact science, making it very difficult. It also means the team has to be thorough in the assessment to make the best recommendations and determination possible.

To start, the team needs to gather background information and try to identify escalating behaviors that led up to the current threat. Every now and then, after some violent crime, news reporters interview those who knew the killer, such as neighbors, and we hear quotes along the lines of, "he just snapped" or "he didn't seem the type." The truth is that good people do not just suddenly turn violent. There are usually warning signs. Often violence is just below the surface and has been growing or building over time.

Part of the background includes learning about any recent changes in the offender's life. Divorce, child custody changes, or financial stresses could spark deep emotional reactions and possibly indicate that the individual feels like there is nothing to lose. Drug or alcohol addictions also contribute to a weakened emotional state. Without a solid platform, a person is more likely to feel like he or she has no support or does not care about the outcome and has nothing more to live for. Lacking balance or worry about the future, a person is more likely to carry out a violent act out of desperation.

The team's next step is to build an understanding of what the individual is angry about or on whom he or she is focused. What type of behavior has been displayed? Very early warning signs even include behavior not normally tied to violence, such as being rude or insulting to others. Next steps may include throwing things, slamming doors, or yelling profanities. Generally, the longer the escalating behavior has been going on, the more emotionally tied into the situation and the higher the risk. If the individual is sending long e-mails at 3 a.m. or calling repeatedly, following coworkers, or demanding meetings to rehash past decisions, then the individual is displaying stalking or harassing behavior that should raise a red flag.

The assessment should include a review of any known violent behavior. Is there a history, such as a DV arrest? Has the person been served with a protection or restraining order (RO)? Look at whether or not the individual seems to have an obsession with violence. He or she may seem to be abnormally fascinated with violent crimes or killings, almost idolizing the murderers.

Often you will hear the recommendation to consider the presence of firearms as a warning sign, in and of itself. Keep in mind that the presence or ownership of guns alone is not a good indicator. For some, target shooting or competitions may be a serious hobby and does not automatically equate to a danger sign on its own. Iceland, for example, has extremely low violent crime per capita while having a high gun ownership rate. Iceland has about one gun for every three people.

Finally, the team needs to look at the threat itself, if there is one. Some event or incident sparked the threat assessment team to start the process.

In a perfect world, managers or employees are well trained to recognize escalating behavior, and the team is activated early to intervene before all-out violence occurs. In reality, no one is alerted until the situation is at, or past, the boiling point.

As we look at any threats, it is critical to remember that not all offenders will make overt threats, at least not directly to the target group. Numerous school shootings have been prevented because suspects posted threats on Facebook or told others about their plans. Law enforcement could then intervene prior to the event. Sometimes, the warnings may be given to an outside party or group. In 2012, James Holmes had telegraphed his violent thoughts to a psychiatrist at the University of Colorado, even threatening her in text messages. Unfortunately, no one knew that his target would be a movie theater in Aurora, Colorado, and would leave 12 dead and dozens injured.

Traditional assessments give strong weight to any known threatening statements. In the FBI model, threats are broken down into four categories. Threats may be veiled, conditional, indirect, or direct. A veiled threat is a disguised or implied expression of harm, such as, "He is going to pay for this." A conditional threat is a menacing statement that will happen only if another event happens. For example, "If I get fired, I'll shoot that son of a bitch." Indirect threats are not as clear, for example, "This place will make someone go postal." Direct is the most obvious type: "I'm going to kill that idiot." Keep in mind that threats can be nonverbal as well. Shaking a fist at someone or pointing a finger like a gun and pretending to shoot could be part of the threatening or escalating behavior of an offender.

Many schools of thought consider direct threats to be the most treacherous. However, any serious threat should be considered very dangerous. Another consideration is how specific the threat is. Obviously, a threat involving very specific information, or that is very detailed, sounds more like a plan than an idle threat. If the individual has given it that much thought, then they are a step closer to carrying out an attack or act of violence.

A detailed threat may mean the act is imminent, and police should be called. "I'm going to make him hurt like he hurt me." That is a direct threat, but not very specific. "I'm going to the kitchen to get the same knife we used to cut his birthday cake. Then when he gets back from his meeting, I'll be waiting across the hall in the copy room, sneak up behind, and jam that knife into his back so he knows what backstabbing feels like." Obviously, the second example is more specific with details, and a statement like this should prompt an immediate reaction.

In addition to any threats, take into account the reaction. If people who know the individual are worried or concerned, it is another reason to take it seriously. Trust the instincts of those closest to the situation. If employees are concerned, even lacking an actual threatening statement, it is possible that they are picking up nonverbal signals or behaviors but are having a hard time expressing it.

There are threats that do not include any type of violence. An employee who argues about a situation and refers to suing the company or reporting them to some oversight group will create an unpleasant scene. However, there is no threat of violence. The situation may cause tempers to flare and be seen as intimidation, but the individual is actually looking at other options, other than violence. In a certain way, that should make everyone feel safer—assuming, of course, that there are no other indicators of violent behavior.

## DOMESTIC VIOLENCE

Police officers understand the dangers of domestic violence (DV) calls. Anger, jealousy, and rage push emotions into the red zone. Often there is alcohol or drugs involved. To top it off, the victim can turn against the officers faster than the suspect in a domestic version of the Stockholm syndrome.

DV can be a powder keg, threatening to explode not only at home but at work as well.

Legally, DV is any crime committed as an act of retaliation, revenge, harassment, or intimidation between partners of an intimate relationship. Many states further define intimate relationship as marriage, including a common law marriage, or having a child together. Unfortunately, outside marriage or a common child, there can be some gray areas.

A responding police officer may simply ask one or both of the parties if they are intimate, which can spark some interesting and graphic answers not fit to be printed here. Many people assume physical intimacy in a "biblical" sense means being intimate. However, there are couples who've dated for some time who might never have had that level of intimacy. A one-night stand where last names are not even known could be considered more intimate than the long-term celibate couple by that definition!

When I was in law enforcement, my fellow officers and I often joked that we needed a checklist to determine if a relationship was intimate or not. Intimate couples should know the names of the partner's mother, his or her last name, birthday, favorite color, favorite type of music, and so on. Alas, we never got that tool, so some of those strange, late-night, drunken ménage-à-trois mix-ups still counted as intimate relationships.

I digress. The important point is that DV is not always easy to see but remains dangerous. DV is not gender specific. In other words, it can be a male against female or female against male; male against male or female against female. There are cases where a female suspect hires or gets a male friend to go after the male partner.

During a DV situation, the police will try to determine who the suspect is and arrest that person (sometimes both go to jail). Victim advocates will contact the victim who may be temporarily moved into a safe house. The suspect goes to jail. Before being released, he will get bond conditions that stipulate no contact with the victim. Once released, he may learn that his spouse or partner is in a safe house and he cannot find or contact her.

The suspect may try to contact family or friends, but doing so could be considered an attempt to contact the victim via a third party and could result in him going back to jail. But he knows when and where she works. A suspect bent on revenge, stalking, or harassing the victim will find her job a good opportunity. Now the workplace is tied in with the employee's home life.

Many confrontations happen in the parking lot as the victim arrives or leaves from work. The suspect can wait or pull up in his car as the victim arrives. Often, there are fewer people around so it may seem like a good spot for the suspect to talk to the victim alone without others around.

## On the Job DV Prevention

It may be obvious, but in order for an organization to take any steps to protect an employee from DV, it must first know about the risk. For that to happen, employees must feel comfortable telling a manager or representative about the situation. That is not going to be easy. Many victims of DV may feel awkward talking about such a personal matter. A victim may believe it will have a negative impact on career advancement.

Often, the first warning signs may be from coworkers. Employees, or at least managers, should have training on signs of victimization. Schools and hospitals train staff to be alert to signs of neglect or abuse. Employees in any business should be aware of signs of domestic abuse.

---

### DV AT WORK

After losing a custody battle over his son, Scott Dekraai had enough. On October 12, 2011, he drove to the hair salon where his ex-wife worked in Seal Beach, California, and walked inside. He immediately shot and killed her and then shot a coworker and friend who had helped her through the divorce. A manager charged at Dekraai with a pair of scissors, but he was also shot and killed.

Dekraai fired at several more people inside the salon, later telling police that they were "collateral damage." He left the store and shot a male sitting in a car, believing that he was an off-duty police officer reaching for a gun. In all, Dekraai killed eight people, including his ex-wife, and seriously wounded another.

Changes in job performance or increases in absenteeism are potential signs. Unexplained bruises and marks, or efforts to hide injuries with makeup or a change in clothing (going from short to long sleeves in the summer) are other signs. Disruptive visits or calls from the partner could be an indicator that the personal life is spilling over to work.

Organizations should have a clear and supportive policy regarding workplace violence. The company should not take actions against a victim employee for reporting a DV situation. Once a legitimate threat is brought forward, the threat assessment team should review the matter just as it would any other threat.

There are a number of steps that can be taken to help protect the victim and her coworkers. If a RO has been obtained, a copy should be provided. This can be helpful to the first responding officers if police have to be called. Also, many victims may confuse bond conditions with ROs. Violations of either could result in an arrest, but in the United States, a RO violation mandates an arrest. The RO also gives details on how far away the suspect must stay from the victim and outlines the exact locations and distance the restrained person must stay. The RO will almost always include the victim's work address as an area where the suspect must avoid.

The victim should be asked to provide a photo of the suspect. With modern technology, that is easily accomplished by having the victim e-mail or text a photo directly from a smart phone or from Facebook. The photo, as well as the suspect's car description, should be given to security or to key employees who act as a gatekeeper such as the staff at the front desk.

When distributing information for any type of alert, keep in mind the victim's privacy and limit the information to an "as needed" group only. Security or coworkers should keep an eye on the parking lots or look for anyone suspicious loitering in the area. In a number of cases, attacks may be made by a third party, where a female suspect hires a male to carry out the attack.

Since victims are often targeted while coming to or from work, changing normal start and end times by even a half an hour can throw off the suspect and increase the chance that he will be spotted. Also, whenever possible, change the victim's parking to a different area, such as a highly visible, close parking spot. Many companies will escort the victim to her car. If a suspect is armed, the escort may become just another victim, as those around the victim in Dekraai's attack. The parking lot should be scouted first or escorts should be armed personnel wherever possible. In fact, it is a good idea to look at local security companies and either set up a prearranged agreement or at least know whom you want to call when a need arises for security (more on this in Chapter 12).

It is a good time to consider other security measures or temporarily increase security. Tighten access control to limit a suspect's ability to get in. If doors use a code, change the code in case the victim told it to the suspect or he found the code at home. Review emergency providers and contacts for police. In some cases, hiring additional security to be highly visible or help with access may be a strong deterrent.

According to data from the DOJ, only a small percentage of workplace assaults are related to domestic relationships, including family members. In fact, only about 2% of all assaults are domestic related. However, 8% of all workplace homicides are domestic situations.

DV is a very real concern to any organization trying to create a safer environment. Take the threats seriously and appropriate steps to protect not only the targeted victim but also innocent coworkers or customers who are not involved at all.

## DISGRUNTLED EMPLOYEE

When we think of workplace violence, the picture most likely to come to mind is the unhappy, disgruntled employee who goes "postal." The stereotype is one of a long-term male employee, frustrated by poor reviews or passed up for promotion, even fired, who comes to work on a violent rampage, targeting those coworkers or leaders who did him wrong—acting out of the blue, without warning. A history of mental illness as well as a lengthy criminal history also seem like part of the picture.

The problem with stereotypes is that they are generalizations at best and do not tell the whole story. *Security Director's Report* published findings from one study that looked at 44 cases of workplace homicides by employees in the United States. Almost one-quarter of the killers had been employed at the company a short time—less than a few months. Most had no criminal history or mental health treatment. The vast majority were male, but not all. More than three-quarters of them lived alone, which indicates little or no family support.

Workplace relationships accounted for 21% of all on-the-job homicides, according to the DOJ. Almost half of those, or 10% of all workplace homicides, were caused by customers or clients while the remainder were caused by current or former coworkers. As you can see, the disgruntled employee may not be the greatest risk but remains the cause of one out of every 10 workplace homicides.

Violence does not just happen. As we noted earlier, people do not just snap. Behavior escalates over time. Any anger or rage over perceived injustices will usually develop or grow over time. The good news is that the time and escalating anger create opportunities to recognize and intervene before a situation boils over.

The first step in prevention starts right at the hiring decision. Every employee should be screened as discussed in Chapter 6. A history of job hopping or a pattern of not being able to get along with coworkers or managers should be a red flag. Not hiring a potentially violent individual is the best prevention of all. Rationalizing problems, not taking responsibility, and blaming others are key indicators of potential problems. A good interview can help pinpoint how the individual reacts to criticism or discipline or highlight the inability to work well with others.

Recognizing early warning signs and reacting is vital to interrupt an escalating cycle of violence. Recognition means training. The members of the threat assessment team should all be trained on the specifics of evaluating threats and responses. But the training should not stop there. Every employee and manager should be able to identify inappropriate behavior and understand what to do about it.

Without training and support, you cannot assume that everyone will notice or heed early indicators. A clear policy and procedure is useful in identifying behavior that is indicative of violent behavior as well as how employees should handle it or react, including whom to notify with concerns.

So what are the warning signs? The very earliest signs may be as simple as rude behavior. A coworker who expresses frustration or disappointment with rude, uncivil, or antisocial conduct could be showing some of the signs that might later lead to escalated acts. Examples include someone who deliberately shuts a door on an approaching employee, hangs up on a manager in mid-conversation, or acts blatantly bored stiff during a presentation. Some people may display some of these acts because they are not thinking. A change or deliberate actions directed toward others show some level of intention or forethought and not just poor upbringing.

The next level of behaviors rises to the level of harassment, bullying or intimidating others. Staring down others during a meeting or discussion is one example of intimidation. An individual who pulls out a notepad to record every decision he disagrees with is using another form of intimidation with the not-so-subtle hint that any mistakes will be "reported" and you will suffer the consequences.

Bullying and harassment can be a bit more obvious. Bumping into someone or knocking over items on your desk are illustrations. Harassment is any kind of action intended to annoy or alarm another and can include any physical contact that does not rise to the level of assault (i.e., no injuries). This can include repeated phone calls or communications that are disruptive and not part of a legitimate conversation.

Next is an assault. Legal definitions can vary from one jurisdiction to another. Typically, a simple assault is any strike or blow that causes injury. Injury may be defined as causing pain, so pinching someone could be considered an assault. Aggravated assault involves injury with a weapon or an assault that causes serious bodily injury (SBI). SBI can be a permanent scar, broken bone, or loss of limb. Even a chipped tooth can be SBI.

Property damage or vandalism may be in the mix as well. Instead of taking out anger on another person, the offender may attack or sabotage company property. It is also another step indicating escalating behavior.

From assaults, the next level of violence is murder, including a mass attack with multiple victims. This is, of course, the level we most want to avoid.

## Intervention

A key part of the prevention is intervention. Anytime there is a behavior that could be part of the escalation cycle it is vital to intervene, address the conduct, and make sure that it is not repeated.

Sometimes, an offender will test boundaries to see what he can get away with. If those tests are left unchecked, the boundary is moved and allows for continued escalation. What was once unacceptable now becomes the new normal. If an individual storms out of a conference room upset and slams the door with a loud profane exclamation and nothing is done, he can get away with it again. Maybe the next time he will direct his profanity at individuals in the room. After that, it could include slamming a chair back with a veiled threat and continue to grow.

Often people do not feel comfortable stepping in. They worry about upsetting or offending the individual. Instead, think of the coworkers who are upset or offended by tolerating that type of conduct. It is unprofessional at best and paves a path to violence at worst. At this point, getting the threat assessment team involved will be very helpful. In addition to the assessment, there may be a chance for early intervention with an employee assistance program as well, if applicable.

Whenever there is some unacceptable behavior, you must immediately be ready to throw out a roadblock to stop it. Roadblocks can be in one of several forms. One way is to ask for clarification. If an offender makes a veiled or indirect threat, ask him, "Did you just threaten me?" Most likely, he or she will make an excuse such as, "I'm just upset." Do not accept that. Remind him or her that it is unacceptable regardless. Next is the challenge. Confront an offender and flat out say, "stop that" or "knock it off." Make it crystal clear that the behavior is not okay and will not be tolerated.

Last, you may need to use threats of your own—the threat of consequences. If behavior rises to this level, you may need to let the offender know that the actions could result in police involvement, HR review, suspension, or termination. Do not make any promises or agreements about any outcomes—just the reminder that his actions are unacceptable.

Remember how boundaries moved? If the same event happens a second time, do not use the same obstacle or intervention. You've already used that once, and it is now time to move to the next level. If not, you are just helping the problem individual move the boundary farther out.

## Zero Tolerance

Not long ago there was a story of a young boy playing army on a school playground during recess. As part of the game, he threw an air grenade at his imaginary enemy. In doing so, he violated the school policy on threats or simulating weapons. There were no other red flags mentioned in the news reports. Due to the school's zero tolerance policy, the police were called and a hearing was held to determine if he would be suspended. This is hardly an isolated case. We've heard about students being suspended or expelled for having a plastic knife in their lunch box.

I find it amazing when a zero tolerance policy is somehow translated into maximum punishment. The two are very different. Why bring this up? All organizations should have a policy to address workplace violence. Violence should never be tolerated, and the policy should establish a zero tolerance of any acts of violence including the early warning signs. The response should be based on the actual situation.

With some of the earlier examples, it seems that the real goal was forgotten. Stopping violence ultimately is about the persons who pose a threat—those that could and will cause harm to others. A kid playing army does not pose a threat in and of itself. The policy and procedure need to allow organization leaders the ability and judgment to tell the difference.

The flip side is that any serious threat should be dealt with quickly. Even minor, but true legitimate, acts of violence may result in termination. If an individual displays a pattern of aggressive or violent behavior, there is no point in allowing the situation to fester or grow. The sooner a violent offender can be removed, the better. The longer the situation is allowed to build, the greater the emotional ties including anger and rationalization to justify an attack. Eliminate true problems as early as possible.

## Eyes and Ears

Who is most likely to realize that one employee may be a loose cannon? That person's coworkers. They will be the first to pick up on subtle, even subconscious clues that make them uncomfortable. Other employees are more likely to see or hear how that offender acts or thinks. To ensure intervention, all employees have to be trained on warning signs as I mentioned earlier. But employees must also feel comfortable bringing those concerns forward.

Open communication is part of that. Employees need to understand and believe that they can bring concerns up without retaliation. Setting up an anonymous reporting system is one way to do that. As we saw with employee fraud, tips can be a great way to start an official look into an individual's behavior.

## Last Word

A disgruntled employee often starts down that path due to a belief that he was not treated fairly. This is another reason why consistency in how promotions, terminations, or discipline are handled is a common complaint by employees and can affect morale. In the case of someone who could be potentially violent, it could be a trigger factor (not the root cause, but a trigger).

No matter how hard an organization tries to be consistent or fair, some employees will almost always see some level of inconsistency. An organization should communicate the reasons for personnel decisions or actions as much as possible. Explaining the "why?" may help avoid some of those issues. It will never be perfect, but striving for consistency and fairness will help reduce the risks of disgruntled employees—even those who will never be violent.

## DANGEROUS CUSTOMERS

It was easy to picture a stereotype for disgruntled employees. Now try to build a mental picture of a customer going homicidal. It is much harder! And yet, the risks are almost as great. Going back to the DOJ data, 10% of all workplace homicides were from customers and 11% from current or former coworkers.

In fact, an Internet search for customer violence does not provide specific examples. However, if you start reviewing past news articles about workplace violence, you do start to come up with examples. In 2008, a male went into a Georgia hospital hunting down the hospital workers who had unsuccessfully treated his mother—two years before! In another case, in 2009 an 88-year-old man attacked the Holocaust Museum in Washington, D.C., and shot a security officer before other guards wounded him. In Colorado, Matthew Murray killed two people in Arvada at a church missionary building and later that weekend went to New Life Church, armed with thousands of rounds, and killed two more people before a security officer shot and wounded him, at which point he committed suicide.

Not all attacks involve guns or shootings. In fact, some customers may be unwilling clientele, as can happen with government agencies. In 2010, Andrew Stack flew a plane into an Internal Revenue Service (IRS) building in Texas, killing a manager, wounding several others, and reportedly causing $36 million in damages following a dispute with the IRS.

Each of these killers had different motives. However, each apparently felt that whatever wrong they perceived, it could only be resolved through violence and, frequently, in their own death.

Understanding how an organization can spark anger in a past client to push him or her to violence is critical if you are going to be able to prevent or mitigate the event. In most cases, lack of basic customer service is the root of the anger, or at least the trigger point. What is often even a minor incident can be handled so poorly as to create a volatile and dangerous situation with the wrong person.

Basic intervention means listening to complaints and trying to work out solutions, without being controlling or condescending. Fundamental customer service skills may actually de-escalate the situation before there is even a threat or hint of violence.

Think about the times you've been most angry with a company. It probably had as much to do with principle as matter. And being able to walk away and take your business elsewhere is usually a resolution. But there are times when you cannot walk away and shop elsewhere. For example, imagine taking a new car in for a warranty repair and being told it was not covered or fixed. A mechanic's lien may be held over your car forcing you to pay. If the dealer aggravates the situation further by not listening or not caring about the problem, your anger will just intensify.

Health care bills are another potential example. Often billing departments are located off-site and so-called customer service people will not provide names or phone extensions, so every call to resolve a dispute results in starting the explanation over again. The message is one of lack of caring, and a consumer is not able to just walk away. In fact, many types of bills can be sent to collections without the consumer having the chance to be heard by a third party. That affects credit scores, and under current law, mortgages, interest rates, and loans are all determined by credit numbers regardless of past credit history or creditworthiness. One claim, wrong or not, can ruin a person's credit and cost them thousands of dollars in interest.

If an individual is suffering under many of the red flags we've looked at before, the situation could reach a violent boiling point. Loss of control, lack of social support, and financial collapse could combine for a dangerous outcome.

Be careful not to have a bureaucratic approach to customer service. Provide people the chance to be heard. Try to work with individuals to resolve issues instead of hiding behind an anonymous bureaucracy. Hold employees accountable to ensure good service is provided.

For employees on the front line dealing with angry individuals, provide training on how to deal with them and respond. First and foremost, employees should be able to identify signs of escalating behavior. Some industries are prone to higher risk and should be especially diligent in training staff. Health care workers, particularly in emergency departments and those dealing with mental health patients, are at a higher level of risk. Police officers and security guards are even more likely to be assaulted on the job, as are bartenders. Teachers and retail workers are also at high risk.

## POLICE RESPONSE

In Hollywood movies, the police always arrive in the nick of time with lights flashing and sirens blaring, just in time for the credits to roll and everyone to live happily ever after. The reality is much different. When the police do respond and have someone to arrest, it is not the end of the story. For most threats and disturbances, even assaults, the crime is a misdemeanor, meaning the suspect will spend the night in jail at the most. If the situation involves a DV case, the suspect may stay in jail until appearing before a judge, usually the next business day.

We've looked at how serious threats should be treated and some of the signs that an individual is escalating in behavior, posing a risk to others. However, from a legal perspective, crimes such as harassment, or making threats, are minor and do not seem a high priority within the justice system. In fact, for some indirect or veiled threats, a crime may not even have been committed. The police officers responding to your call will not be able to do anything. Even if a disgruntled employee or violent customer is arrested, the outcome will likely be anger management classes.

The point to understand is that law enforcement may not be the best resource when trying to be proactive about a potentially violent person. The police will not wave a magic wand and have your problem vanish, perhaps not until a serious crime has been committed and it is too late and someone is hurt.

To make matters worse, when you call to report that someone may have made threats, unless it is an in-progress disturbance, the officer will get the call as a "cold" harassment. Cold means that it is not in progress and the suspect may not even be there, and the harassment is usually translated as a minor (okay, boring) crime to investigate. Often, these calls result in the officer having to arbitrate a name-calling contest.

You have to understand the mindset and be able to plead your case on why you are concerned and why the individual may pose a legitimate threat. Officers can check for past criminal history or calls with the individual in that jurisdiction and find out if there have been similar reports in the past. Police officers can also be present as a peacekeeper during tense conversations or terminations on what, in police vernacular, is called a civil standby.

Keep detailed notes with dates and times of escalating behavior for documentation. Even if no other action is taken, you can ask the police officer for a report number. If the officer will not take a report, at least note the officer's name, date, and time, and ask if there is a dispatch call number as a reference. If you suspect that the officer is not taking the situation seriously, you can always politely ask for a supervisor or call the police dispatch center back and ask to speak to a sergeant or supervisor.

Often when a situation has been growing worse over time, organizations start thinking about getting a restraining order (RO) against the problem individual. In general, I do not recommend taking this course. For one thing, if an individual employee or manager is seeking the RO, then he or she must remember that the RO is public information and will be provided to the suspect and contains personal information, including home address, on the form. Sometimes serving a suspect with a subpoena to appear in court for a RO can further escalate the situation and provoke the suspect even more.

I attended one seminar on workplace violence and back-to-back speakers had completely opposite views of ROs. The first speaker, a well-known specialist in threat assessment, recommended against organizational ROs for many of the same reasons I have mentioned. The second, a compliance attorney from a hospital, had the opposite view and felt that ROs were definitely appropriate. Looking from the compliance avenue, it makes sense to have an additional legal tool as part of the overall protection process. In most cases, a RO will keep individuals away just as you want. However, for those most prone to violence, it may not serve a purpose at all.

Last, a RO is just a piece of paper and is not a force field that will keep a dedicated evil doer away. A RO is a tool that serves a purpose in some cases, such as a DV, gives the police a reason to arrest someone just for being nearby, and is useful for a stalker or an ongoing harassment. For most organizations, you can warn or have the police warn a suspect that if he or she returns, he or she will be charged with trespassing. For most would-be offenders that is sufficient. For one serious about a deadly violent attack, the consequences of either a RO or trespass charge would be insignificant.

Talk to your local police before an incident occurs and build a relationship with them. This will help get a better response in most cases when you do need assistance and also helps you learn more about how the police respond so you can make an informed decision on when to involve them.

## HOW TO SURVIVE AN ACTIVE SHOOTER

When all the prevention and mitigation fails and acts of violence do occur, you must be mentally prepared in advance. The Department of Homeland Security (DHS) sums up what to do during an active shooter situation with three words: run, hide, or fight. Sounds simple, but the reality can be much more complicated.

We have heard of the idea of "fight or flight" and often believe the instinctive response to danger is one of the two. However, when confronted with a life-threatening risk, one never encountered before, a third reaction may occur: freezing. In shock, as our minds try to grapple with a new and stressful event instead of responding or fleeing, it is common to take no action at all.

When faced with an active shooter, it is very likely that many people will freeze up and not know what to do. To avoid that there are a few things that individuals can do ahead of time. Make a plan, imagine "what if" scenarios, and physically practice your plan.

First, make a plan. That means deciding right now what kind of response you will take during an event, in this case an active shooter. If you heard gunshots down the hall right now, what would you do? For that matter, would you react if you are unsure if it is gunshots? What would you do if in doubt? Once you decide to react, you must have a plan.

Second, imagine various scenarios and picture your response. Maybe you have a plan for your office, but what if you are in a conference room or the cafeteria? This is not idle daydreaming; this type of visualization can help you respond in a crisis. Studies have shown that athletes who visualize their performance before a race or game will be more likely to outperform their competitors. In addition to the physical practice, the mental picture is another way to help train the body.

Third, practice the plan. Visualizing your response is great, but actually trying your plan can expose problems or obstacles you did not anticipate. For example, if you think that you can move a desk in front of a door, try it. You would hate to find out too late that the desk is bolted down or cannot be moved for some reason. If the plan includes turning off lights to hide, be certain you know how to turn off the lights—try it. Other ambient light in the room could affect how you would hide.

Going back to the DHS model, the first suggestion is to run. What escape routes can you use and what are the alternatives? Think of where a shooter might be and what his or her line of sight and fire is. Can you escape undetected?

For most people, getting away really is the top priority. There are exceptions. With others to think of, teachers or nurses may not be able to escape as easily. The idea of leaving children behind, especially when in a position of responsibility, is reprehensible. Escape for a teacher may only be possible if the class is away from its room in another part of the building or even in a separate building across campus. Nurses with bed-ridden patients will not be able to evacuate either, not without leaving the patients behind. In some cases, such as these, it is essential to hide or shelter in place.

If escape is not possible, you must hide. Even hiding is something to think about before a crisis arises. How would you barricade yourself in place? Lock or block your door, silence cell phones, and hide under a desk. Can you and coworkers block a door with furniture and desks to delay an attacker? Think about which direction the doors open. If they open inward, it may be easier to barricade the door. If it opens outward, you can still block the door with chairs or tables.

Most active shooter cases are over in a few minutes, sometimes in 90 seconds. If you were unable to escape and forced to shelter in place, every second equals a better chance to survive. Since the shooting at Columbine High School, police officers have trained to deploy teams into an active shooter situation immediately. The first few responding officers will enter and begin searching for the shooter(s).

The longer you are able to shelter in place, the greater the chance to survive. Even turning off lights can throw a gunman off into thinking the room might be empty and send him searching for targets elsewhere. You may even consider playing dead, especially if in an area the shooter already attacked or if near other victims. It is a chilling prospect, but a possible way to hide in plain sight.

As a last resort, when you or someone else faces imminent danger, you may have to fight back. If the gunman enters your hiding area, you will have to react to survive. Chairs or tables near the door could serve as a distraction or block the view into a darkened room. Attack the shooter as he enters with anything you might have as a weapon. A letter opener, pocketknife, scissors, even a pen or pencil can be used to strike the shooter. Throwing objects or chairs can be a distraction to allow for escape or a close in attack. Even a fire extinguisher can work as a weapon to blind and incapacitate the gunman. Look around your room right now and think about what could be a weapon. Picture your office and take an inventory of what could be used to protect yourself at work. Where would you hide and wait or position yourself if discovered or if the shooter enters? Look for spots where you can surprise and ambush a gunman as he or she enters the area with the weapons you have available.

Once you are fighting with the suspect, do not stop. Give it your all and never give up, even if wounded. Do not stop until the suspect is down and unable to hurt you or anyone else anymore.

When leaving the vicinity of an active shooter, be ready to follow the commands of any police officers. In the confusion and chaos, officers will not know who the shooter is and may not even have a description. Anyone could be a threat. Keep your hands empty and visible as you exit the area. Follow any commands the officers give, whether to get on the ground, stop and spin around so they can look for weapons on you, or if they direct you to another location. Once out, try to give the best information you can on the number and description of any shooters, as well as victims. How many weapons did the shooter have? Do you know if he mentioned explosives? Be ready to be a good witness for police once out of the danger.

Recovery from any type of workplace violence can be difficult, even insurmountable, for small businesses. Some estimates put the cost of a workplace homicide at $800,000. There is also publicity that could turn into lack of support from the community and victims' families if warning signs or preventive steps were ignored.

## CONCLUSION

Workplace violence usually appears in the form of assaults or threatening behavior and, less often, murder. No matter the extent of the violence, it is disruptive to employees and can affect productivity even in relatively minor cases. Training staff to identify warning signs is a key step in the prevention process. Assessing and analyzing threats with a team helps direct the organization's response and identifies security measures needed.

When it comes to workplace violence, an ounce of prevention is truly worth far more than a pound of cure. Take warning signs seriously, put the right security measures in place for the specific threat, and practice how to respond to an active shooter.

## BUSINESS KARATE BELT LEVEL

Test your company's karate belt level in the discipline of awareness/stance. If your organization meets each belt level and all the standards of the lower belts as seen in Figure 8.1, you have then achieved that color level.

**White**
- Create a policy on workplace violence, including how to deal with domestic violence situations, as well as escalating employees or customers

**Yellow**
- Train all employees on warning signs of escalating behavior
- Use a reporting system to allow employees to report concerns

**Green**
- Create a threat assessment team with HR, security, legal, and management
- Take action when a threat or concern arises - never ignore a real threat

**Purple**
- Develop written intervention plans to outline response and additional security measures that may be utilized during an elevated threat
- Support strong customer service, with personal interaction and accountability

**Brown**
- Provide police with floor plans for use during an emergency
- Use consistency in discipline and promotions to build a "fair" environment

**Black**
- Create a plan on what you would do during an active shooter
- Train all employees how to survive an active shooter

**FIGURE 8.1**    What is your belt level?

# Further Reading

Bachman, R., July 1994. Violence and Theft in the Workplace (NCJ148199). United States Department of Justice, Washington, DC.

Harrell, E., March 2011. Workplace Violence, 1993–2009 (NCJ 233231). United States Department of Justice, Washington, DC.

National Institute for the Prevention of Workplace Violence, Inc., n.d. The Financial Impact of Workplace Violence. Retrieved from: http://www.workplaceviolence911.com/docs/FinancialImpactofWV.pdf (accessed 22.11.13.).

Security Director's Report, November 2012. Shootings Defy Certain Stereotypes (What Are the Stereotypes?). Institute of Finance and Management, Greenwich, CT.

Truman, J.L., Planty, M., October 2012. Criminal Victimization, 2011 (NCJ 239437). United States Department of Justice, Washington, DC.

Workplace Violence Prevention and Response Guideline, 2005. ASIS International, Alexandria, VA.

# Freestyle Sparring: Learning to Fight Back—Emergency Operations Planning

## KARATE SPARRING

The primary goal of learning martial arts is to learn how to defend yourself. Learning forms and basic moves all help develop technique, balance, fitness, and muscle memory. The drills that develop reaction and test the instincts that have grown during practice are the sparring drills. Sparring is free-form fighting, where the rules are defined and then two or more karate students practice what they have learned to try and "defeat" the other.

During sparring, an opponent is free to move around and will use feints, strikes, or blocks to attack you. In a true self-defense situation, you could strike an attacker anywhere. However, in classes, attacks are generally limited to above the belt and even sometimes to the front part of the gi or uniform top.

To beat an opponent, you have to be able to attack from any direction and be able to respond or move quickly to seize an opportunity. For example, if an attacker tries a spin kick, you may be fast enough to block the kick and stop the attacker's spin, exposing his or her back, including kidneys. A quick punch can score a point or end a fight on the street.

In short, sparring matches train students to instantly recognize an attack and react instantly to block it. Some sparring drills even pair two or more attackers against one student, increasing the likelihood that an attack will come from any quarter from anywhere around her. The student must also be able to switch tactics swiftly, going from a block to a kick to a punch, without even thinking consciously about it. Basic skills, such as balance and footing, remain important, especially in a competitive match where the space could be limited and stepping off the mat or out of the ring could count against you.

## BUSINESSES IN THE RING

Fighting is a last resort and should only be done on the street in a true emergency. Businesses, like our karate students, could face devastating emergencies as well. The threats can come from any direction in a 360° circle around the organization, even from within. Just like karate students use combinations of tactics to beat an attack, organizations have to be able to bring all the right tools and skills to the table to best protect against what could be a shattering experience as well.

For organizations, surviving a disaster is all about emergency planning and business continuity. Dealing with catastrophic events, responding immediately, protecting employees, and keeping the business productive is crucial. According to some studies, businesses forced to close during a natural or man-made disaster remain closed, forever, in one-third of the cases. One out of three businesses shut down for an emergency situation will never open again.

That idea alone should motivate most people to develop the organization's emergency plans. However, it often does not. Why? For some reason, we humans are very good at rationalizing away the risks. In fact, there are several layers of denial that stop leaders from making emergency plans. I do not know who originally said it, but somewhere I heard the denial described as four layers:

- "It won't happen."
- "If it does happen, it won't happen here."
- "If it does happen here, it won't be that bad."
- "If it does happen here and it is really bad, then there is nothing that could have been done anyway."

At some point, we have probably all rationalized some sort of potential emergency in the same way. Would you drive across town without a spare tire? Probably. You think the odds of getting a flat are remote. Or if you do get a flat, it won't be that bad. You'll call a friend to pick you up and go home and get the spare fixed and put it on the car. Or you'll call AAA, the American Automobile Association. Or if the tire goes flat and you don't have cell service, no one is around, it is pouring rain, and it is midnight, you might justify your decision by thinking that you would not have been able to put the spare on anyway under those circumstances.

Each of these denials is false. Disasters do happen, could happen to you, and could be very bad or dangerous. Last, even if it is bad, there are steps that could have been taken to reduce the risks or minimize the impact. In our tire example, having the spare is one step toward mitigating the risk of being stranded in the middle of nowhere. Beyond that, packing a raincoat, keeping a flashlight in the car, and checking that the right tools are there could all help get you back on the road as quickly as possible.

# BACKGROUND OF EMERGENCY PLANNING

The best emergency plan in the world will fail without leadership. Setting up the right structure to keep the response on track during a disaster or emergency is the first step to success. Fortunately, a great model has already been well tested and proved effective. The Incident Command System (ICS) is the structure developed that allows for flexibility while defining clear roles and functions to help navigate through a tough situation.

The ICS was first developed by the military and later adapted by crews fighting wildfires. As you can imagine, there were difficulties in coordinating response, allocating resources, and even planning what should be done. Crews were spread out across wilderness areas, each facing different challenges or needs. Multiple agencies were also involved, from local firefighters to sheriff's departments as well as groups of firefighters brought in from out of state or other areas. Information from aerial surveillance had to be analyzed, strategies developed, and then the right resources with specific goals sent to the various areas around the fire to help contain it and protect homes or forests.

The basic structure consists of an incident commander who is ultimately responsible for all decisions. The incident commander is directly supported by a team, including a safety officer, security officer, public information officer, and liaison officer. There are several sections, each one in turn supported by a section chief who reports to the incident commander. The sections include operations, planning, logistics, and finance/administration.

The incident commander has the overall responsibility to determine what goals need to be accomplished and the steps to reach those goals. The liaison officer coordinates with any external agencies or groups that may be involved or have asked for help, such as the local office of emergency management or local police. The safety and security officers may be combined into one role and are, as the name implies, responsible for the overall safety and security of those involved with the emergency response. The safety/security role is to identify any threatening situations that could jeopardize responders and make recommendations to adjust for risks. The public information officer, or PIO, is responsible for any media statements or communications, as well as internal communications to employees or affected groups.

Once the incident commander has outlined the overall objectives, the other sections each take on specific roles to achieve those objectives. The planning team is focused on information: what is happening around the organization or externally, as well as gathering information on what resources are available. The planning team takes that information to develop a timeline outlining what needs to be done in the immediate future as well as down the road, even into the recovery phase.

The logistics group is responsible for finding out what resources are on hand, where the resources are, or how to get them. A large piece of this often involves getting a labor team set up. Depending on the type of emergency and the response needed, a labor team can help by providing runners to get information to the right people in the midst of chaotic communications. The labor team may need to help move internal equipment, evacuate customers or patients, direct traffic, or secure the facility.

The operations team is responsible for the "doing." This team has to carry out the planned tasks and may be dependent on the supplies procured by the logistics team. This is where the rubber meets the road. If the emergency involves damage to a critical building, the operations team will be responsible for assessing and repairing the damage. Specific team members may include a cross section from across the organization, such as information technology personnel, especially if the disaster affects data servers or equipment. In a hospital, operations may be focused around clinical care, especially if the emergency is an influx of patients or involves the evacuation of patients to other care sites. The labor team put together by the logistics crew may be put to work in a needed role.

Next is the finance or administration section. This group is responsible for tracking expenses, purchases, payroll issues, time sheets, or any other item that reflects a cost to the organization. For example, during a blizzard, hospital staff may be forced to stay overnight to continue caring for patients. Nearby hotel rooms may be used to give everyone a chance to get some sleep and rest between shifts. The finance team tracks those expenses as well as who was working at what times. The administrative side also includes keeping a log of decisions made at the incident command level as well as collecting and keeping any related paperwork.

The Incident Command System is designed to be flexible. That means for some situations you may not need to assign a person to each and every role. For example, if the scope of an emergency is smaller or temporary, the same person may fill the role of the operations section chief as well as the logistics chief.

In law enforcement, the first police officer on a scene becomes the incident commander. His responsibilities include making sure the scene is safe, identifying what additional resources will be needed and what immediate goals need to be established, and beginning to work towards those goals. As other police officers arrive, he will assign them as needed, similar to how the operations chief would work. In short, the initial response and preliminary ICS may be one person and grow to include other officers, supervisors, and even other agencies, such as the fire department or paramedics.

Fire departments routinely use the ICS in an even more formal way. The initial fire truck on scene quickly becomes the command center and even uses that term as the radio identifier. Eventually, when a battalion chief arrives, that person becomes the incident commander and takes on that radio designation to provide continuity of communication for everyone in the field reporting back or requesting instructions from the incident commander.

The United States' Federal Emergency Management Agency has numerous free courses available online that help train individuals on ICS. These courses are a great way to get those in your organization familiar with the type of command structure that should be used to deal with emergency situations.

## EMERGENCY PLANNING

The emergency plan is the guiding tool that the incident command team needs to best address disastrous situations. The plan should focus on four areas: prevention, mitigation, response, and recovery. Obviously, the planning needs to start long before any emergency actually happens.

The first step is to identify an emergency planning team. The team should include senior leaders or an organization executive to act as sponsor and provide key leadership where needed. Other members should include security, information technology, facility leaders or building engineer, and human resources. The team should be a cross section of critical aspects within your organization and include any departments that do have, or should have, some expertise in the emergency planning arena.

Once the team is formed, it should start by identifying potential risks or threats to the organization. For us, it is already done. Pull out the security risk matrix we conducted in Chapter 4 and review the list of threats. The list included security risks, such as criminal events, which may or may not rise to the level of an emergency planning need. However, some criminal events, such as an active shooter, bomb threat, or hostage situation will definitely be part of the emergency plan.

Other threats may include weather, such as hurricanes or blizzards, and even strikes or work stoppages in vendor locations if that would essentially shut down the organization. Some of these topics will fall under business continuity and the steps that an organization should be prepared to follow to continue operations or business functions.

There is a concept called all-hazards planning, in which the emergency planning process takes a generic approach to develop the response for a wide range of threats, rather than a specific plan for each and every risk. While there are similarities in responses, the emergency response may be vastly different for each event. The first stages, such as forming the ICS, and gathering information, determining goals, and planning how to deal with the emergency may be similar. The actual details of the response will change.

I prefer looking at all the likely hazards and creating checklists outlining what needs to be done for each scenario. There will be some similarities with many of the hazards. For example, both hurricanes and blizzards will impact how employees, suppliers, and customers get to and from the organization and both could result in power outages. In fact, utility failure is another potential hazard, so there will be common ground as you create your list. The shared responses only have to be created in one plan, making the process simpler. And having a response checklist clearly identified for the emergency facing the organization will make it much easier to start the response.

Planning for the various potential disasters should revolve around several common themes: loss or damage to the enterprise's buildings; lack of access to the organization; loss of utilities such as electricity, water, or heat; and injury or loss of life.

Damage to the organization or buildings can occur due to severe weather such as tornadoes, high winds, hail, earthquakes, or even blizzards where heavy snow could collapse a roof. There are man-made events, such as terrorism or accidents, that could result in damage as well. Whether the loss of the buildings is due to an explosion, weather, or a truck accidentally colliding with the side of the building, the result is the same. The common elements of the response should include an assessment of the damage, identify and relocate critical functions, determine the length of time the area will be out of service, and set up operations in another location to resume business.

After Hurricane Katrina, some experts recommended businesses set up a spare or backup facility in order to continue operating after a disaster. A separate site, located about 200 miles away from the original, would be accessible by car in case air travel was not possible, as we saw after 9/11. The site should include phones and computers with backup access to any servers or data needed to function. Presumably, during a disaster vital staff would drive to the location, set up in hotel rooms, and continue working.

A plan like this sounds good in theory, but I do have concerns that would have to be worked out in advance. One is the cost. It is hard to imagine very many organizations being able to afford equipping and setting up, plus securing and maintaining, a second location just for emergencies. Some companies will have satellite offices that could serve that function and could base their plans around that. For other companies, the idea may not be suitable. However, even a school may set up arrangements for transporting students to another facility if the school is not available. For a long-term disruption, a school may arrange to use local churches or send students to surrounding schools.

Part of the planning should definitely include making arrangements in advance and getting a memo of agreement or memo of understanding (MOU) before an emergency occurs to ensure that external resources will be available during a disaster.

Another central theme to consider in planning is the lack of access to the business. This could be due to weather, such as blizzard, with roads closed, or due to an evacuation caused by a bomb threat or even tied to the first theme and damage to the building that create an unsafe environment. Planning should also focus on how to continue functions for both a short-term situation and a longer-lasting event. A key planning concern is how to access vital data or technology. If it is a quick evacuation, planning also needs to include accounting for all employees and customers (patients, students, etc.) and confirmation that everyone is out.

For both damage and loss of access, security should be a high priority (see Figure 9.1). Looters move into disaster areas quickly realizing that no one is present and valuables are exposed. When homeowners are forced to evacuate large areas due to wildfires, it is amazing how quickly come the reports of looters getting into the area, burglarizing homes, and stealing property from people already suffering. Business evacuations are no different.

FIGURE 9.1   Empty or damaged buildings quickly become a target of looters or other criminals.

Emergency planning must include a secure operations component on how to secure the building whether with internal security or MOUs with local security companies to provide the right level of coverage to secure a facility. During a long-lasting event, fencing, locks, or other measures may be needed for complete protection of the property.

Utility failure is a very real risk. Some areas are served by aging infrastructure and utilities are increasingly targeted by cyber criminals attempting to hack and tamper with systems. Losing electricity, water, or gas can quickly turn a workplace into a useless shell. An assessment on how long the outage will last is one of the first steps to be taken. If it will last for a length of time, then you are in a situation where the building is essentially damaged and relocation may be necessary. Again, there must be access to virtual data or servers. In the case of power failures, access to retrieve hard copies of paperwork or other documents will be possible. In some circumstances, you may choose to continue to operate in the main location, such as during a loss of water. Water bottles can be brought in. Even toilets can be flushed with buckets of water. However, there is still planning to be done to determine the resources needed and the best course of action.

The last impact to consider during a disaster is injury or loss of life. In recent years, we've seen this in many forms. Letters containing anthrax or other powders cause disruption. Even if the powder is not anthrax or harmful, the threat is present and the situation has to be handled as an imminent menace. Bomb threats and actual devices, even a small pipe bomb, are another concern. In the last chapter, we talked about the risks associated with workplace violence, including active shooters. The planning process for a comprehensive emergency plan needs to include all possible serious violent acts.

During some violent acts, such as an active shooter, the best course of action may be for everyone to shelter in place. These incidents are often over in a few moments. There may not be any opportunity to assemble the incident command team, at least not during the incident. In this case, the planning should focus on prevention, mitigation, and recovery. The response is there, but it will be up to individuals or groups throughout to implement the plan, so advance training and practice exercises are critical to make sure the response works per the plan. During an active shooter situation, the incident command team may still be able to communicate but will have to rely on phones or conference calls, if it is safe to do so.

Accidents or fires are a common form of life-threatening situations. The emergency plan should focus on those types of hazards and the related risks. If there is a serious accident or fire, the plan needs to address coordination with first responders, such as the fire department, and provide information on what hazardous materials are on site and where potential victims might be located. The response also needs to include accounting for employees to make sure no one is left in harm's way.

# THE WRITTEN EMERGENCY OPERATIONS PLAN

When everything goes haywire, trying to remember what to do amid the chaos is not going to be successful. The emergency operations plan (EOP) must be written and accessible. The plan is fundamentally a guide to deal with and overcome any disasters, so it should focus on the hazards, what to do, how to respond, and who will be doing what.

A plan can be as detailed as an organization wants. It may include the scope, list the planning team members, and outline authority and executive sponsorship. Since the heart of the plan is to be a tool during emergencies, I like to keep the EOP direct and on track. It can include specific appendices that list the detailed steps to follow for a given emergency, but somewhere there should be a practical guide.

Key parts of the plan include:

- Scope: i.e., address or locations covered by the plan identified here.
- Identified hazards from the security risk assessment.
- List of critical functions or assets: to help establish guidelines for recovery, organizational survival time may be listed here. For example, if a company has cash on hand to meet expenses for 17 days, then it becomes imperative to resume operations within that time or shut down.
- List of resources, including aid agreements or MOS with external resources.
- Trained incident command team leaders: some individuals may be specifically trained for certain sections, such as logistics. Every role should have at least one other person who can fill in. Larger organizations may have three or four people available on different shifts to create the ICS.
- Communications plan covering how teams and individuals will relay information during emergencies; includes how information will be provided to employees with updates on the situation.
- Media plan addressing how information will be relayed to local news agencies. Remember, "no comment" is not a viable media plan.
- Checklists: an appendix or supplemental tool kit that provides detailed goals and steps to follow for each leader in the ICS to guide the team through the emergency and ensure that critical steps are not overlooked or resources forgotten.
- Recovery plan: this will be covered in more detail in the next chapter.

The plan should be useable, practical, and realistic. Remember that the plan is for situations that are out of the norm; there will be chaos and perhaps even some panic among employees. A plan that is too complex or too detailed will not be read, understood, or implemented with the best results.

## Trouble Spots

In every real emergency or disaster and every drill there are always problems. No matter how well the plan was prepared or thought out, nothing ever goes smoothly. Each situation is different and there are unexpected obstacles.

The most common problem, one that I've seen in every emergency, is a breakdown in communication—not necessarily a technology problem with radios, cell phones, static, or dropped calls, but more often the right information not getting to the people who need to know. When that happens, the wrong decisions are made based on faulty input, or critical steps are not carried out.

Communications will break down largely due to the "fog of war" mentality. Often in the incident command center so much information and feedback is being sent or received that the chain of command starts to fall apart. All decisions should strictly follow the chain of command and go through the incident commander. However, leaders in the field or even section chiefs start bypassing the incident commander in an effort to resolve problems quickly. The problem is that other section leaders are not aware of the change in the situation, available resources, or new problems encountered.

I remember one incident involving a mass casualty influx at a hospital. The command center was very calm and quiet, and it did not appear that anything out of the ordinary was going on. I began to worry about what was going on in the emergency department where the incoming patients were being treated. One of my team members came in to relay information and confirmed that the situation on the front line was extremely busy and chaotic and none of the sense of urgency or need for additional clinical support was being relayed back to the incident command team. The emergency department had begun calling other hospital units to send staff, completely bypassing the incident command (IC) center.

The reason this is a problem is that the incident command team and sections have no idea what resources are where or whether or not they are needed. On the flip side, I've also seen situations where those in the field are relaying vital information only to have it ignored. If that places others in danger or harm's way, individuals will quickly work together changing the plans without passing the information back to the incident command center. This happened during one hazardous material spill when I was a police officer. Based on the information from those on the scene about the chemicals involved and the wind direction, officers realized that other officers were being sent into the "hot zone" to divert traffic. When incident command could not be persuaded to change the decision, officers communicated between themselves to change the plan, affecting the entire traffic pattern as defined by the incident command team.

The best way to mitigate some of the communication problems is through training. Everyone involved in the execution of the emergency plan should be well trained on the expectations and the communication portion of the EOP. The communications plan and training should include details on the types of information to pass through incident command and how to request additional resources. All involved individuals need to understand the specific roles and tasks and how that fits into the overall strategic goals of the emergency response.

During one evacuation drill, the plan had been trained to the labor teams that would be carrying out the drill with specific directions on where to move evacuees. Some of the units were assigned to move evacuees from one point on the floor to the elevators, but they were to wait for the next unit to take over at the point. The elevator teams were only supposed to transport people to the main level where another unit would meet them and escort them to the exit. However, once put into action some of the teams decided not to follow the plan. The floor unit decided to go ahead and transport people down the elevator. The elevator team meanwhile missed them and was waiting for the unit that had now left the area entirely, leaving more people behind on the floor who still needed to be evacuated. The idea may have seemed like the best course at the time to those individuals, but instead created confusion and unnecessary delays. It was also frustrating to the logistics section chief who was being asked by the operations chief where the units were that had been sent to the area to carry out the evacuations.

Another common obstacle is hesitation or failure to take action. Depending on the situation, there may be only a few minutes to start the EOP, including setting up the incident command team. Even in drills with a high sense of urgency, the acting incident commander was slow selecting team members and trying to gather information rather than providing early and clear instructions on what steps everyone needed to take.

For example, during a bomb threat a search should always be carried out. If there is a suspicious device on the grounds, it is obviously much better to find it as early as possible. The incident commander should quickly set up the team and set goals, i.e., searching the entire area, coordinating with law enforcement, and documenting or recording which areas were searched.

A mass casualty incident is another example where urgency is needed. As soon as information comes in that there are numerous patients due to an explosion, bus accident, or another hospital forced to evacuate, there are only a few moments before the first patients may begin arriving. The emergency plan for that type of situation needs to be implemented immediately, without delay.

Another common obstacle is a failure to fully debrief an emergency situation. If the incident command team was activated, a careful review of what happened, what went well, and what did not should always be done. The debriefing should include everyone involved and get the perspective of different groups involved in the response. As noted earlier, the view from the front line of the operations section might be very different from what the finance section was facing.

The review should be facilitated by someone looking to get constructive feedback. The findings should be documented. Perhaps most important, the findings ought to be used by the planning team and adjustments to the emergency plan or response made to correct any issues.

# CONCLUSION

Each emergency or disaster will present unique challenges and problems. The response will never go perfectly, and everyone needs to be able to adjust and remain flexible. Fortunately, with careful planning and willingness to learn and adapt, supported by training, the employees will be prepared to support the emergency response and help shift the focus back to recovery as soon as possible.

# BUSINESS KARATE BELT LEVEL

Test your company's karate belt level in the discipline of awareness/stance. If your organization meets each belt level and all the standards of the lower belts as seen in Figure 9.2, you have then achieved that color level.

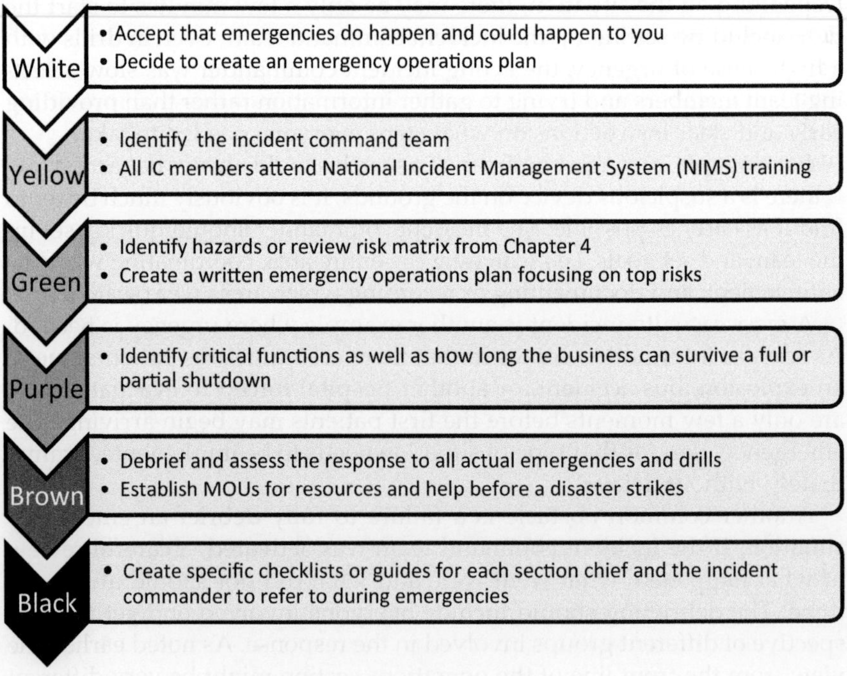

**White**
- Accept that emergencies do happen and could happen to you
- Decide to create an emergency operations plan

**Yellow**
- Identify the incident command team
- All IC members attend National Incident Management System (NIMS) training

**Green**
- Identify hazards or review risk matrix from Chapter 4
- Create a written emergency operations plan focusing on top risks

**Purple**
- Identify critical functions as well as how long the business can survive a full or partial shutdown

**Brown**
- Debrief and assess the response to all actual emergencies and drills
- Establish MOUs for resources and help before a disaster strikes

**Black**
- Create specific checklists or guides for each section chief and the incident commander to refer to during emergencies

FIGURE 9.2   What is your belt level?

# Down, but Not Out: Disaster Drills and Recovery

## MARTIAL ARTS: SPARRING AND GROUND FIGHTING

Karate students focus on balance and footing throughout almost all drills, forms, or basic exercises. The purpose is to be able to stay on one's feet during a sparring match. However, as we saw in the last chapter, there are times that even the best martial artist will end up on the ground.

Even in the police academy, recruits are taught basic techniques of ground fighting. The intent is to protect yourself while down, but also to reach a point where you can get back on your feet as quickly as possible. Standing means greater mobility and speed. If a suspect flees or brings a weapon to bear, a standing position offers more flexibility on how to react than being on the ground.

Karate students, just like police officers, must learn how to defend themselves while down but also be ready and focused on getting back up as quickly as possible. Recovering to a standing stance is a crucial exercise. Some karate experts like to demonstrate fancy techniques for standing. You've seen those individuals lying on their back, arching backs, and flipping feet underneath them to get back to a standing position in a second—fancy, but effective. For most of us, the technique may be a little simpler, but the end result is the same.

## GETTING YOUR BUSINESS BACK ON ITS FEET

Often when businesses are knocked down by a disaster or emergency, it is a real challenge to get back to operational. We've seen some of the challenges and talked about how one-third of businesses that close during an emergency never reopen.

Creating an emergency operations plan as we looked at in Chapter 9 is a great start. But will the plan work? That is another issue entirely. It is very easy to talk about and put together a plan that sounds good on paper only to find that in a real emergency, vital pieces were overlooked or the response did not work as thought.

Karate students have to practice moves to get back on their feet as quickly as possible. That could be falling into a forward roll, a fancy back flip, or a simple matter of getting feet down and pushing up with hands in a fighting stance, ready to block an attack. All require practice. I have heard that for something to become instinctive or natural, 1500 repetitions are necessary. In that case, the karate student must repeat getting back up 1500 times to do it instinctively in a fight.

Businesses need the same level of practice to make sure that any emergency can be dealt with and the business can remain standing at the end, even when competitors remain down and out—out of business, that is. For an organization, 1500 reiterations aren't practical, but preparation is.

The only way to create that natural response is practice. That means training everyone involved on what the emergency plan is and how the organization will respond. After training, the plan and the training are both tested with drills and exercises, hopefully before any real emergency puts the plan to the test.

## TRAINING

The best emergency operations plan is useless if it cannot be implemented. For the plan to be effective, everyone must know the plan and what to do when disaster strikes. To make certain that everyone does know the plan and what to do, there must be training.

The training needs to be targeted to the audience. If different groups or people within the organization have different roles during an emergency, then the training should be geared to those roles, rather than a general approach. Training also starts with learning the basics and progressing to more advanced levels.

If you just created an emergency plan to address active shooters, you would not immediately give everyone the plan or the policy and procedure and then ask them to perform during a realistic drill. Training should start with the basics, including an explanation of active shooters, then move on to cover more details about how to react, how and where to hide, how to barricade doors and rooms, and how to fight back if necessary. The training may even include information on warning signs and escalating behavior to watch for.

Some groups may have roles that are more specific and need more in-depth training. For example, the security team may need additional training on interacting with arriving law enforcement, as well as how to secure the building, reviewing any video surveillance systems, or gathering information about an ongoing event. During some emergencies, such as a fire or hazardous material spill, the facilities personnel may need to be trained on how to shut down the plant or when and how to cut off gas supplies. During a hostage crisis, IT staff may be asked by police to shut down Wi-Fi access to limit the suspect's ability to see news about the situation he or she created.

Some of these tasks may seem straightforward, but in a stressful situation will be easily forgotten or overlooked. Training is one way to begin building the instinctive response staff needs during an emergency.

The topics are just one way that training can vary. The format, or way training is delivered, is another one. Training can be conducted online, such as through a course watched via a computer. There is also generic online training available through Federal Emergency Management Agency (FEMA), such as National Incident Management System training, mentioned in Chapter 9. For internal training, classrooms could be set up with instructors to provide the training to a live audience. The instructors are then available to handle follow-up questions or generate discussion about some of the emergency responses. Another form of training is actual practice in the form of drills. Drills are more of a practical exam to see both how well the plan is implemented and how well it works.

Each format has advantages and disadvantages. Selecting the right process to match the training objectives is important in order to have a successful training program.

Online or computer-based training (CBT) is often a more cost-effective way to reach employees. Once the training is created, it can be used repeatedly. Employees can go through the training by taking the course every year or on some other predetermined schedule. CBT courses also offer the ability to test the students at the end of the session with some basic questions to make sure key objectives are understood. Usually these courses are shorter or can be taken at any time, so it is easier to work them into an employee's shift and does not create nonproductive time, where an employee's entire time is spent on the training and not on normal business functions.

The disadvantage is that there is no instructor and no chance for the learner to ask questions or get additional information. To be honest, many of these types of courses are simply endured by the employees with just barely enough learning to get through any tests at the end. This is especially true when the learning is required and there is no effort made to explain the benefits to the students/employees, and the course is just seen as another task to get through as quickly as possible and then get back to the "real" work.

CBTs are best used to introduce basic concepts or ideas. In other words, plant a seed. The ideas should be fairly straightforward and simple. The goals should be geared to the learning audience as well. So if the goal is to train security personnel how to respond to a workplace violence incident, do not require other employees to watch the same training. If the primary goal is to introduce all employees to a new workplace violence policy or provide an overview of warning signs and escalating behavior, then the course will be applicable to everyone.

Classroom training is a great way to train employees and reach the next level of comprehension. Instructors can cover topics in more detail and, more importantly, answer questions and solicit feedback from the students. It is easier to tailor the training to the audience. When training the emergency response plan for a utility failure, the focus can shift to the departments or groups represented in the class. Information technology employees may be responsible for the portion of the response designed to set up remote operations at another site and protect servers or databases. Human Resources may need to secure physical copies of employee files and continuity of payroll during the utility failure. Each group should understand the overall purpose and objectives of the emergency operations plan, but the individual roles and responsibilities will vary. An instructor can adjust the training to cover the details of the groups in the class, or even the classes themselves can be scheduled for specific departments or groups to focus entirely on that unit's response. Another advantage is that students are more likely to focus on the training rather than the computer course.

Of course, the downside is the time of the employees and the instructor. There is more preparation time needed on the part of the instructor. When the employees are in training, they are not doing their normal work so there is a cost associated with the training. Scheduling the time for the class is another challenge for many organizations. None of us feels like we have "free time" to spend on a training class.

Drills are ultimately the best way to train everyone involved on the emergency operations plan, the incident command system, and the actual responses. Drills are a practical exam as much as they are training and offer the chance to test the plan itself. Gaps or discrepancies in the plan can be identified and the appropriate response taken to address the deficiencies.

Drills or practical exercises are so beneficial that they are required for many organizations. Fire drills in schools and commercial buildings are a requirement of local fire codes and are a simple example. Hospitals that are accredited by The Joint Commission in the United States are required to conduct four emergency management drills every year.

There are several different types of drills. A tabletop drill is one in which key stakeholders come together and are given a scenario, then determine and discuss the response. Tabletops generally involve at least one facilitator and can involve one group working together or several groups working independently. Usually, the facilitator will provide the initial emergency scenario and let the groups work in breakout sessions with a report back at the end of each session. The facilitator will likely add more details or injections about the emergency situation and have the groups break out again and so on, until the drill objectives are completed.

Next is the functional exercise. The functional exercise or drill simulates a real situation, and the reaction and response is designed to be as close to a real event as possible. Sometimes there are components that are simulated. For example, if a hospital is conducting a mass casualty incident with an influx of patients, the number of volunteers available to act as patients may be limited. In those cases, simulated patients may be used to test the overall response of the plan. Sometimes the simulated patients could be a file or paperwork on a gurney, stuffed animals, or even dolls. In other drills, the same "patients" may rotate through the triage cycle more than once to add to the patient volume.

The full-scale exercise is the most complex type of drill. This is one carried out in real time with minimal simulated activities. When you see a news story about a large-scale exercise involving the National Guard, local police, and firefighters and carried out across large areas of the community, you are looking at a full-scale exercise, one that usually involves dozens, even hundreds, of participants, including volunteers. Even in these cases, although they are supposed to be in real time, there is usually some stretch in regard to time. My experience with these types of drills has been that all the various resources are on scene almost immediately. In real disasters, it could take government support much longer to set up and respond.

## PLANNING A DRILL

Of all the types of training that we've looked at, drills are by far the most involved and the most complex. Naturally, carrying out a successful drill takes a great deal of preparation and planning. Even a tabletop exercise will involve a large cross section of the organization and may include outside resources, such as law enforcement. It is important to get it right and make sure it is a valuable learning experience and does not waste everyone's time.

Planning an emergency response drill takes a coordinated effort, and even this phase needs to reflect different parts of the organization as well as support. Once the decision is made to conduct a drill, the next step should be to decide who needs to be on the exercise planning team. This could include members of the emergency management committee or planning team or may involve others. The initial planning team may be just a few people, but the team could decide to bring in others or ad hoc members later as the details begin to come together.

There are several key decisions to be made almost immediately. One of the first has to be the overall focus of the drill. Should the exercise focus on an active shooter? Or the response to a tornado? What about a hazardous material spill? Maybe a loss of the IT servers?

The most effective drills are those that are realistic, and they should be based on the top risks discovered during the risk assessment matrix, going back to Chapter 4. If you plan a drill that is out of the norm, it will be very hard to build support and interest. For example, if you are in Kansas, a drill covering a tsunami certainly seems pointless, whereas that might be completely appropriate for an organization in Hawaii near the shore.

Another consideration is past experience with a threat or hazard. If the facility has dealt with blizzards fairly routinely and that is high on the list, the drill may focus on something else, such as bomb threats. The priority may change due to other factors as well. If there has been a recent wave of bomb threats to similar organizations in your industry or area, then that may make the drill on that topic more critical.

Once you have the hazard to focus on, the real planning starts. First are the objectives that you want to test or hope to see in the response. The common areas targeted as objectives of the emergency operations plan will include communications, resources, safety and security, response by staff, utilities/facilities, and ongoing business functions.

Objectives need to follow the same guidelines as most other business performance measures and should be S.M.A.R.T., or Specific, Measurable, Attainable, Realistic, and Timely.

Imagine that we are planning an exercise to test your organization's response to an active shooter. One objective under the safety and security category will be to test the plan to lock down the facility. The idea is to keep others out of harm's way. Many organizations, such as schools and hospitals, have plans to lock down or a restrict access plan, if you prefer. If your organization has five open doors or entrances, the objective might be that security is able to lock down all five entrances within 10 min. Perhaps your organization is set up with card access and magnetic locks and can be locked down with the push of a button. The objective might be to accomplish it in 1 min. In either case, the objective has to be realistic. One minute may not be realistic for a large hospital with doors that have to be manually locked and secured.

Another objective for an active shooter drill may be to see if employees follow the procedure. A goal then would be to verify that all associates close and lock or barricade doors in their areas. Observers can walk through the organization and see that these specific goals were achieved in a given time, such as within 2 min of the initial announcement. Speaking of the announcement, a communication goal might be that a broadcast is immediately made on overhead speakers.

Keep in mind that you do not need an objective for each of the focus areas, but you should be able to come up with a few specific examples that are critical to a successful emergency response. Each type of drill or scenario may require very different objectives. For example, in an active shooter situation with a violent shooter on the loose, setting up incident command could be a tragic mistake—especially if the shooter is a disgruntled employee familiar with the plans and who would love nothing more than to get all the top leaders in one room together. However, other drills may be set up to test the incident command system and the allocation of resources, such as a labor team to support operations.

As the objectives of the drill start to take shape, you can begin developing the actual scenario. The scenario should be something that is realistic and even based on real events where possible. Going back to the active shooter drill, imagine that your organization is an urban hospital with a history of family disturbances in the labor and delivery unit. With custody issues, changing family dynamics (i.e., the father or mother of the newborn has a new boyfriend or girlfriend), and even family members with gang ties, the potential for violence is very high. It is easy to create an active shooter scenario out of one of the many disturbances that has occurred and use it as the basis to test the active shooter response.

Severe weather is certainly grounds for a drill scenario as well, especially if you operate in a part of the world where there has been flooding, tornadoes, or hurricanes. Even wildfires pose risks. In urban areas, it does not seem like a viable threat, but if there is a fire in the region, smoke can limit visibility and result in road closures as well as requests to stay home. There is also added impact on any employees who might suffer from breathing difficulties.

The planning team also needs to look at logistics and resources needed. This could be as simple as setting up a room for the drill. The planners may realize that external resources would help with the drill and be able to provide valuable feedback. The local office of emergency management may be interested in evaluating or even helping plan exercises. Local police may be able to participate in the active shooter scenario, either as a liaison to help evaluate the response, as well as explain what the police response would look like. For a fully functional drill, police departments may be able to provide actors to play the key roles during an active shooter or hostage situation.

Earlier, we briefly mentioned the role of observers. Planning includes identifying the people who will help evaluate and observe the drill. The feedback from the observers is absolutely vital to make the drill successful and a true learning experience. The evaluators should be provided information in advance, including a checklist for the specific objectives that they are hoping to observe. Different evaluators may be looking for different objectives. If one is assigned to incident command, he or she may be looking for very different outcomes than one observing the front line response. Clipboards are extremely helpful for taking notes, as well as safety vests to help all the role players quickly identify them.

Other planning considerations include communications. What information will be announced prior to the drill, if anything? The drill could be unannounced and a "surprise" to the organization. This can be one way to help assess a more realistic response to an emergency. There are considerations as well. Obviously, a drill that affects business or jeopardizes safety could be a problem. Typically, I like to announce some minimal information in advance, although it does depend on the nature of the drill.

You have probably heard of some active shooter drills that were unannounced and set up to appear realistic. Suddenly, students or faculty could be faced with what seems to be real gunfire and an actor yelling and waving a fake gun. This is a very realistic test, but also puts people in a state of very real fear and creates the potential for panic. What lessons are being taught by a drill like this? Even police officers who go through extensive instruction are not trained by using drills that are presented as real events. Officers know when they are in training sessions and thrown into scenarios with actors playing the parts of bad guys. Guns are left behind or cleared to ensure no live ammunition is in the training environment. Scenario training is set up in a way designed to be safe while mimicking real life. Why would we treat students or employees differently?

There are some exceptions. Fire drills are not normally announced ahead of time, although can be. Drills to test staff's response to missing children are not always announced ahead of time either. Both can be somewhat stressful but involve relatively straightforward responses. Carefully consider what objectives you are testing and the potential concern of creating more fear than learning.

One challenge is how messages are relayed to employees during an emergency. Imagine your organization suffers through an event like Hurricane Sandy, which left parts of New York and New Jersey and surrounding areas without power for a long period of time. How do you reach employees and tell them how they can help? Should they arrive at work? Work from home? Remember, in a widespread situation employees may be without power as well. During September 11 and the Boston bombings, cell phones did not work, either due to excessive traffic and loss of antennas, or in the Boston case, because law enforcement shut down the cell companies to limit the chance of someone using cell phones to detonate other bombs.

There is also the communication to customers to consider. After Hurricane Sandy, one supplier was able to send e-mails to customers to let them know that the company was unable to ship purchases. The company provided several e-mail updates over the next couple of weeks to let customers know what progress was being made. Clearly, the organization had some means of accessing the client e-mail list and sending out the communications even during the power outages following the hurricane. Also, the idea of keeping clients informed seemed like a great way to retain customers who, I am sure, were largely understanding of the circumstances. Not keeping customers informed could have chased clientele to competitors, perhaps not to return.

Another communication piece to consider is whether local media should be alerted ahead of time. Media may be interested in the exercise, or at the very least, a heads up could avoid surprises if media show up curious about extra police or other activity. Depending on the type of drill and the organization, media coverage could be good publicity.

As the drill scenario develops, you may want to think about how the scenario could change during the drill or what surprises the incident command team should be ready to handle. These injections should be planned in advance along with how the changing scenario will be communicated to those carrying out the response. In general, it is a good idea to have a lead facilitator in the incident command center to add the injections and keep the drill on track.

The injections are called MSELs (pronounced like "measles"; Master Scenario Events Lists). They are chronological scenario events that help shape the drill and change the response. For example, during a tornado response drill, the first injections may be that there is a strong storm developing and a tornado watch in effect. This should start the organization's early response and mitigation plans, such as tuning into local weather alerts. The next injection may be an escalation to a tornado warning to test the plan and the response. From there, the next injection could be that there is damage to the building or a loss of utilities. By using these injections, you change the response and test different components of the emergency operations plan.

The exercise planners need to include a debriefing in the allotted time. The debriefing is the ultimate learning tool during an emergency exercise. As soon as the drill ends, all those who participated should gather to recap what happened. This can really shed light on potential problems. Often, for people working on one piece of the puzzle, everything seemed to go smoothly, but others may have experienced a completely different perspective. Be certain to have someone record the findings and go over both what worked well and what did not. Finally, the outcome should be captured in an after-action report. The report helps the emergency planning or management team reevaluate the emergency plan and make the necessary adjustments or changes.

Last, most drills focus on some exciting emergency event, such as an active shooter. As soon as the simulated bad guy is caught or stopped, the drill ends. Keep in mind that recovery from a disaster can be as important as the response during the emergency. At least some drills should test the recovery portion of the emergency plan. That may include utilizing employee assistance programs or setting up backup operations to simulate business continuity from another site. Do not overlook the recovery part of the plan.

## USING LESSONS LEARNED

Emergency planning is an ongoing process. It never really ends. The emergency operations plan is a living document, one that will constantly need revision and adjustment. It grows and changes as the organization changes and improves after testing and real-life experiences.

The continuing cycle starts with the planning, followed by testing, including emergency exercises. After any test, the plan is assessed or analyzed and, hopefully, improved upon. As improvements are identified, this leads back to planning, and then the cycle starts over again, as you can see in Figure 10.1.

Emergency management, or business continuity, is a vital business function and should be an ongoing part of all organizations.

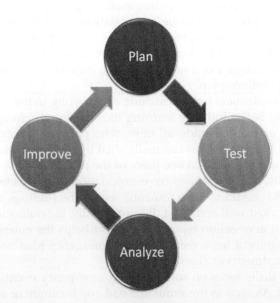

FIGURE 10.1   Emergency planning is a never-ending cycle.

## CONCLUSION

In Chapter 9, we looked at the development of an emergency operations plan, which could also be called a business continuity plan. Once a plan is in place, everyone involved in the response needs to be trained on the plan and the expected response in a disaster. Training comes in several formats, but the best training format of all is the emergency drill or exercise. This trains and tests not only the employees but also the plan itself. After the drill, the response should be reviewed and areas for improvement identified, leading to a revision of the emergency plan in an ongoing cycle.

## BUSINESS KARATE BELT LEVEL

Test your company's karate belt level in the discipline of awareness/stance. If your organization meets each belt level and all the standards of the lower belts as seen in Figure 10.2, you have then achieved that color level.

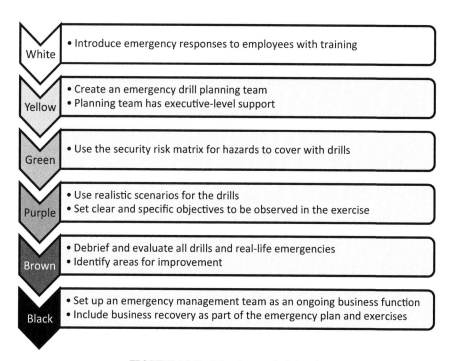

White
• Introduce emergency responses to employees with training

Yellow
• Create an emergency drill planning team
• Planning team has executive-level support

Green
• Use the security risk matrix for hazards to cover with drills

Purple
• Use realistic scenarios for the drills
• Set clear and specific objectives to be observed in the exercise

Brown
• Debrief and evaluate all drills and real-life emergencies
• Identify areas for improvement

Black
• Set up an emergency management team as an ongoing business function
• Include business recovery as part of the emergency plan and exercises

FIGURE 10.2   **What is your belt level?**

# 11

# The Do's and Don'ts of Self-defense: Understanding Your Premise Liability

## THE LEGAL SIDE OF SELF-DEFENSE

Learning the punches and kicks and escaping from choke holds and grabs are all vital to martial arts. However, in a modern society, there is another element as well. Karate students need to know something of the legal aspects of when and how individuals can protect themselves. Knowing how to attack is not always as important as knowing when to attack.

Police officers go through extensive training on the use of force and appropriate response to violent attacks or threats. Martial arts students need to understand the legal ramifications of self-defense and what is appropriate under the law. There is no one perfect standard that covers every situation. However, the underlying legal element is that the person believed there was an imminent threat of harm or injury from the attacker and the force used was reasonable.

A good instructor will cover legal issues with students as part of the karate lessons or self-defense techniques. Students should learn to balance the response with the threat. For example, if a stumbling drunk attacker punches at a karate student, the response may be a block and a counterstrike to stop the attack. The response should not be some potentially lethal strike. On the other hand, an attacker armed with a knife or gun certainly creates a situation of imminent threat, so the defender may need to use any and every attack available to survive. In legal cases, courts may even look beyond the force used, but also how the individual got into the situation, and whether he or she had the opportunity to avoid the confrontation.

## THE IMPACT OF LIABILITY

Just as karate students need to understand the legal aspects of self-defense and the use of force, organizations need to understand their exposure to liability and the related risks. Businesses can be held legally accountable for activities, including crime, that occur on the premises. Organizations need to understand the potential impact on the business, both in the United States (a very litigious country) and around the world.

The average verdict for a tort, or lawsuit, involving a premise liability case is over $600,000, according to a study by Jury Verdict Research. Total civil tort cases in the United States cost more than $260 billion each year. Obviously, there are very real risks, and it is imperative that businesses include liability costs in the overall security management plan.

Premise liability relates to the physical condition of the organization's property and any unsafe situations, ranging from slips and falls to criminal events. More specifically, you may see the term *negligent security*, which, as it sounds, is a protection program that is deficient or overlooks common, but vital, security measures, such as lighting or adequate security personnel. A successful lawsuit is one that demonstrates that the property owner should have foreseen a problem and taken steps to reduce the risks.

## HISTORY OF PREMISE LIABILITY

Property owners have not always been held liable for the occurrences on the property. Civil tort law in the United States is based on traditional English common law or the court cases that filled in the gaps left in the actual wording of written law. In other words, common law reflects the court's interpretation of the spirit of the law.

Originally, under English common law, a property owner did not have any level of responsibility or obligation to persons on the property. However, in America, courts began to develop the concept that landowners did owe a certain onus or a legal duty to someone on the property who could not provide for his or her own security. By the middle of the last century, courts had expanded the obligation of landowners and expected a greater level of responsibility to provide for the safety of any invitees on the property. This includes employees, visitors, customers, vendors, and so on. In some cases, the definition of invitee has gone so far as to include the "never invited," such as burglars or other criminals. I recall hearing of one case where a would-be burglar fell through a skylight and broke a leg, and the property owner was held liable for allowing an unsafe condition.

According to the U.S. Department of Justice, there has been an increase in cases where victims of crimes claim that the owner failed to provide adequate security, which in turn contributed to their victimization, whether injury or loss. At an average cost of over half a million dollars, it quickly becomes apparent that organizations have a strong business reason to protect everyone on the property in addition to any moral obligation to protect the same individuals.

## ELEMENTS OF NEGLIGENCE

What is negligence? Obviously, it sounds like some type of lack of caring or poor or neglected property. In short, it is the failure of property owners to provide reasonable care for the safety of others or their property. That raises the question as to what is reasonable. *Reasonable* is a word found throughout court cases and criminal laws. It is described as the standard that most people would apply to a given situation. The courts have given us a set of four elements to determine whether or not there was any negligence.

First, there is the element of legal duty. Did the property owner have a legal obligation? As we discussed, courts have created more of an obligation of duty to ensure the safety of those on the premises. That means that anyone lawfully on the property can expect a level of safety while there. In some jurisdictions, that duty may even include persons unlawfully present.

Second, is there a breach of duty? If there is a duty to protect individuals on the grounds or in the building, was there a failure by the organization to take reasonable steps to protect the persons on the property? A breach of duty may include a variety of possibilities, which we will look at in more detail as we go through this chapter. Some examples would include having inadequate lighting around a parking lot. As we saw in Chapter 7, lighting is a great way to deter crime, so an organization that does not maintain or repair lights or will not add lighting and has a lower standard than other similar organizations in the neighborhood could be found to have a breach of duty.

The third element of negligence is proximate cause. Was the breach of duty the catalyst or cause of some harm? Back to our previous example of poor lighting, was the poor lighting the proximate cause of the crime? If the crime occurs during the daytime in a surface parking lot, then lighting would not be a direct or proximate cause of the crime.

The fourth and final element of negligence is perhaps the most challenging to define. This is the element of damage. Did the breach of duty actually lead to some harm or loss? That is generally easy to determine, at least where there is physical injury or loss. The hard part is whether or not the premise owner should have known or been able to see the risk. The question is whether or not the damages or injury was foreseeable or apparent. Again, this is an area where courts are taking a different approach in determining what a business has seen in terms of risk before a loss occurs.

In the past, foreseeability was a relatively simple question. If a similar event had happened before on the premises, then it was foreseeable. However, this gave property owners a sense of a "free" pass for the first time an event occurred and no sense of obligation or duty to make changes until after someone was hurt or there was loss of property. Under this model, courts usually look at the previous three years or so for similar crimes.

Instead of foreseeability, courts are using a standard of totality of circumstances. Businesses have a responsibility to look at area crime rates and surrounding neighborhoods. If sexual assaults or robberies have been happening in the surrounding area, then there is an expectation that the business would be able to foresee the risks and take some reasonable steps to prevent any harm. Courts will look at industry standards and compare what security measures are typically found within that industry to see if the defendant was lacking. Courts will also look at the organization's knowledge and experience at its other locations. If a hotel has several locations and has dealt with parking lot robberies at one and taken preventive steps, then there will be some expectation that the hotel owner should have been able to foresee the risks of robberies at another of its locations.

Under the totality of circumstances doctrine, the courts will determine if the security measures in place were reasonable or were inadequate as compared to generally accepted standards, as well as the owner's own experience. Courts will try to answer the question about what the property owner should have known and should have done.

There are some business leaders and even security professionals who seem to believe that there is no liability exposure if the business acts as if there is no problem or risk. This is the ostrich approach, where some might think that by hiding their heads in the sand, there would be no exposure or liability risk. This leads some businesses to think that conducting a risk assessment or tracking criminal incidents at a site actually increases its liability. However, ignorance is not a defense. If reasonable standards are not followed, security measures not taken, or complaints ignored, then there is not a valid defense.

From a morale standpoint, an approach to security risks based on the total circumstances actually is a realistic and reasonable way to create a safer workplace and provide a secure work environment for employees, customers, and vendors.

## UNSAFE CONDITIONS AND BREACH OF DUTY

If there is a duty to protect people on a property, then the question follows, what are we protecting those people from? The security risk matrix created in Chapter 4 is a great starting place in terms of identifying hazards. The top risks were those that would cause the greatest impact or harm, or were most likely to occur, and factored in how well prepared the organization was to deal with the particular danger. The harm, the likelihood, and the prevention—all are components of liability. The risk matrix then is the natural starting point when looking at security-related risks. These risks are the basis for a breach of duty if not addressed in a reasonable way.

Before looking at some of the security risks, we need to remember that not all unsafe conditions are due to lack of security. For example, one of the greatest sources of premise liability is due to slips and falls. Icy parking lots, wet floors, loose carpets, or broken tiles all create risks to people on the grounds and could put them at risk of tripping or falling. If the property owner was negligent in dealing with these unsafe conditions, there could be liability if an individual is hurt or harmed by a fall. Grounds should be well maintained and spills or water cleaned up as soon as possible. If there are other issues, such as damaged sidewalks that create the risk of tripping someone up, then those should be repaired as well.

If your organization has a security force, the security guards or personnel can help reduce unsafe conditions by serving as the eyes of the facility. Part of the security department's regular duties can be to identify unsafe conditions, such as icy areas, that need attention. The security team can report hazards to the grounds or facilities department or may fix the problems themselves. Often security is the only department on duty 24/7 and may be in the best position to fix problems, such as after-hours snow removal, to ensure the property is safe when visitors or employees begin arriving.

Of course, the downside is that security personnel may have other duties, and the time spent on maintenance tasks could be detrimental. As with any use of resources, it is important to analyze the pros and cons and plan for the best use of all personnel. Occasional safety concerns related to weather, such as snow, may be considered of higher importance in the short term than normal security patrols or visibility and deterrence.

Another consideration with premise liability is the presence of any hazardous materials or activities. Some thought should be given to any chemicals or hazardous supplies kept on the site. For example, many hospitals have large oxygen tanks to be used for patients with respiratory problems. Liquid oxygen also happens to be used for rocket fuel, creating a potentially explosive situation. Basic measures to protect property and people (and limit liability) could include traffic bollards to reduce the risk of a vehicle hitting the tanks, as well as fencing, inspection, and separation from flammable materials or combustible sources.

Again, hazardous materials at a location should be part of the overall risk assessment and should already be identified. In the United States, the Occupational Safety and Health Administration (OSHA) requires facilities to keep safety data sheets (SDS, formerly MSDS) of all hazard chemicals used or kept on site.

Security issues are another area where there is the potential for a breach of duty if reasonable measures are not in place to protect people on the property. We have looked at some of the risks already, such as workplace violence. Robberies are particularly dangerous and account for the majority of on-the-job homicides. If your organization has cash, isolated locations or employees, or other high-value goods, such as narcotics, the risk of robbery is greater and therefore the courts will look closely at what measures were in place to protect employees and customers. Ignoring the risks and failing to exercise due caution increases the chance of a successful lawsuit.

In 2008, Troy Anderson was parking his car at the Hilton Embassy Suites hotel in Orange County, Florida. He was attacked by a car-jacking suspect who shot Anderson several times, leaving him with life-threatening injuries. Anderson subsequently sued the hotel and the contract security company, winning $1.7 million. A key consideration included a spotlight that was out and would have lit the parking area. Hotel management had been notified of the broken light but had not repaired it. Also, the security personnel assigned to patrol exterior areas were routinely used for customer service functions, and according to daily security reports, were delivering carts to hotel guests at the time of the robbery. In addition, there was another robbery 10 days prior to the shooting. The actual court proceedings included much wrangling about who knew what and when. In the end, the jury believed employees, who testified that they had alerted management to the previous robbery and the lights that were out, leading to the award of damages of $1.7 million (*Troy Anderson v. Hilton Hotels et al.*, Case No. 2009-CA-040,473-O, Fla. 9th Judicial Cir.).

Sexual assaults are another type of crime that involve high risks and could easily result in liability. The case of *Bonds v. Abbeville General Hospital* involved a hospital employee who was abducted and sexually assaulted. Kaylon Bonds arrived for her shift at the hospital a few minutes late. Normally, a security officer was present to escort her in, but he left the parking area when she did not arrive on time. As Bonds got out of her car, a male approached her and forced her back in the car at gunpoint. She was taken to a remote location and was beaten and raped. In the subsequent lawsuit, the subject of foreseeability came up as there had not been a previous sexual assault like that on campus. However, an expert witness testified about the higher-than-average rate of sexual assaults in the area as well as the lack of lighting and perimeter access control around the parking area. The victim also testified about the dim lighting and her complaints about the poor lighting and limited security coverage. She said that she was told that it would not change due to budget constraints. The hospital successfully moved for summary judgment, meaning that there was no legal basis for the claim. However, the security company was not granted summary judgment, and the lawsuit was allowed to move forward.

The legal cases are very complicated and will look at a wide range of testimony, expert witness statements, and reports, as well as try to establish the facts of a case, such as whether a light was out or not or for how long. The question of whether or not there was a breach of duty is potentially very involved as is the question of foreseeability.

Certain factors or security measures will be reviewed during a negligent security case. Each will be evaluated to determine if they were adequate and if the property owner provided reasonable levels of protection.

- Lighting: The property's lighting will be reviewed to determine if there were any inadequacies, including dim areas. The Illuminating Engineering Society of North America has outlined very clear guidelines in regard to adequate lighting. You do not have to be an engineer to determine lighting levels though. A simple guide is that you can read newsprint or the face of a watch throughout a parking lot. Any area where the light is too dim for that should be reviewed and lights added.
- Access control: Another common consideration is the level of access to an area. This can include the types of locks on doors, as well as perimeter access, such as fencing.
- Lines of sight: In several cases, the issue of visibility has been a key factor. In one robbery, the cashier was located at the back of the store, and others could not see a robbery in progress until the suspect was confronted inside the business. Convenience stores and liquor stores have been taught to limit large posters or signs on windows, which block the view and give a suspect a sense of invisibility while inside the store. It also makes it harder for employees to see potential suspects "casing" the store.
- Security personnel: The role and duties of security personnel will be closely reviewed. If there were no security personnel, the question will be if there should have been. All security paperwork, including routine daily activity reports that outline where and how officers spend their time, will be reviewed, as in the case of *Anderson v. Hilton Hotels*, and the paperwork showing that security personnel spent much of their time on guest services.
- History of security incidents: Of course, past security incidents will be carefully reviewed and taken into consideration in the question of foreseeability.
- Maintenance: The condition of the grounds and security measures will be taken into account in many lawsuits. Grounds that are not maintained and issues that are not repaired can be a contributing factor to a crime and show a breach of duty. Broken or damaged doors or windows could allow entry to unauthorized suspects. Defective lights left unrepaired are a critical oversight. Even graffiti left untouched creates a sense of lack of caring or feeling of unsafe environment, which could be a factor that sways a court against a property owner.

# NEGLIGENT HIRING AND SUPERVISION

Premise liability is not the only thing that can generate a lawsuit. Negligent hiring and negligent supervision are common sources of liability for businesses. Negligent hiring torts come about when an organization hires an employee who is unqualified or unsuited for a position. Imagine a day care center that hires an employee without conducting a background check. An employee molests a child, and in the aftermath, it is discovered that the employee was a registered sex offender with a history of sexually assaulting children. Courts would find that a routine background screening would have uncovered that fact, the employee would not have been hired, and the child would not have been harmed.

A negligent hiring case can be very expensive, both in terms of money, such as legal costs and punitive damages, and also directly impacting the company's public image, resulting in loss of customers. Going back to the example of the day care center, would you want your children there after learning that background checks were not done?

Negligent hiring cases often focus on background screening as well as qualifications for the job the individual was hired for. Qualifications may include driving ability and record for someone hired as a driver. A surgeon hired or contracted by a hospital would be expected to have certain qualifications and experience before operating on patients. Courts also look at the element of foreseeability and whether an employee's actions should have been anticipated based on what was known when the individual was hired.

In the legal case of *Kase v. Unnamed Trucking Co.*, Kase sued a trucking company after its driver, Ebert, bumped his truck. The two argued and Ebert assaulted Kase. The lawsuit brought up an assault conviction against Ebert more than 20 years previously. The trucking company was aware of the previous assault when Ebert was hired, but the court ruled that this did not make the assault foreseeable due to the long period of time separating the incidents. The court also ruled that the trucking company was not liable as Ebert was out of the truck and acting beyond the scope of his employment when he assaulted Kase. In this case, the trucking company was not successfully sued.

In 2008, truck driver Roger Reagan was killed when another truck, driven by Morgan Quisenberry, crossed the center line and hit him in a head-on collision. Reagan's family sued Quisenberry's employer, Dunaway Trucking Co. A background screening, including a check of Quisenberry's motor vehicle driving history, had not been performed. A check of his driving history would have shown that his license had been previously revoked twice for driving violations. Due to the lack of screening and Quisenberry's history of unsafe driving violations, the court ruled in favor of Reagan. In total, the court awarded the plaintiffs $7 million.

Clearly, the background screening process is vital to protect organizations, as well as customers, other employees, and the public at large. Most businesses would not survive a lawsuit of this magnitude.

Negligent supervision is another potential source of liability. Negligence can be a very broad topic. Supervisors or managers, for example, who fail to take action on a complaint of workplace harassment, set the company up for a negligent supervision case. From a security perspective, negligent supervision will frequently focus on security personnel. Often security personnel are provided by contractors, an industry typically with low profit margin and high turnover. If not careful, that can translate to lack of training and minimal supervision of personnel, especially in remote locations or after normal business hours when most employees are not around. I read of one case where the overnight security personnel had to periodically phone into a central number to confirm that they were on the site. The two overnight guards drank and smoked marijuana, then attacked two people parked nearby. They killed the male and sexually assaulted the female, then stabbed her and left her for dead, and still called in as required. Clearly, supervision was lacking for employees to be able to get away with such a disregard for the job and tasks to be performed.

Ongoing training and performance management are vital for all personnel once an employee has been hired, and to address, rather than ignore problems. It is easy for managers to ignore discipline issues rather than confront the individual, but that creates a risk of liability. In multiple cases, organizations that failed to address reports of workplace harassment have been held liable in court rulings. It does not have to be a case of harassment either. If a manager or supervisor is aware, or should be aware, that an employee has been drinking on the job, and that individual is allowed to drive at some point for a work-related task and is involved in an accident while under the influence, the repercussions on the organization could be huge.

Security personnel are often involved in situations that people are not usually involved in and need additional training to react appropriately. Loss prevention is one area that has prompted numerous lawsuits over the years. Any employee involved in loss prevention should be well trained on the best practices related to identifying and apprehending shoplifters. Falsely accusing an innocent customer and detaining him could create accusations of false imprisonment, battery, and emotional distress.

Training built on best practices and reinforced on the job by solid supervision will help companies avoid negligent supervision liability. Performance management includes testing the employee's training and also is a way to track ongoing issues and identify behavior that could put others in harm's way.

## CONCLUSION

Learning martial arts includes learning about the legal issues related to self-defense and the use of force. Martial artists must be able to understand the concept of what a reasonable person would do and be careful not to use excessive force even when legitimately protecting themselves, such as using a lethal attack to stop a simple slap.

Organizations are exposed to various legal risks and need to understand those risks and how to best protect themselves. Premise liability is one form of liability and can be tied to negligent security. Poor lighting, inadequate locks, and insufficient security personnel are all potential causes. Organizations also need to understand the concept of foreseeability and have an accurate view of what the risks are. Failure to ignore hazards does not mean an organization will escape a lawsuit.

Background screening and reasonable supervision are other ways that a business can protect itself from liability and, more importantly, protect the people it employs and the customers it serves. Developing a realistic understanding of liability and the potential risks is a must for any organization serious about protection.

## BUSINESS KARATE BELT LEVEL

Test your company's karate belt level in the discipline of awareness/stance. If your organization meets each belt level and all the standards of the lower belts as seen in Figure 11.1, you have then achieved that color level.

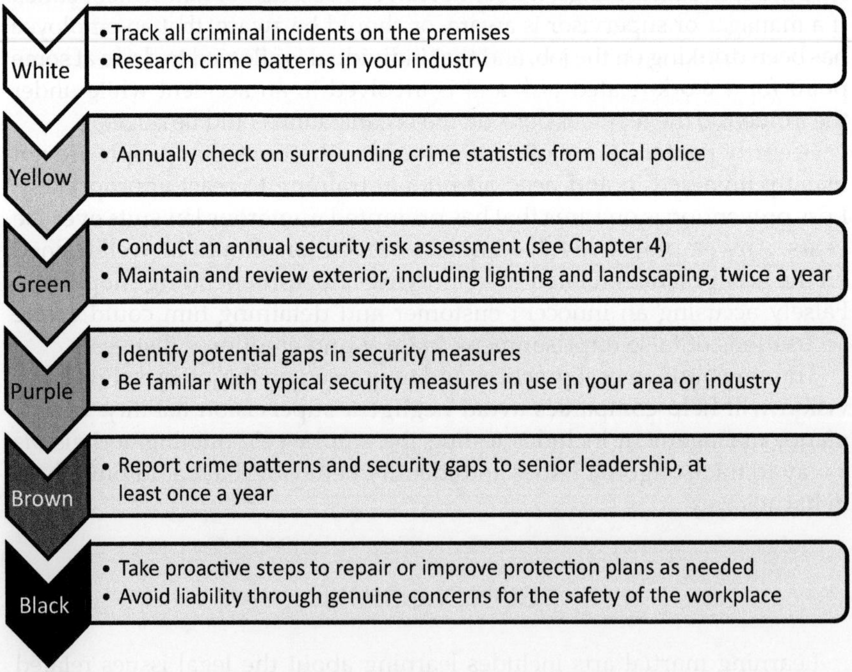

**White**
- Track all criminal incidents on the premises
- Research crime patterns in your industry

**Yellow**
- Annually check on surrounding crime statistics from local police

**Green**
- Conduct an annual security risk assessment (see Chapter 4)
- Maintain and review exterior, including lighting and landscaping, twice a year

**Purple**
- Identify potential gaps in security measures
- Be familar with typical security measures in use in your area or industry

**Brown**
- Report crime patterns and security gaps to senior leadership, at least once a year

**Black**
- Take proactive steps to repair or improve protection plans as needed
- Avoid liability through genuine concerns for the safety of the workplace

FIGURE 11.1   What is your belt level?

## Reference

Bonds v. Abbeville General Hospital, April 4, 2001. Kaylon Delaine Lisenby Bonds and Odie Bonds, Individually and on Behalf of Their Minor Daughter, Kodi Bonds v. Abbeville General Hospital. No. 00-1462. Retrieved from: http://caselaw.findlaw.com/la-court-of-appeal/1083740.html (accessed 14.09.13.).

## Further Reading

Gordon, C.L., Brill, W., April 1996. The Expanding Role of Crime Prevention through Environmental Design in Premises Liability (NCJ 157309). United States Department of Justice, Washington, DC.

Hospitality Industry Security Risks: Florida Hotel and Management Company Ordered to Pay $1.7 million to Victim of "Car Jacking" in Parking Lot; "Inadequate Hotel Security and Burned out Lights in Parking Area". November 7, 2012. Retrieved from: http://hospitalityrisksolutions.com/tag/hotel-parking-lots/ (accessed 14.09.13.).

Jury Awards $7 million to Farmington Family of Truck Driver Killed in Accident, November 11, 2011. Channel 4 KMOV. Retrieved from: http://www.kmov.com/news/local/Arkansas-jury-awards-7M-in-fatal-truck-accident-133724583.html (accessed 20.09.13.).

Marcinak III, C.F., n.d. Negligent Hiring in an Assault Case: A Rare Trucking Company Victory. Retrieved from: http://www.smithmoorelaw.com/pubs/xprPubDetailSmithMoore.aspx?xpST=PubDetail&pub=697 (accessed 21.09.13.).

Miller Jr., R., October 27, 2010. Average Premises Liability Verdicts. Retrieved from: www.marylandinjurylawyerblog.com/2010/10/average_premises_liability_ver.html (accessed 22.11.13.).

Reagan et al. v. Dunaway Timber Company et al., n.d. Retrieved from: http://dockets.justia.com/docket/arkansas/arwdce/3:2010cv03016/34497/ (accessed 21.09.13.).

Webster Systems LLC, Data 360. October 6, 2006. Legal-Civil Trials and Tort Costs. San Francisco, CA. Retrieved from: www.data360.org/graph_group.aspex?Graph_Group_Id=268 (accessed 09.02.07.).

# 12

# Weapons of Organizational Self-defense: Security Protection Systems

## SELF-DEFENSE WEAPONS

When we normally think of weapons and self-defense, we picture a karate expert kicking a knife out of an opponent's hand or using a swift crescent kick to knock a gun aside. Learning how to protect oneself from various common weapons is definitely part of a comprehensive karate program. Military and law enforcement self-defense training also focus on disarming an attacker, as well as weapon retention.

Even though martial arts are focused on unarmed self-defense, weapons cannot be ignored. In addition to learning how to stop attacks from someone armed with a knife or gun, some types of martial arts also teach students how to use traditional weapons in attacks and blocks. Kendo, for example, is one that, like fencing, is built around learning how to use a long sword in combat.

An expert twirling a nunchaku around his body and over the shoulder is an impressive and intimidating image and a classic example of how martial arts use weapons. A bo or staff is another example that comes to mind. There are many other examples of martial arts weapons, such as sai and tonfas. At the very least, a well-rounded martial artist will almost certainly have a basic familiarity with some of these weapons and how to use them.

## BUSINESS WEAPONS

Throughout this book, we have talked about protecting businesses and people. The idea of weapons seems out of place. However, weapons are not just for aggression but also for protection and defense. Law enforcement officers often carry some variation of martial arts weapons. The escrima stick has evolved into the expandable police baton, the tonfa into another police baton, the PR-24 (a side-handle baton), and even nunchakus are used by some departments.

For organizations, the kinds of weapons that we will talk about are those tools that can be used to thwart an attack or stop a crime. Burglar alarms, panic buttons, emergency phones, firewalls, video surveillance systems (VSS), and even security officers are all examples of tools that a business can use to deter or stop criminals. These tools are the weapons available to businesses.

Too often, when a business decides to improve security the first step is to contact someone about alarms or cameras. Sometimes, the lowest bidder is selected. Other times, it is whoever has the best presentation or even the vendor with some type of "brother-in-law" connection.

Security measures can be very expensive and sometimes complicated. The wrong decision can be costly. In Chapter 11, we talked about premise liability and how a victim may sue an organization as well as its security guard company. Faulty or broken cameras, alarms, or emergency notifications can be a source of liability as well as injury. Selecting the right contract security services and the security measures that will best fit your organization is crucial to a comprehensive security management plan.

## CREATING A STRATEGIC PLAN

It can be overwhelming if you are building security measures from the ground up. Most likely you will not have the budget to put in all the measures at one time. The costs for different security measures such as access control, video surveillance, and alarms all add up very quickly. Most organizations that do not have any measures in place and have made the decision to improve security will not have a budget for the improvements or at least not enough to be able to install all the desired systems at one time.

On the other hand, installing components in a piecemeal manner can be useless in the long run. When different systems are added over time, there is the risk that the components will not be tied together. Often the hardware is even in different locations, so security personnel have to use one computer in one location for some video cameras but go to another office (often an IT closet) to view different cameras. Access control may be entirely monitored from yet another location. With different systems, maintenance becomes tricky. The suppliers or vendors may be different for each component, and over time the employees who are familiar with how to use the systems leave and commonly no one in the organization knows how to use the security systems effectively. As a police officer, I was often surprised when a business would have a video system but was unable to download any footage or provide copies to the police. After moving into security management, it quickly became evident why that could happen.

The best approach before taking any other action is to create a plan for what security measures are needed and at what locations. You should be the one deciding how you want the security measures to work. Later, when you begin talking to vendors, you may start to learn about the limitations or challenges and have to make changes, but if you do not have a plan to start with, you will end up with systems that do not meet your needs.

Where to start? Refer back to the security risk matrix again and look at the top security risks. Once again, this should be your guide to moving forward with your security planning. If crimes in parking lots are at the top of the list, cameras and lighting will likely be the priority, or possibly security officers to patrol and monitor areas. Much of this will depend on the industry, the size of the organization, and the general environment. A school may have very different priorities than a small business office with a few employees, which in turn will be different from the needs of a manufacturing firm or warehouse.

The starting point will also depend on what measures are already in place. This ties into the risk matrix as well, where we took into account the steps an organization has taken to mitigate threats. That means the items that scored the highest in the matrix are the most likely to happen and could have a higher impact on the organization, with little preparation or measures in place to deal with the threat. Clearly, the highest concerns on the matrix should be the focus of the security strategic plan.

If one of the top concerns is related to suspicious persons in the building, then access control may be the top priority. Hospitals and schools often have many access points and higher risk of unauthorized persons on the grounds or in the buildings. Other businesses may have more concerns with parking lot safety. In that case, the business may focus on cameras to cover outdoor areas or add security personnel to patrol the exterior.

The important aspect of this planning process is to prioritize what steps should be implemented first, along with the timeline to add additional security measures. This allows the organization to plan and budget for the new actions. The other benefit of creating a long-term plan is to define what outcomes the company would like to see from the different security measures. For example, if access control is a priority, this plan outlines the doors that will be locked and what types of systems will be used, such as card access and doors with magnetic locks set to timers to automatically lock at the close of the door, as well as the ability to audit all who enter after hours. This is the chance to explain where visitors will be directed, so signage could be a component of the overall access plan. The same process applies to cameras, including defining what areas will be covered and what type of image is needed. The goal may be to see everyone entering or exiting a specific location or even each entrance of the building. In that case, the image should be of sufficient quality to identify facial features. If the coverage is a parking lot, then the focus may be on vehicle choke points to identify all vehicles entering the area, in which case the ability to read license plates may be desired. Or, the plan may be a broader coverage to see activity in the parking lot and monitor for suspicious persons or activity. In that case, the view would be a much larger field and reading license plates will not be feasible.

Other considerations are how the systems will work together. Ideally, the access control system will be tied to door contact alarms that will send an alert if there is forced entry, such as someone entering without using a card for access (i.e., the door is forced open in a burglary). Of course, the question of who receives notification and what to do about it is another deliberation. Also, the access control should also be tied to video surveillance in order to capture alarm events and provide a clear image of what caused the alarm.

At this point, do not worry if your ideas or prospective desires are or are not really feasible. The next step will be to begin looking at vendors who will provide the systems, training, support, and expertise that will help you meet your goals or adjust them to more realistic levels.

Last, even if you have the budget and support to put everything in place at once, it is still a good idea to have an overall plan for the measures needed and what you are hoping to achieve with those components. It gives you direction, and more important, will keep the project on track. Vendors will have a better understanding of what you are trying to accomplish. For those unscrupulous vendors that will try to sell you items and services you do not need, the plan also keeps you from falling for the unnecessary products.

## A WORD ON SYSTEM INTEGRATORS AND VENDORS

Once you have an idea of what you what to accomplish, the next question becomes a matter of who will carry it out. The phone book and Internet are full of security services promising to provide cameras, alarms, guards, and an array of other services. How do you pick the right one?

The best place to start is with references. If someone has had a good experience working with a security provider, then that is a great place to start. However, a word of caution—be careful of a "I know a guy" or "friend of the family" type reference. He or she may be great, but you still need to be diligent when making a selection. A vendor that has done some work in homes or small offices may not be suitable for a larger organization, such as a large commercial building, school, or hospital. A good rule of thumb, passed on by a security design consultant, is the rule of six. Make sure that the vendor has installed the system proposed for you for at least six other customers that are similar in size and scope or industry to you. Also, be sure that the systems have been in place for at least six months. Sometimes vendors will include experience of work to be done, or not quite started, or even components in a beta testing mode. Last, be sure to get six good references from each of those clients.

If you do not have personal references as a starting point, take a look online. There are various free magazines for security professionals, including several specifically related to electronic security systems. Look at some of the advertisements, or better yet, do a little research and see which integrators have been recognized within the industry. Another option is the nearest chapter of associations for security professionals. Perhaps the largest is ASIS International, with tens of thousands of members around the world. A quick check of the website for the association will provide information on local chapters and usually a contact number for the chapter head who can point you in the right direction.

It is important to understand the different roles and types of companies in the security services. First, you have the manufacturers. These companies actually make the door-locking hardware or the cameras and VSS. Typically, these companies license dealers to sell, install, and support the products. Sometimes, the suppliers only allow dealers to install certain systems, and I have heard of cases where the dealer has had its license revoked because it sold a competing system to a client. Many security providers will only sell certain systems and may not have a comprehensive product line to meet your needs.

Then you have system integrators. An integrator is a company that has a range of products and services and can provide a comprehensive electronic security program, from door-locking hardware to cameras. Sometimes, the system integrator acts as a liaison with dealers so the integrator will subcontract a dealer for installation and support.

If you have several different systems, such as alarms and video and card readers for access control, an integrator is my preferred approach. A good integrator becomes a partner who helps you achieve your goals. In some cases, the integrator will guarantee support within a certain amount of time to minimize downtime that affects the security of the organization. The integrator also represents several product lines and assists in making sure you get a system that matches your requirements.

Again, be sure that the integrator has the experience to meet your needs. Check references. Ask about how problems during install were handled. Also, ask about the response time when something goes wrong. Do they respond as promised? Many have online or phone support, which can fix a number of issues without a site visit. Ask about ongoing training and support. I've learned that training is critical to get the most out of a system and really look at what training and support is offered to ensure that security personnel have the help needed, even at 3 a.m. on a weekend. Be certain to get all the details of any service-level agreements in writing as part of the overall contract.

As I mentioned, an integrator should be a valuable partner. If you are not comfortable when you meet with representatives during early pitch meetings, be sure to find someone you will be comfortable working with. I've had a few vendors who want to sell something and show up using a wide range of technical terms, slogans, and acronyms that mean nothing to me. In the end, you want someone who makes life easier, not one who confuses you with jargon.

## ACCESS CONTROL

In your security strategic plan you will have decided on priorities and the best way to get started. Your starting point may be video surveillance or alarm systems. However, a common starting point is access control. The ability to keep unauthorized people out of vital areas is a fundamental security issue.

Access control brings to mind card readers or keypads that operate on codes. Of course, the most basic and common access control system consists of traditional locks and keys. Keys work fine for homes and perhaps even for many smaller organizations. However, there are disadvantages. If an employee loses a key, or is fired but doesn't return the key, there is the potential loss of security. Replacing all the lock cores in doors can become very expensive. Another disadvantage is that there is no way to audit who accessed what doors or when. The ability to audit access can be very useful during internal investigations.

However, it is almost impossible to imagine an organization that has no key-operated locks. Even businesses that use card readers for access control will have too many doors. Some, such as inner doors at offices or closets, will still rely on traditional keys and locks for security.

With keys, it is common to have a grand master that will operate all the locks within a building. The locks can be broken down further to include a master and submaster keys, which only open a limited number of doors. A master may open all doors on one floor or in one area, and a submaster may only open certain suites or offices to further restrict access.

Controlling and tracking all the keys can become a logistical headache. A list of who has keys and what type or level key needs to be constantly updated. Every year, an inventory should be done to confirm that all keys are accounted for, especially the grand master keys. Another issue is to identify who will have the grand master, who will have masters, and so on. Key inventory and control needs cooperation between facilities, human resources, and security. Facilities will be responsible for replacing or fixing damaged locks or keys, while human resources needs to keep an inventory of equipment issued to employees. Security should be aware of who has access to different areas to help monitor for unauthorized entry.

Also, security personnel may be the first to identify broken doors or locks that are not securing properly.

If you are serious about access control, you are most likely thinking of some type of card reader system. Access cards are easier to manage than keys. If a card is lost, it can be cancelled immediately. Likewise, if an employee is terminated or changes positions, the individual card can be cancelled or access levels changed to meet the new needs. Access cards also create an audit trail, so you can find out who entered specific doors or areas and when. You can also track an individual employee's access throughout the facility. Both are useful tools during an investigation of a theft or other suspected activity.

In order to run audit reports or update access levels of specific cards, the information about the card usage, or even whether it is still authorized or not, must be transmitted from the input point to the door and vice versa. In other words, the doors, cards, and software have to be able to talk to one another. There are various ways that access control systems relay this information.

Many access control systems are connected directly to the central computer software by cables or wire. The door lock is wired to a card reader, which is also wired to a magnetic lock that releases the door for authorized entry. The card reader is also attached via wiring to a central control point or computer somewhere in the building. Since every point has some type of connection to the system, one of the most expensive components may be wiring or running cable. In addition to the software, card readers, and locks, the cost of installing the wiring across buildings can really add to the expense of the system.

In addition to the hard-wired option, there are stand-alone locks. Often stand-alone locks are a keypad on one door that only opens when the right code is entered. Updating or changing the code means someone has to go to each and every keypad and reprogram the code, such as after an employee termination. There are also stand-alone locks that work off of access cards. Since the locks are not tied directly to the control computer, changes in access level do not get to the door right away. In many systems, someone still has to go to each door and update the individual doors and locks with a laptop or special device that plugs into the lock and reprograms the stored information.

I have seen at least one system that uses a different method to spread information to the doors. Each card must be used at a main entry point. These entry points transmit any changes to the card, which in turn spreads the information to other locks every time it comes into contact with a stand-alone lock. The information spreads like a virus from the control computer to all the outlying doors. Some remote locations may not get the information immediately, but the system has built-in checks that would still restrict access by a lost or terminated employee.

Some stand-alone systems also work on Wi-Fi. That allows information to get transmitted from the control point to the locks in a timely manner. Since it is wireless, it reduces the cost of running cables through the building but may not be as viable for a large organization with outlying buildings that do not have a Wi-Fi system in place.

Stand-alone locks are a great solution for many organizations and can be more cost effective. It is important to understand how each system works and how information is transmitted. A stand-alone system may sound like a better value up front, but over a length of time, employees' hours spent updating information on each lock and door could quickly eliminate any savings in wages and salaries.

Stand-alone locks that are not connected in any way also mean that audits are not an option or take much more time. You may be able to get the information from each specific door, but a comprehensive investigation is much more difficult. Also, someone has to go to each door and download the information, which could trigger an alarm to someone engaged in criminal activity.

Another consideration is the control software. Some systems charge licensing fees, and the software can be difficult to use or learn. As part of the overall plan, identify exactly which locations, including which departments and individuals, will be able to monitor and update the access control system. Common examples are human resources, facilities, or security. HR may issue access cards to new employees so may also need a special printer and Webcam to take a photo. The access cards also double as company identification and can include names, titles, or other information. Some organizations may have facilities or security take that responsibility. Security should certainly have access to track and audit activity and be able to deactivate a card upon a termination. If photos are taken when the card is issued, security can also use the photo to be on the lookout for that person after a high-risk termination, such as when threats are made.

The access control system can also act as a burglar alarm. If a door is opened without an authorized card, an alarm can be triggered. This type of alarm would occur if someone pried open a door or broke a window to push the door open after reaching through. The system can also detect if a door is propped open for too long and then trigger an alarm. It is important to understand exactly how the alarms are transmitted to security or whoever else would respond and check the door.

## VIDEO SURVEILLANCE SYSTEMS

After access control, VSS are a common security measure to consider. Like access control, one of the expensive pieces of a VSS is the cables that connect the cameras to a central server. That means that the areas to be covered by camera should be given some careful thought so the system provides what you hope once it is installed and running. Adding another camera later can be costly, so it is typically better to define the areas to be covered beforehand.

In general, cameras should cover all parking areas, doors, or entry points into the building, and any high-value areas. The specific areas to be viewed can come from the security risk matrix. For example, if internal theft at a warehouse is a concern, then camera coverage on the rows between shelves may be what is needed. If parking lot concerns are a top risk, then more focus should be on the exterior environment. Cash registers are another high-value area, both for crimes such as robbery and also for internal theft.

Another consideration is how the video will be used. Will video be primarily for forensic purposes, such as investigating crimes after the fact? Or will the VSS be monitored for immediate information about what is going on in real time?

Once you decide how the system will be used, you will have to decide on what system to install. Technology is constantly changing, and it can be difficult keeping up with and understanding the differences. This is where a good system integrator becomes an important ally. An integrator who understands your needs and the technology and has experience with similar locations can make the difference between having a successful VSS or one that is barely used and confusing.

As you look at video options, you will hear terms such as *analog, IP, NVRs, DVRs,* and *MP.* Analog cameras are not digital. The trend is more toward digital cameras, but analog still has a place in VSS. IP refers to Internet protocols, which really just indicates digital cameras that have an IP address to tie into the VSS. NVRs and DVRs are network video recorders and digital video recorders. These refer to the location where video images will be stored and recorded. This can be on a network server or on its own stand-alone server. MP refers to mega pixels. Just like your cell phone or digital camera, the number of mega pixels refers to the level of detail recorded in the image. The higher the number of MPs, the more memory will be needed, but also the higher the image quality.

## DUMMY AND INVESTIGATIVE CAMERAS

I sometimes find it amazing how often a business or organization does not want to invest in a working VSS but would rather put up a dummy camera. A dummy camera is a fake or nonworking camera. It does not record any images, nor offer someone else a chance to view the area remotely. It is a complete bluff.

*(Continued)*

## DUMMY AND INVESTIGATIVE CAMERAS *(cont'd)*

The consensus in the security industry is to avoid dummy cameras completely. A fake, nonworking camera can actually increase the risk of liability. It creates a false sense of security rather than being seen as a way to prevent or reduce crime. Stay away from using this trick as a security measure.

Video systems can also be used in temporary situations, such as to conduct covert surveillance in certain areas to investigate a specific crime or incident. If an office area repeatedly has thefts over the weekend, then a camera could be used to help identify the weekend bandit. Numerous outlets sell covert cameras disguised as wall clocks, pencil sharpeners, and so forth. Be sure that the one to be used has sufficient memory to record the area under investigation. Motion-activated recording helps in areas that are not used frequently for the time in question. A busy area will require much more memory. Also, if the suspect recognizes the covert camera and steals it as well, you will not have any recording of what happened. I am still searching for a covert camera that records images to a Web-based cloud via a public Wi-Fi to avoid that problem. It would also allow a view of what happened without going to the camera and retrieving it, something that could draw attention and alert the suspect.

Last, with covert cameras, never record areas where there is an expectation of privacy, such as inside a restroom or locker room. Recording individuals in those settings could quickly lead to lawsuits and negative publicity.

Some technical considerations will be whether or not a digital VSS resides on the organization's IT network or is a stand-alone system. The advantage of being on the organization's IT network is that the camera cables only have to tie into the network, such as in an IT closet. With a stand-alone system, the cables have to be able to connect back to the main server that will be used for that system. Depending on the type of system selected, this decision could have an impact on where and how cameras are viewed. If you want several different locations to be able to view cameras, or at least some of the cameras, the network solution may be more feasible and cost effective. The main disadvantage of being on the network is the concern about bandwidth. Most IT personnel will be very concerned about how much virtual space your cameras will use and if that will slow down the ability to transmit other data over the network. I've seen some cases where IT choked down the bandwidth by limiting the number of frames per second recorded by the cameras, which greatly reduces the effectiveness.

Storage and memory space is another key issue. At a minimum, you should store at least 7 days of recorded video. Ideally, a month of video is even better. There are many times where someone delays reporting something or a theft isn't even discovered right away, so being able to review stored data going back to 30 days is extremely useful. Memory usage will depend on how much is being recorded, but if video only records on motion, you will not record empty rooms. As memory becomes more affordable, it is fairly easy to get a terabyte (TB) of memory or more for video recording.

These decisions should be carefully worked through with the integrator, the IT department, and the security personnel who are responsible for the day-to-day use of the system.

## EMERGENCY ALARMS

Security measures may need to include ways for employees or visitors to get help during an emergency. This usually comes in the form of emergency help phones around the exterior of the building or property or duress alarms for staff.

Emergency phones are typically found in parking lots and garages. The phones should be located near main travel paths or points. In garages, the phones should be mounted near stairwells and elevators. These are convenient locations as they typically are distributed at opposite ends of the garage and in high-traffic areas where someone might need assistance.

The big question for emergency help phones is who answers them. If you have a security department or dispatch center, then it is easy enough to tie the phones directly to security. If not, is there another department or unit that operates 24/7 that could be responsible for the phones?

Ideally, the help phones can be connected to the VSS, so images of who triggered the alarm are immediately available. But someone has to be able to respond to the alarm or it is nothing but a false sense of security.

Help phones should be tested routinely, ideally at least once a month. Having a phone that doesn't work can create liability if there is a reasonable expectation of help by activating it but nothing happens. Also, like any other property, help phones should be maintained and look operational. It will not create a sense of safety if the help phone is neglected and covered with graffiti, for example, as the phone in Figure 12.1.

Duress or panic alarms are another type of emergency alarm. Duress alarms are used by employees in high-risk areas who may need to summon help in an unobtrusive way. Typically, when we think of duress alarms, banks come to mind. Bank tellers have used duress alarms for years to notify police during a bank robbery.

The use of duress alarms has become much more common. Hospitals, schools, as well as offices are adding duress alarms for staff. A teacher can hit a duress alarm when dealing with an aggressive student, or hospital nurses can trigger an alarm to get help with combative patients or even visitors. Some reception areas have duress alarms that alert managers

**FIGURE 12.1** Security measures that have been neglected do not create a sense of safety and could create liability. Would you rely on a help phone covered in graffiti and rust and surrounded by weeds?

or directors in other parts of the office about potential problems at the entrance.

Businesses with higher risk of robberies often use duress alarms. Taxi drivers in many areas have duress alarms. The driver can trigger the alarm, which alerts the taxi dispatchers and activates a GPS device. The dispatchers can notify police and provide the taxi's location to police as a way of protecting drivers.

Just as with help phones, you must think about who will respond and how the responders will receive the message. Duress alarm systems, like many of the other systems we have looked at, come in different formats. There are virtual duress alarms tied to desktop computers, which can trigger an alarm by hitting a certain button or combination. Some have external buttons tied to a USB port. Other alarms are wired in place, sending a message through a dedicated phone line to a central monitoring or dispatch center. Wireless systems are also becoming more common. The systems either work with specific repeaters, which use an algorithm to triangulate the location of an activated duress alarm, or are tied to the company's Wi-Fi.

With duress alarm systems, recognize what areas or people you are protecting and have a clear understanding of how the system works and what the limitations are. Most important, test them regularly and have a response plan in place so there is always assistance for a person who needs help.

## SECURITY CONTRACT SERVICES

The last type of security component you may consider is a security guard service. Security personnel either are proprietary or contract. Proprietary personnel are your company's own employees, with the same benefits as other employees and typically better paid. The general belief is that proprietary security has lower turnover, higher retention, and are more dedicated and in tune with the organization and are more loyal. Contract services often have high turnover and are seen as less loyal to the organization. I am familiar with contract services where the full-time security personnel work at dedicated client locations and are just as loyal as any employee would be as that client becomes their full-time position. It is where they work day in and day out, with the same individuals.

When making a decision about contract services, there are a number of considerations to take into account. The cost or price is an obvious one, but I would strongly recommend against making a decision based on the low bidder. Instead, look for the best value. By value, take into account the quality, training, supervision, and experience of the contract guard service.

Find out if there are local licensing laws for security personnel. Often that is a simple matter of talking to several potential contractors. Those that operate legitimately will be only too happy to tell you what steps it has taken to meet all requirements. Also, look at the turnover and retention of the different security services you are considering. Excessive turnover will affect you, as the security personnel you may rely on will have limited experience with your organization and specific needs. Check into the training new employees receive and find out what ongoing training is performed as well. Find out what type of background screening is done before someone is hired. Is the company diligent in checking for criminal history, work history, and education?

You want to look at supervision as well. In Chapter 11, we mentioned one case where security personnel were not supervised and engaged in criminal acts. That may be more of a rarity, but you do want to know who ensures that the officers correctly perform the expected tasks, especially in the middle of the night when few people are around.

For larger organizations, you may have a mix of fixed posts and patrol positions. Be careful about having too many officers in fixed posts, for example, in a lobby monitoring the entrance. Officers in fixed posts need breaks and time to check e-mails, read pass-on information, and complete training on occasion. Often patrol officers have to relieve the fixed posts, which takes away from the areas those patrol officers should be covering. Also, if the patrol personnel are the responders to alarms, you are reducing the response force.

Be certain that the security personnel, whether contract or in-house, have clear guidelines and training on how to perform security duties and how to handle the various situations that will be encountered. Often, these are called post orders and should be based on the organization's policies and procedures.

It is a good idea to establish some agreed-upon metrics when selecting a contract security company. The company should provide monthly reports that include crime totals and the number of calls for service or response time. These reports are based on historical or lagging information. There should also be proactive goals, such as 90% of crime reports include a follow-up or that any downtime of security systems is repaired. Some proactive metrics may be less frequent. An annual risk assessment might be one goal, assuming that is a defined role for the contract security team. However, it is only done once a year so would not be a monthly proactive metric. Employee surveys on how safe employees feel or of the customer service levels provided by the security officers are other examples of measures that may only be done once a year.

Another consideration is whether security should be armed or not, or equipped with nonlethal devices such as Tasers and handcuffs. This should be based on what the primary objective of the security role is. If a security role is to respond to an active shooter, then clearly the officer should be armed. If the role is to monitor cameras or access, then that position may not need to be armed. Carefully review any training procedures and background screening process for officers who will be armed.

Tasers are a popular choice for security in settings with a high risk of combative, but unarmed, individuals. Health care security is equipping security with Tasers on an increasing basis as the risks and number of assaults against health care workers receive more focus and attention. Many people think, however, that a Taser is also a suitable replacement for a firearm and have the misconception that security equipped with a Taser is sufficient to stop an armed shooter. That is false. Law enforcement training stresses the difference between Tasers and firearms. Police officers may use a Taser to try and stop an armed individual, but they are trained to have an armed cover officer in case the Taser fails to stop a suspect.

## CONCLUSION

Selecting security measures can be a complicated affair. There are different stakeholders, from the IT department to frontline staff. There are also technical aspects to understand, as well as overall goals and objectives of what the security measures will do.

Have a clear plan on what the security devices will do, how the system will improve the protection of the organization and address realistic security threats. Develop partnerships with suppliers, vendors, or system integrators who will help you understand and deal with the technical issues, as well as maintain systems once in place.

Your security systems often are the fundamental way that the organization protects itself, just like karate students learn to use various weapons for self-protection. Choose your weapons carefully and be sure you know how to use them effectively in order to get the desired results.

## BUSINESS KARATE BELT LEVEL

Test your company's karate belt level in the discipline of awareness/ stance. If your organization meets each belt level and all the standards of the lower belts as seen in Figure 12.2, you have then achieved that color level.

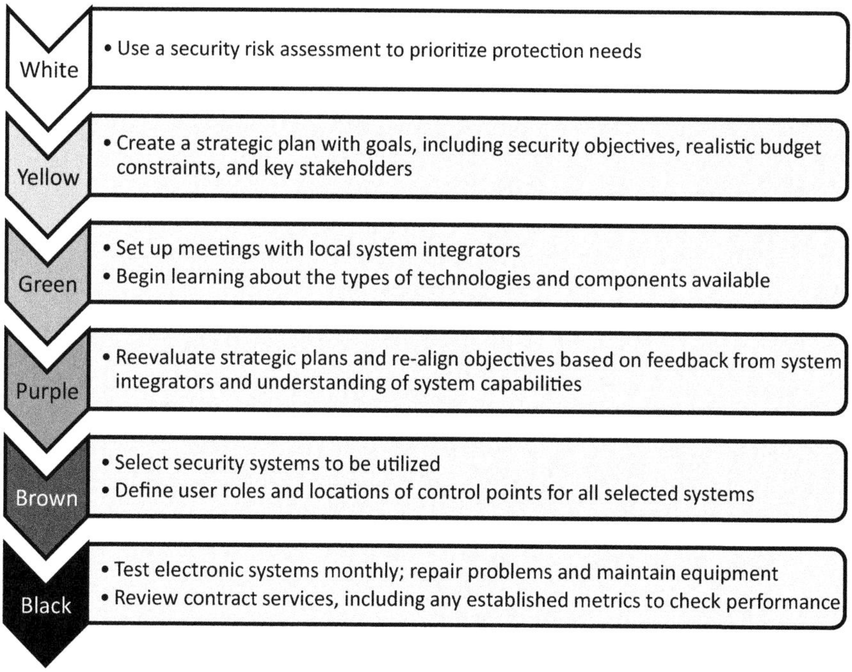

**White**
• Use a security risk assessment to prioritize protection needs

**Yellow**
• Create a strategic plan with goals, including security objectives, realistic budget constraints, and key stakeholders

**Green**
• Set up meetings with local system integrators
• Begin learning about the types of technologies and components available

**Purple**
• Reevaluate strategic plans and re-align objectives based on feedback from system integrators and understanding of system capabilities

**Brown**
• Select security systems to be utilized
• Define user roles and locations of control points for all selected systems

**Black**
• Test electronic systems monthly; repair problems and maintain equipment
• Review contract services, including any established metrics to check performance

FIGURE 12.2  **What is your belt level?**

# 13

# Personnel Safety
# Is Personal Safety

## KARATE AND SELF-DEFENSE

Why are karate, tae kwon do, jujitsu, and Krav Maga so popular? The main reason that people take up a martial art is to learn self-defense and how to protect themselves. Fitness and even entertainment are certainly part of the reason for sticking with a class, but self-defense is undoubtedly the top reason for most people. There are certainly other ways to exercise and many other sports or activities to get involved in.

There has been a growing interest in martial arts over the past couple of decades. There is hardly a strip mall now that does not have a karate school as one of its tenants. The interest in concealed carry permits for firearms and even disaster preparations are also increasing in popularity. People feel the need to be self-sufficient or at least able to protect themselves and their families.

Most people learning self-defense will never need to use those skills in a real situation. However, even so there are many benefits. Fitness is one obvious benefit. Martial arts can be very aerobic and help maintain flexibility and strength. Confidence is another definite benefit. Martial arts training helps develop a winning mindset and helps build confidence that a student can handle a tough situation.

So, of all the potential benefits, at the core, martial arts are truly about learning the art of self-defense.

## BUSINESS AND SELF-DEFENSE

If, at its heart, karate is about self-defense, then how does that correlate with the business world? Organizations do not exist for the sake of learning how to protect themselves. Organizations have other, broader goals, such as educating students, selling merchandise, repairing equipment, or providing services. However, businesses are comprised of people and those people may feel concerned about personal safety. Security is a fundamental concern and an important benefit, perhaps even comparable to other benefits such as health care or time off, or at least part of the physical work environment, such as office furniture and location.

The personal safety or security of all personnel brings a true value to the business, some obvious benefits and many that are less apparent. Work-related injuries, including assaults, have an immediate cost in terms of worker's compensation. There is also the risk of liability in the case of negligent security.

Less evident are some of the other benefits. For example, information related to personal security, even home security, mentioned in a company newsletter can help create interest and support for corporate security programs. There are even information security compliance guidelines that require organizations to send out quarterly newsletters to build awareness on security issues. By including topics related to personal security, employees may be more likely to read the newsletter and pay attention to the other articles in the newsletter, which in turn builds awareness about corporate security concerns. An article on how to secure a home wireless network or how to protect your wireless devices on a public Wi-Fi may incorporate tips that also protect proprietary data on computers or tablets used for work projects.

In addition to building interest and awareness around security topics, training or promoting personal security also shows care and concern for employees. Throughout my career in both law enforcement and corporate security, I have seen numerous cases where some crime happens, not necessarily even a serious one, but it creates fear and drives rumors and concerns about employee safety. The fear turns into frustration and anger if concerns are not addressed or dealt with. If an employee is threatened or harassed by an aggressive panhandler in the parking lot, others will hear about the situation and often rumors run wild. Even when the facts are known, employees will expect their concerns to be addressed, such as increased security in the parking lot. If these worries and requests are ignored or not addressed, employees will feel resentful.

Employees who feel unsafe at work will leave and find work elsewhere. Think about your competition and how competitors' locations are viewed or whether the buildings seem more secure or not. In one security survey that I conducted, about 15% of employees considered leaving due to crime at that location. That is a lot of turnover, and if some of those individuals are key players in your firm, your competition may well hire them, along with their knowledge, skills, and experience—all at your expense.

## CREATING A CULTURE OF PERSONAL SECURITY

In Chapter 1, we looked at security awareness and ways to build education and awareness around best ways to protect businesses. Corporate communications such as newsletters were one way, and as mentioned before, is a good place to include tips on personal security.

Beyond newsletters, there are other ways to alert employees to issues or threats that could harm not only the organization but individuals as well. A good way to do that is to send out periodic security reminders. For example, before the Christmas holidays, a reminder to employees on ways to stay safe while shopping or how to protect their homes from burglars can be very timely and much appreciated. Your creativity is really your own limitation. Adding humor or an unexpected twist is a great way to get employees to read it. Add pictures or clip art to spruce up the communication. Be sure to use real crime prevention tips—practical and something that people do not always think of or know about.

---

## HAVE A SAFE AND MERRY CHRISTMAS!!

Twas the week before Christmas and all around town
People were bustling and shopping and scurrying around
On top of it all, over the noise of the traffic, all across the city
Carolers could be heard with a happy holiday ditty
Most of them had a heart full of cheer
But there were a few, a dark few, with a Grinch-like leer
For their thoughts were on thievery and robbery
Car break-ins, burglary and other nefarious skullduggery
But don't worry or let your holidays be ruined with fear
Simply follow a few of the security tips presented here
Remember if going out for the night
Set a timer to turn on a light
Christmas decorations hanging from the rooftop with care
When turned off, tell a burglary 'no reason to beware'
If someone tries to take your wallet or purse
Trying to fight them may make it worse
But if your life is in danger, then fight tooth and nail
Yell, scream, kick and bite and don't stop until you prevail
In a busy mall, tell your kids, if lost, find a store clerk
Teach them to seek help rather than some perverted jerk
Identity theft is always a popular scam
So be alert to fraudsters on the lam
Since I am running out of rhymes
And this may be a waste of your time
Read the additional tips lower down
And don't let security worries make you frown
In any case, while you're out and about at play
Have a Merry Christmas and a Happy Holiday

*Reprinted from www.blog.businesskarate.com*

---

In addition to security reminders, security alerts are another tool to help increase safety. Alerts are a warning or update about a specific situation. Going back to our earlier example in the parking lot, an alert sent out to employees right away lets everyone know what happened, as well as a description of the suspect and reminders on specific actions employees can take to protect themselves. The reminders may include the phone number for security in order to arrange an escort from the parking garage or to report suspicious people. Checking surroundings before getting out of the car and being alert to anyone in the area may be another reminder. The alerts serve as a reminder to specific situations, help dispel rumors by providing an official account of what happened, and let employees know what to do to protect themselves.

Unfortunately, some organizational leaders will not want to share alerts or information about security events. A common excuse includes worries about stirring up fear or rumors. Privacy may be a worry as well. My experience has been that the vast majority of employees will appreciate honest and open communications about crimes that have happened nearby, especially when accompanied with solid crime prevention recommendations. Any communications about recent crimes do not have to include specific information about who was involved, or the name of employees, in order to respect the victim's privacy. Failure to tie alerts and recommendations into recent crimes will let the rumor mill run wild. I have seen cases where minor vandalism and damage to glass was transformed into a major gun battle hitting the side of the building. Attacks and sexual assaults quickly generate fodder for rumors as well. A quick and proactive communication actually avoids the very issues that some leaders fear. Rumors will generate more fear than the communication. Failure to share information and provide prevention tips could even lead to liability if another employee is hurt in a similar crime and was never warned about the risks.

Training is another key element when building a culture of personal security. Training related to personal security can be voluntary. Generally, local police or even the district attorney or federal investigators will be more than happy to come to your business and talk about crime prevention tips. The individual may be an expert on identity theft, online sexual predators, or local gang activity. Any of these topics may be of value and interest to employees. Some employees may want to learn about Internet safety if they have children surfing social media sites. Other employees might attend the session on identity theft and learn how to protect themselves from becoming victims.

To make these sessions effective, you need to schedule the sessions when employees are most likely to attend. Breaks, such as lunch, are popular in the form of "lunch and learn" classes or "brown bag" sessions. The class is voluntary, but available when employees have time to go and are on a break. Letting them bring lunch to the class (or even providing it) gives employees a chance to attend while not feeling like time is wasted or that the class adds stress to an already busy schedule.

Be certain to advertise any classes. Having a great speaker and topic of interest but failing to let everyone know in advance about them is a sure way to have a small audience. Each organization will be different, but using e-mail reminders or fliers in the cafeteria are good ways to get the word out. I like to have attendees sign up in advance whenever possible. That creates a level of commitment by those who signed up to help attendance and also makes sure that there is enough space for everyone who does want to come to the session.

## DEALING WITH VIOLENCE

Personal security topics may cover a wide-range of issues, as we've mentioned, from identity theft to preventing home burglaries. There are times, however, when personal safety and safety at work overlap. In Chapter 8, we talked extensively about workplace violence, and that is one area where the organization and the individual employee's interests are definitely intertwined.

For those industries where violence is more prevalent, it is almost negligent not to offer training on dealing with aggressive or violent individuals. One of the best ways to prevent violent behavior is for employees to be able to identify warning signs and take steps to de-escalate the situation. One of the industries with a high risk of assaults is health care—in particular for emergency room care providers as well as those who deal with mental health patients. Due to the higher levels of risk, employees in those areas should be specifically trained on what to do, what to look for, and how to reduce the risks.

Failure to provide the tools for staff to be able to deal with violence in these situations will lead to frustration and dissatisfaction. Of course, there are costs. There are a number of training programs specifically designed to teach staff how to handle aggressive behavior. There are costs for the classes, and perhaps more relevant are the costs of nonproductive time and/or employee salaries and wages while staff are in training. However, the benefits, in terms of reduced worker's compensation, staff injuries, and improved morale, outweigh the costs.

When selecting a training program to address violence faced at work, consider the time for the class itself, as well as the effort to remain current or to recertify, a requirement for most recognized training programs. Also, be certain that the training content meets your needs and addresses the type of violence or situations faced by your staff members.

What should the training cover? First, it should address the risk factors that contribute to escalated behavior. In health care, that could be stress or worry over the health of a loved one, worries about expenses, family dynamics, mental illness, and substance abuse. Policies or procedures related to dealing with violence should be reviewed as part of the training. Next, identify early warning signs. A patient with a history of violent behavior is at increased risk of becoming violent again, and the history itself, if known, is a risk factor. The same could apply to other organizations, such as a student with a history of being violent or an unhappy customer who has been threatening or aggressive in the past.

Other early warning signs include raised voices, clenched fists, or tightening muscles. Body language can be an indicator that someone is getting defensive or no longer listening. Some examples include crossing arms, especially high across the chest as compared to crossing arms lower across the stomach. Tight lips or closed mouth and jaw jutted out can be a sign of stress. Another common behavior is fidgeting, such as pacing back and forth, or frequent glances or looks around the area. The quick looks can indicate that someone is looking for an escape from the stressful situation. In law enforcement, it often means that someone is about to run and this is a warning to intervene to prevent a foot chase.

As behavior escalates, a person may get extremely close, pointing fingers and yelling. Slamming objects or throwing things is another warning of imminent trouble. Of course, one of the most obvious warnings is the use of threats. Agitated individuals frequently tell you exactly what they are going to do and will make threats. This is a very dangerous point as the situation is at the boiling point and about to become physical. Whenever possible, steps to calm the situation should be taken earlier to avoid reaching these levels. Of course, escalation does not always follow a perfect cycle as the situation intensifies.

Intervention must be part of the training. Early intervention is often as easy as showing empathy and willingness to listen to an upset individual and offering to help and reassure them. This correlates to the customer service behavior discussed in Chapter 8. Never tolerate threats, whether physical or verbal. As situations escalate, employees should know what to do to get help, such as the use of duress alarms, or what escape paths are available to get away from the situation. Training should show management support and let employees know that their safety is first and that violent behavior should never be ignored or accepted.

It is amazing how often the warning signs are ignored or employees justify or excuse the behavior without taking any steps or measures to intervene. Training should stress the point to be aware and to respond to escalating behavior—never ignore it!

Another way for many organizations to help prevent violence is to identify suspicious people who do not belong. Some businesses are not open to outsiders, but many are. Sometimes, even with restricted access, there are ways for outsiders to get in, either through doors left open by employees, or tailgating behind someone else, or even pretending to belong, such as someone pretending to be a service technician.

Employees may become the "eyes and ears" of security and be the front line to protect each other as well as the business from suspicious outsiders. Of course, a common question is how to identify a suspicious person. What makes someone suspicious? It could be as simple as a lack of employee identification or badge. It may be odd behavior that makes someone suspicious, such as trying to avoid contact with others or loitering in areas away from other visitors or customers. The quick answer, though, is that if you are wondering whether or not someone is suspicious, then he or she is. Something has triggered a worry or attracted your attention to the suspicious person. I believe very much in trusting gut instincts in that regard.

## CARS AND PARKING LOTS

If you were pressed to pick the one spot where employees feel the most concerned about their safety and security, it would have to be outside the actual office or building. In almost every business, the majority of security concerns are in the parking lots or around the exterior of the building. Unless the grounds have high security, such as fencing and proactive security patrols, employees will feel the most vulnerable once they leave the building and are walking to their cars.

Throughout this book we have talked about parking lot concerns and ways to improve security. When it comes to teaching employees about staying safe and protecting themselves, the focus should be on being alert and paying attention to one's surroundings.

Distractions abound and often take our focus off the details of where we are and what we are doing. Cell phones, text messages, or hands full of paperwork, briefcases, and even the occasional coffee cup all demand attention and leave us ignoring what is going on around us. Crooks in parking lots will be looking and waiting for a victim in order to carry out a crime of opportunity. Someone who is alert and paying attention should see them or be aware of hiding spots while walking to or from her car.

How many times have you caught yourself crossing a street with barely a glance for traffic while messing with a cell phone or checking e-mail messages? Or walking through a parking lot with little or no thought to anything other than checking your smartphone for a new text or an update on Facebook? We have all done it at some point, but it really does distract from paying attention.

If you are serious about personal security, then it is vital to put away distractions and pay attention. Imagine if we lived in the past and worries included risks of being attacked by a saber-toothed tiger; you would certainly be on high alert walking home to your cave knowing that the danger is real. The news is full of stories about abductions, sexual assaults, missing persons, and murders, and while these serious crimes are relatively rare, attacks do happen. Not all attacks are as serious as some of these—such as aggressive panhandling or purse snatching—and are unlikely to make it to the news, but they are still extremely scary to the victim.

Military and law enforcement training puts high emphasis on remaining aware and being alert. There are different ways to look at awareness, but a common method is to use color codes that equate to the level of focus or attention. White is the least aware. In this zone, you are basically clueless regarding what is going on and not paying attention. You might be in the white zone while at home watching TV or otherwise in what should be a completely safe environment. This is not the level you want to be at when walking through parking lots or down a city street. If you are attacked while in the white zone, you will be caught completely by surprise and your mind will have to not only react but also take in what is happening, and then overcome the shock and surprise before even starting to respond. A victim or target caught in the white zone will most likely not be able to defend herself or be able to escape the attacker.

The next zone is yellow. In the yellow zone, you are aware of surroundings and paying attention to what is going on around you. This is where a person should be when out and about or the level a police officer should be at when on patrol. There is no specific threat or concern to attract attention, but it is a level of awareness about who is around you and potential problems. If you are walking through a parking lot, you should develop the routine of looking around for people loitering, or in vehicles watching others, and be aware of potential hiding spots as you walk as in Figure 13.1. There is not a specific threat drawing your attention, but an overall awareness of surroundings.

FIGURE 13.1 Parking garages can be very isolated and offer numerous hiding spots, even between parked cars.

The next alert level is the orange zone. At this point, your attention is drawn to a particular person or issue. It could be that you noticed a van start up and slowly make its way toward you. Or you heard a noise behind a parked car, but do not see anyone there. Something has drawn your attention; some potential threat is coming into focus. At this point, you should begin planning various responses. If the van stops or slows down when it is close to me, I will dart to my left between parked cars and into the next lane and run back toward the building. Your response can even be more proactive. Instead of waiting to see what the potential threat does, change the circumstances first. After hearing a noise behind a parked car, take a detour and completely circumvent the area before finding out if someone was hiding there or not, when you will be closer and it will be harder to escape.

The last level is the red zone. This is the fight or flight zone (you won't freeze because you already have a plan in mind). The threat has materialized and has turned into an actual attack. The van stopped and someone jumped out and rushed at you, or a crook tried to grab you from between cars. Obviously, this is exactly what we want to avoid. The best way to win a fight is to not get into one in the first place.

There are times when the risk is higher than normal and you should be at a higher level of mental preparedness. For example, the Christmas shopping season creates more opportunities for crooks. In one case, a former coworker's wife was Christmas shopping at a suburban mall in a low crime area. As she was walking to her car with an armload of presents, two males pulled up nearby and hit her with a stun gun, grabbed her bags, and drove away. She was unhurt, but the shock and fear will stay with her. In another case, at an upscale shopping mall, a customer had just bought an iPad and was walking to his car. A suspect attacked him and grabbed the bag, pulling on it so violently that the victim's finger was ripped off as the bag was wrapped around the finger. Smartphones and tablets like the iPad are becoming a popular target for crooks, so the risk is greater when carrying or shopping for such items.

Personal security training should also include recommendations for what to do once someone is in her car. Again, it is easy to get distracted and check voice mail or e-mail before starting off. Always start the car and lock the doors first in case you need to make a quick getaway. Keep your head up and look around while checking texts or on the phone. Stay alert. Police officers are taught to do the same kind of thing while on traffic stops. Wise officers keep the ticket book up higher, against the top of the steering wheel, and can easily just glance over the top to see the stopped car and make sure no one gets out or attacks them, as well as glancing in the mirrors to check for others stopping behind the police cruiser.

While driving, keep an eye on the rearview mirror as part of the overall level of alertness. If you believe you are being followed, turn down some side streets in safe areas and see if the car continues to follow. If you suspect you are being followed, do not go to your house. Drive to a crowded area and use a cell phone to call police. If you do not have a cell phone, you could try going through a busy drive-thru and asking the clerk to phone police. Be careful to pick a drive-thru that allows vehicles to get out of line. You do not want to get trapped if someone does try to attack you.

Always know your location and approximate street address. As you are driving, if you need to call the police from a cell phone, the dispatchers will not have an exact location. To get the quickest response, you may need to provide the address or at least block, such as the 1100 block of Main Street.

The idea of someone following you in a car may sound like something out of a spy story and not very realistic. It does happen on occasion, such as following a road rage situation where one driver wants to follow another. Sometimes, it is domestic related when a spouse follows or attacks the partner while he or she is in the car. There have been several reports where members of motorcycle gangs will follow police officers home from work to attack them or to break into their homes to steal firearms.

As I write this, there is a current news story of a driver in New York City who was surrounded by a group of motorcyclists known to the police for various disruptions and dangerous driving stunts. One of the motorcyclists can be seen on a video trying to block in the driver and instead got bumped. The driver stopped, but was quickly surrounded by the group. According to news reports, the driver stated he left the scene out of fear for his safety and that of his family. After a chase of 50 some blocks, the driver was stopped in traffic and the motorcyclists surrounded the vehicle and broke out windows with their helmets, dragging him out of the car and beating him.

One lesson to take from this is to remember that if you are in danger and in your vehicle, do not stop—keep moving. I was involved in one police pursuit that went on for a long time and the driver kept managing to escape the attempts to stop him. After the pursuit, when he was finally in custody, we learned that he was a former Marine and had attended an executive protection driving course where he learned to never stop, no matter what, and to always keep the car moving.

You should not have to teach your employees how to evade police or even pursuit driving techniques. However, many of us spend a great deal of time in our vehicles and a personal security program can certainly spend time on awareness of some of the related security issues and how to stay safe, whether in a vehicle or walking to one.

## HOME SECURITY

There are a number of practical reasons why home security should be important to businesses. First, how many employees are conducting work from home? That means there may be work devices or computers at home, documents, company credit cards, or other items that could be lost or stolen and might not have the same protection as at the worksite. Second, information about protection and security at home will be of more interest to many employees and help increase awareness in general about security issues. Last, it also helps to show concern for employees and, from a cold business perspective, improves productivity if employees are not worried about, or dealing with, issues at home such as burglary.

Identity theft and Internet safety are both topics that usually generate a lot of interest among employees. Offering training on how to avoid being a victim of identity theft can be very popular. Many people have heard of the risks but do not know exactly what steps to take to protect their credit or identity. Victims can spend huge amounts of time trying to correct or recover from identity theft. That is a worry and time-consuming issue that will have an impact on the workplace.

A good training session may teach employees how to monitor their own credit for signs of abuse. There are paid services that will monitor credit reports, but employees can also do much of the same on their own for free. In the United States, federal law requires that each of the three credit reporting agencies provide a free copy of a person's credit report once a year. By asking for a copy from each, throughout the year, you can check for any new, unauthorized activity, such as someone opening an account or credit line that you did not initiate.

There are also limits on losses, especially with credit cards. In my experience, most credit cards will not charge the holder for any unauthorized charges on a lost or stolen card if the loss or theft is reported promptly. By law, the maximum a cardholder could be liable for is $50.

Understanding the types of information or items that can be used by identity thieves can be eye opening. Offering training on identity theft and practical advice on how to prevent or manage fraud is also useful to the business as employees develop a better understanding of the importance of protecting vital information.

Identity theft often happens via online data collection or theft. ID theft prevention should cover how to protect oneself on wireless networks and the potential dangers of insecure data. Even passwords can be easily stolen, sometimes without any high-tech devices. With the number of passwords everyone is expected to remember and know, it is easy to leave key passwords written down in close proximity to desks or computers. For offices located near street-level windows, perpetrators may be able to view usernames and passwords, as well as capture screenshots from outside the business, on a public sidewalk.

Home burglary may be another concern of employees. Offering training on home security and protection is another way to reinforce security awareness with a personal connection. Again, there is a definite benefit to the organization if employees have company computers or data at home.

Furthermore, company executives could be specifically targeted for business intelligence, so a company may specifically take steps to ensure an appropriate level of home security for key leaders.

In a recent study, individuals arrested for burglaries were asked about target selection and what would drive them to pick another target (Blevins et al., 2012). Some of the top factors that would scare away a would-be burglar were people in the area or intrusion alarms. From a prevention standpoint, reminding employees to make it look like someone is home is perhaps one of the best deterrents to a burglary. Suggestions can be simple, such as stop mail when out of town, have neighbors park in the garage and pick up newspapers, as well as leave lights on timers to create the appearance that the house is occupied. Burglar alarms were a strong deterrence as well. Many burglars reported that they would specifically check for alarms and would pick another house or business if there was an alarm.

Burglars were also concerned about traffic in the area. People in the vicinity pose a risk to burglars and increase the chance of a crook being seen, the police called, and an arrest made. Also, most burglars entered through open or unlocked windows and doors; only a few actually picked locks to gain entry. Homeowners who get rid of or limit hiding spots around the house help increase the chance of a burglar being seen. Trimming back bushes and low tree branches increases lines of sight. Securing doors and windows with solid locks, including strong frames, is another key way to protect a home.

Safety and security outside of work and at home is a great benefit to associates in the workplace, as well as to the organization, and can help protect both personal and company assets.

## SELF-DEFENSE BASICS

There are times when all the steps to prevent crime from happening fail and you could become the target of a violent crime. Notice that I said target and not victim. The two are not necessarily the same. Learning a few basic defensive techniques is not hard and could come in handy in a tough situation. There are various courses that range from a couple of hours to several sessions over a span of a few weeks to teach individuals basic self-defense moves, including how to escape from common holds and evade an attacker.

Often, businesses will sponsor or offer a seminar or course on self-defense. This is a great way to support associates and help create a safe workplace. Staff will feel more confident and able to protect themselves.

If you want in-depth instruction and the chance to fully develop self-defense skills as well as fitness, taking a martial arts class may be the right choice. However, choosing a class can be somewhat intimidating, especially for someone new to the idea. First, there are a number of different martial arts with different philosophies, styles, and techniques. You must do some research and pick the one that fits best for you. Jujitsu is popular and is great for learning about holds, escapes, and grappling. Many street fights or attacks revolve around grappling and holds, so jujitsu may be the best one for practical self-defense, if that is your primary goal. Other martial arts, such as tae kwon do, emphasize kicks, punches, and blocks—in essence, meeting force with force. These might be more physically demanding than you want to take on. Aikido focuses on deflecting attacks, so may be more suitable.

In addition to deciding on the style of classes, there are other considerations. You will want to look at the instructor's teaching style and make sure that you feel comfortable and that it will be a suitable learning environment and one that you will enjoy. After all, if you do not enjoy the class, you will not stay with it. You should also check on the instructor's experience and make sure that he or she has the background and experience to draw from as an instructor. See if the instructor will let you sit through and watch a class or two before signing up or making a payment. That way, you can see firsthand how the class is run, the exercises involved, and the types of skills that will be learned. You also have to consider whether the focus is on self-defense or more on showy moves that are not practical in a real situation. Fancy jumping kicks and even spin kicks might look great in class but are not effective on the street.

Also, consider cost. Not just the initial costs for joining a class, but all the associated charges and fees. Many martial arts schools have an excessive number of belt levels and very high fees to test and pass on to the next level. I am wary of classes structured like this as they feel more about income than learning. Along those lines, find out how long a dedicated student normally takes to obtain a black belt. I've seen some advertisements boasting that students can get a black belt within a year of starting. Traditional martial arts are built on extensive practice and repetition. A short time to get a black belt is an indicator that the training may be lacking. I prefer instructors or schools that require long times at the different stages to ensure solid and well-grounded abilities. In the tae kwon do school I participated in, it took about five years to reach black belt. A minimum of two years was required at the brown belt level alone to guarantee that the forms and related techniques were instinctive and natural.

Find out about what types of sparring exercises are done during the class. I've seen some classes claim that students participate in full contact sparring. Full contact sparring would result in serious injuries if techniques are performed effectively at 100%. Even with use of pads and protective gear, that level of sparring can still cause injuries. Classes that make these types of boasts seem to be more about machismo rather than true self-defense skills. I would recommend staying away from them.

Last, you need to look at your goals and dedication. Learning karate sounds like fun, but it is hard work, and to excel takes time. Do you have the level of interest to stick with it? You can always try it and see if you enjoy it, but if you are serious, plan on doing it for the long haul. Of course, there are benefits in terms of confidence, physical fitness, strength, and flexibility. Martial arts can become a lifelong exercise and a great way to stay in shape and boost your health.

## FIGHTING FIT

Many organizations are focusing on wellness as part of the overall benefits offered. Wellness programs encourage employees to make better choices about eating, exercise, and be more active in general.

Self-defense programs can be tied in with the wellness program. But beyond work, you can take steps to stay in shape whether for general health or with a self-defense mindset. Of course, before starting any new fitness regime, check with your doctor to be sure that you are able to handle the exercises.

Self-defense is very much about short, intense bursts of energy and activity. Building your fitness around fast bursts is a great way to build the stamina for protecting yourself on the street should the need arise. One of the toughest drills I went through was in the police academy, when two cadets were placed in a ring for two minutes. The object was to push the other out of the ring. Those two minutes of just trying to push each other around the ring was one of the most intense anaerobic workouts ever. That is about the closest you can probably come to feeling like you were in a defense situation without being in one. There is a renewed interest in circuit training workouts, which alternate between tough exercises for a minute or two, then a very brief rest, followed by moving on to another intense exercise.

Even if you are not interested in that level of exercise, staying fit will help if you are thrown into a bad situation. Walking every evening around your neighborhood may not seem like an intense workout but does build up your overall stamina and is easy on the joints. No matter your current level of fitness, taking up some basic activity that you enjoy and sticking with it will boost your endurance and stamina and could possibly make a difference between life and death. Plus it is good for you!

## CONCLUSION

Too often, when we think about business security we only think of the physical workspace and protective measures such as video surveillance or alarms. However, true business security also means protecting employees and keeping them both aware and engaged in security issues. Addressing and focusing on personal security promotes a more secure environment overall. In short, personal security is the foundation for a company-wide personnel security program. A safe and secure workplace cannot be created without a focus on the safety of employees, both at work and away from work.

## BUSINESS KARATE BELT LEVEL

Test your company's karate belt level in the discipline of awareness/stance. If your organization meets each belt level and all the standards of the lower belts as seen in Figure 13.2, you have then achieved that color level.

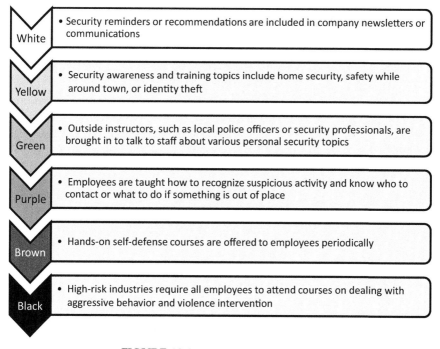

White
• Security reminders or recommendations are included in company newsletters or communications

Yellow
• Security awareness and training topics include home security, safety while around town, or identity theft

Green
• Outside instructors, such as local police officers or security professionals, are brought in to talk to staff about various personal security topics

Purple
• Employees are taught how to recognize suspicious activity and know who to contact or what to do if something is out of place

Brown
• Hands-on self-defense courses are offered to employees periodically

Black
• High-risk industries require all employees to attend courses on dealing with aggressive behavior and violence intervention

FIGURE 13.2   What is your belt level?

## Reference

Blevins, K. R., Kuhns, J. B., Lee, S., 2012. Understanding Decisions to Burglarize from the Offender's Perspective. University of North Carolina, Charlotte, NC. Retrieved from: http://www.airef.org/research/BurglarSurveyStudyFinalReport.pdf. (accessed 15.10.13.).

## Further Reading

Candiotti, S., Foley, V., Botelho, G., October 10, 2013. Prosecutor: Off-duty Officer "Terrorized" Family as SUV Driver was Beaten. CNN. Retrieved from: http://www.cnn.com/2013/10/09/us/bikers-attack-video/(accessed 29.10.13.).

# 14

# The Wrap: Good Security Is Good Business

## RUNNING A KARATE SCHOOL

Karate students may be completely focused on learning self-defense skills. The school's instructor, as passionate as he or she may be about karate, has to remember the aspects of running his or her own business. The owner of a dojo has to think about the location of the school, expenses such as rent and utilities, marketing and attracting new customers, as well as keeping current clients and managing the financials. The owner may also need to hire help or assistance with teaching or other office tasks. Even the security of the business location may be a concern. A break-in could leave the gym damaged or missing critical supplies.

In short, a karate instructor has to think beyond self-defense training. He or she must treat the school as a business. Ignoring the business aspects will almost certainly guarantee failure, and the karate school will not last long. Advertising, human resource functions, and accounting are all part of the process of running a self-defense school as a successful enterprise.

## BUSINESS CONNECTION

Just as an owner of a karate school has to remember the business side of the dojo, a business leader has to remember the protection side of her organization. Security is not just electronic devices such as video surveillance or alarms. It is more than locks, gates, and keys. Security is more than policies and procedures. Security is a management process.

A comprehensive security management program is not just a necessary evil or unavoidable cost. It actually is a business-enabling service. Security protects critical assets and employees and helps the company manage and recognize risks and survive during emergencies or critical incidents.

Most businesses would not operate without a marketing department or a financial group. Even a small business, including a single entrepreneur working alone, must have some plan for marketing the idea or managing expenses and income. As businesses grow, human resource departments, information technology, facilities, or even legal departments are common. Yet, too often, companies operate without any type of security management program.

## THE CASE FOR SECURITY

Throughout this book we have looked at some of the ways security benefits the various parts of an organization, understanding the different risks faced and the methods to minimize those risks. Left untouched, the risks can translate into a real business loss, from low employee morale, high turnover, loss of proprietary data, lawsuits and litigation, damage to company assets, theft, loss of income, bad publicity, and loss of customers. Any one of these concerns would keep a business leader up at night. Security management is a function and partner that helps the individual department leaders manage and address those concerns and help take away the worry.

Screening applicants and checking backgrounds is one way to protect the business. Screening helps avoid hiring employees who would be more likely to steal or act violently. The focus on safety and security, including personal safety tips and recommendations, contributes to employee morale and can help reduce turnover. Paying attention to the work environment and ensuring that steps are taken to reduce crime is another way to help employees feel safe.

When there are any threats or concerns, security is a vital part of the threat assessment program and outlining ways to reduce the risk. Even when the threat is brought to work from home, such as domestic violence, security planning can help address those worries.

Even with screening and ongoing checks, there is still the chance that employees may commit crimes on the premises or outsiders may be involved in crimes. Security leaders can help drive those investigations and provide recommendations on the best steps to take moving forward. Even in high-risk terminations, security comes into play, both in the termination process itself as well as the proactive steps to take following the termination to protect any employees or assets that may be targeted by the ex-employee. Each of these security processes helps support the human resources department in managing employees, turnover, retention, hiring, and terminations.

In addition to concerns about employees, organizations have to think about public image and how potential and current customers see the business. Bad publicity can occur if a customer is attacked or hurt while on the premises of a business. Certain events are so bad that the organization involved will be connected with that negative situation for years to come. Columbine High School is remembered across the world for the school shooting that took place there. Many people will remember Luby's Cafeteria for a shooting that took place in the Texas restaurant. The World Trade Center in New York will be remembered for generations to come for the terrorist attacks of September 11, 2001.

While situations like the ones just mentioned are not always the fault of the organization involved, no business will want to be connected to them. Even graffiti left on the side of buildings or neglected, run-down buildings can contribute to feelings of the business being unsafe. That will not involve the media or negative stories but can contribute to a more subtle form of negative publicity and scare away customers. If there is any type of emergency situation at the location, a solid emergency operations plan will include details on how to coordinate with the media to help with the story rather than be dragged along, including becoming the target of negative press. The security management team plays a role in helping create a safe environment, not just for employees but also for the public, and is vital in developing emergency procedures as well. An organization with solid plans, procedures, and a focus on security and safety will be much less likely to become the target, or victim, of negative reporting. These are all ways that security contributes to the marketing goals of an organization.

With the threat of negative publicity comes the threat of liability. Neglecting or ignoring security may come at a price. Failure to identify potential risks and take reasonable steps to protect the property can be very costly in the long run. Perhaps nothing will happen, but you are giving up control of your organization and its future to the unknown. The costs and impact of lawsuits should be an ongoing concern, one actively addressed, not ignored. Hand in hand with liability is compliance. Many industries have specific compliance issues that must be met to stay in business or, at least, avoid expensive fines and penalties. The Sarbanes–Oxley Act has very specific compliance measures for publically traded companies listed on U.S. stock exchanges. Background checks on corporate officers with fiduciary duties and the ability for employees to report suspected fraud are just a couple of the requirements. Health care in the United States has numerous compliance guidelines to meet as well. Most hospitals are accredited by The Joint Commission, which has very specific requirements for both security and emergency management designed to protect both employees, as well as patients. Employee screening, annual security risk assessments, reporting and tracking of security-related incidents, as well as checking for faulty security systems are all requirements to be met. Again, the security department can be an integral partner in meeting compliance demands as well as mitigating the risk of lawsuits.

If an organization has a manufacturing department or even requires basic supplies to keep operations going, then the supply chain is a vital piece of the business. The supply chain can be quite extensive, including understanding where vendors are located and what supplies the vendors depend on. Suddenly, a domestic business with local customers can find itself tied to international markets and impacts. Storms, strikes, political issues, and even foreign legislation can have a consequence. Closer to home, theft of goods during transport may be a concern. Understanding the myriad of hazards along the entire supply chain is crucial if a business wants to be prepared to deal with these potentially unexpected challenges.

Information technology and information security usually get close attention, and there are well-documented, serious threats to any online data. Aside from the information kept in online databases, there are physical aspects of information security and physical hardware as well as paper copies of proprietary information. In one unique case, thieves apparently obtained a security vulnerability report completed by ADT. The gaps were then exploited by the thieves who broke into an Eli Lilly & Co. warehouse in Connecticut and stole about $60 million worth of pharmaceutical drugs. The insurer is suing ADT for $42 million, and the two suspects are currently awaiting trial after being arrested by the FBI. Clearly information of all sorts needs to be protected, including information on physical devices such as tablets, flash drives, or laptop computers. There is a definite physical side of information security, one where security should work closely with information technology to ensure that all forms of proprietary and company information are well protected.

Many of these examples seem like natural partnering between security and other business units. Perhaps the most important connection is the one between security and the company leadership. Management should have a very clear and comprehensive view of both the challenges and risks facing the organization as well as a realistic assessment of how those risks can be mitigated or avoided. Security management should be in tune with strategic goals, as well as the threats looming, sometimes beyond the horizon, and provide leaders with practical recommendations and advice on dealing with the problems that may lie ahead.

## GOOD BUSINESS

As we've seen, security concerns run throughout an organization in every type of operation. Failure to consider security hazards or challenges can jeopardize the entire organization. Remember the statistic from the United States Chamber of Commerce that one-third of all businesses fail due to security concerns? Another third that shut down during an emergency never reopen. The risks and the outcomes are very dangerous. Failing to have a security management program or plan is tantamount to playing

Russian roulette. You may get lucky for a while, but eventually the threats will catch up.

No one would run a business without the usual components, such as marketing, finance, accounting, information technology, and human resources. Even small companies need these services, whether these functions are contracted out or one person wears several hats, like the home office or small business entrepreneur. Ignoring security will eventually be about the same as ignoring customer service or ignoring the importance of having well-trained and motivated employees. A business may survive for a time but eventually will lose customers or not have the talent necessary to compete in the marketplace.

Integrating security into each of the different business units helps to make each more effective and more valuable to the company and better able to meet goals and strategic outcomes.

Security is important not only from an organizational perspective but on another level—you deserve it. You, and every employee, should feel safe at work, free from worry about violence, theft, and other crimes. Security is not only good business but it is the right thing to do. Everyone deserves to be able to go to work and focus on the task at hand, rather than distractions and fears about crime and security issues.

Security management should be an ongoing, proactive process, focused on current safety as well as long-term planning and goals. Security should be a key partner in business decisions, such as opening new locations, remodeling existing buildings, layoffs, and fast-paced hiring. New vendors and new sources of goods should be reviewed. If employees travel, then the security concerns related to traveling or the destination should be taken into account, with specific information provided to the employee ahead of time to protect him or her, as well as protect company information.

## CONCLUSION

We have covered a wide range of topics throughout this book. Security awareness followed by a security risk assessment and matrix, internal and external threats, workplace violence, premise liability, and selecting electronic security systems. Throughout, there have been many recommendations and suggestions, designed to help you make your own organization and business safer and more secure. You may not be able to implement every one immediately. Building a security program will take dedication and time. However, for each recommendation that you can put into place, your business will be that much safer.

Start with the items you can change. Often some simple changes can make drastic improvements in security. Be persistent and do not lose focus on the security topics or concerns that threaten your business or employees. We have looked at security in the same way a karate student learns a martial art, focusing on the different skills needed. Each chapter includes the specific guidelines to reach the next belt level, just as a karate student moves through the ranks by earning the next step closer to a black belt. Follow these recommendations and you will earn a business karate black belt.

## BUSINESS KARATE BELT LEVEL

Test your company's karate belt level in the discipline of awareness/stance. If your organization has met each belt level and all the standards throughout the book, then you have successfully obtained a business karate black belt, as shown in Figure 14.1.

Black

- Follow all of the recommendations from each chapter to earn a Business Karate Black Belt

**FIGURE 14.1    What is your belt level?**

## Further Reading

Swiatek, J., April 2, 2013. Lilly Insurer: Insider Information Led to Drug Heist. The Indianapolis Star via USA Today. Retrieved from: http://www.usatoday.com/story/news/nation/2013/04/02/eli-lilly-drug-theft-lawsuit-insider-information/2045142/ (accessed 19.10.13.).

# Index

Note: Page numbers with "*f*" denote figures; "*t*" tables; "b" denote box.

Printed and bound by CPI Group (UK) Ltd, Croydon, CR0 4YY

08/05/2025

01864771-0001